LITERATURE ACTIVITY BOOKS

An Index to Materials for Whole Language and Shared Literature

MARYBETH GREEN
AND BEVERLY WILLIAMS

1993
Libraries Unlimited, Inc.
Englewood, Colorado

LIBRARIES UNLIMITED, INC.
P.O. Box 6633
Englewood, CO 80155-6633

Library of Congress Cataloging-in-Publication Data

LB
1515
.G73
1993

Green, Marybeth.
  Literature activity books : an index to materials for whole language and shared literature / Marybeth Green and Beverly Williams.
    viii, 203 p. 22x28 cm.
    Includes index.
    ISBN 1-56308-011-7
    1. Children's literature--Bibliography. 2. Children's literature--Study and teaching (Elementary)--Bibliography. 3. Activity programs in education--Bibliography. 4. Reading (Elementary)--Language experience approach--Bibliography. I. Williams, Beverly.
  II. Title.
Z1037.G8   1993
011'.62--dc20   92-40996
                                                   CIP

Contents

Preface

As language arts curricula move away from a strict basal reader approach, shared literature, whole language, and critical thinking strategies are becoming increasingly important. Children's literature is a fundamental part of the contemporary elementary language arts curriculum. Its inclusion can and should benefit students in a variety of ways. Literature is used in reading programs to expand student experiences, encourage independent reading, and provide a base for future reading experiences. Literature develops the critical thinking skills necessary for children to be productive, life-long learners.

Books that children love can be the basis for a whole language curriculum. Children's natural language is a motivational vehicle for learning. When given the opportunity to explore the challenge of answering questions and participating in activities using higher-level thinking skills, students move from the passive to the active role in learning. The most effective way to motivate children is to use the experiences, materials, and literature they love.

The whole language approach concentrates on children's efforts to express and gain meaning. This approach provides meaningful experiences with relevant stories and books. Children are expected to write and communicate in practical ways that arise from genuine language needs. Teachers of whole language often do not use specific texts or they adapt textbooks for their own purposes. They constantly need materials that are interesting and appropriate for children and they need activities that are consistent with the integrated use of language.

Many children are currently taught to read using a basal program in which each series has a research-based definition of reading and a scope and sequence of the consistent skills. Word lists are generated for different levels and stories are written for these words. These series are available with workbooks and assessment tools. Basals alone, however, cannot provide enough experiences for all children learning to read their language. Controlled vocabularies and contents can limit the imagination and motivation of learners.

Regardless of the approach to teaching elementary reading, educators in recent years have used more children's literature than in the past to enrich their reading programs. Two of the strongest reading approaches, the basal series and the whole language method, have literature integrated into their curricula. As teachers preparing children for the twenty-first century, we must be equipped to use a variety of materials and seek successful ideas and techniques.

One of the many challenges facing us today is the need to improve literacy and develop higher-order thinking skills. Numerous studies conducted in the past few years substantiate that American school curricula need to be more stringent and challenging, and greater attention should be focused on improving children's analytical and inferential skills. Just as important as developing the cognitive domain is the need to assist children in the development of the affective domain.

Every teacher of reading hopes to give children the power and desire to read. Literature is a tool that cannot only empower children to learn, but can enrich the lives and education of children. Literature can be used to promote a love of reading and can allow children to relate to characters and ideas. Literature can encourage deeper understandings and promote critical thinking.

This book surveys the abundance of literature activity books on the market and provides quick, efficient access by subject, author, and title to ideas and activities for more than 1,000 children's books. Because many teachers are including studies of illustrators in their literature curriculum, we also have included references to many prominent illustrators. Teachers wishing to move into a literature-based curriculum will find ideas and activities quickly through this index and will save hours of searching for materials or writing a curriculum to accompany a literature selection.

As we examined each literature activity book, we were concerned that the ideas and activities did not mimic the basal programs. We examined each book for its emphasis on critical thinking, whether it provided opportunities for integrated language arts, whether it provided opportunities for interdisciplinary studies, and whether the activities provided a meaningful extension of the children's title. Each literature activity book is, therefore, rated according to how closely it is able to meet these criteria.

How to Use This Book

This book is divided into four major parts: Subject, author, and title indexes of children's titles found in literature activity books, and a literature materials guide that analyzes the literature activity books.

Following each title in the subject, author, and title index is a suggested grade level in parentheses for each children's title. The letters P and K indicate preschool and kindergarten. Numbers indicate grades. The letter A indicates that the title may be appropriate for all ages.

1. Subject Listing

If you are looking for thematic materials, check this index by subject. Suggested books are listed alphabetically by author, followed by title, grade level, and resource book codes that lead to idea books listed in the Literature Materials Guide.

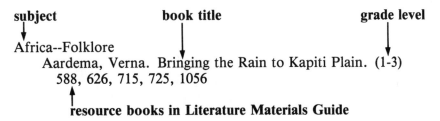

2. Author Listing

If you are looking for a specific author, joint author, or illustrator, check this section under the author or illustrator's name. Folktales and fairy tales illustrated by a particular artist are included in addition to a generic title such as "Cinderella." Following the author and book title are the grade level and resource book codes that lead to the activity books listed in the Literature Materials Guide.

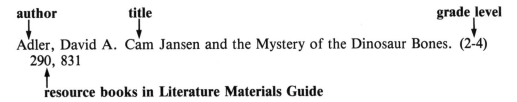

3. Title Listing

If you are looking for a particular children's book title, check this section under the title. Following the title are the grade level and resource book codes that lead to activity books listed in the Literature Materials Guide.

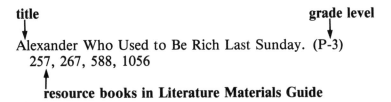

4. Literature Materials Guide

Materials in this section are arranged alphabetically by publisher and then by author. Item numbers correspond to indexed numbers in the indexes. Each activity book entry includes the title, author, publishing information, a brief description of the contents and objectives, and the books covered. Materials were rated with one to four stars according to how well they meet the criteria discussed in the preface.

Dedication

I would like to dedicate my portion of this book to John, Catheryne, and Travis for their enthusiastic support and encouragement. Thank you for always believing in "Mom."

—Marybeth Green

I would like to dedicate my portion of this book to Pat, Barbara, and Brandi for their enduring patience and support which allowed me to write this book.

—Beverly Williams

Acknowledgments

We would also like to thank the teachers of Margaret Wills Elementary for their enthusiastic support of shared literature and whole language and without whose urgent need, this book would never have taken shape.

And to the children of Margaret Wills Elementary who have always encouraged us to look beyond the horizon.... May you always find your dreams!

We would like to thank the staff of Amarillo Computers, especially Shawn Walsh, Doyle Hoover, and Gerry Jubang, for its unflagging support of our endeavor and numerous rescues of our files.

Finally, we would like to thank the Youth Services staff of the Amarillo Public Library for its support and encouragement.

Subject Listing

If you are looking for a topical book and wish to find teaching ideas, check this index under subject. Suggested books are listed alphabetically by author, followed by title, grade level, and resource book codes that lead to idea books listed in the Literature Materials Guide beginning on page 171.

AFRICA — WEST — FOLKLORE

Aardema, Verna. Why Mosquitoes Buzz in People's Ears. (1-3)
1, 14, 145, 255, 269, 407, 666, 712, 1010, 1045

Cendrars, Blaise. Shadow. (1-3)
1, 269, 415

McDermott, Gerald. Anansi the Spider. (1-3)
422

AFRO — AMERICANS — BIOGRAPHY

Adler, David A. A Picture Book of Martin Luther King. (1-3)
416, 588

Aliki. A Weed Is a Flower: The Life of George Washington Carver. (3-5)
588

Altman, Susan. Extraordinary Black Americans from Colonial to Contemporary Times. (5-6)
588

Clayton, Edward Taylor. Martin Luther King: The Peaceful Warrior. (4-6)
413, 1024

Davis, Burke. Black Heroes of the American Revolution. (5-6)
588

Ferris, Jeri. Go Free or Die. (5-6)
588

Ferris, Jeri. Walking the Road to Freedom. (5-6)
588

McGovern, Ann. Runaway Slave, the Story of Harriet Tubman (2-4)
11

Meltzer, Milton. Mary McLeod Bethune. (5-6)
588

Petry, Ann Lane. Harriet Tubman, Conductor of the Underground Railroad. (4-6)
411, 914

Scioscia, Mary. Bicycle Rider. (2-4)
11

Sterling, Dorothy. Freedom Train. (4-6)
405

Yates, Elizabeth. Amos Fortune, Free Man. (4-6)
2, 269, 417, 588, 750

AFRO — AMERICANS — FICTION

Armstrong, William H. Sounder. (5-6)
90, 99, 225, 269, 399, 405, 406, 419, 574, 612, 688, 722, 892, 941

Blume, Judy. Iggie's House. (4-6)
260, 275

Brenner, Barbara. Wagon Wheels. (2-4)
411, 417, 588

Boyd, Candy Dawson. Charlie Pippin. (5-6)
417, 588

Caines, Jeanette. Just Us Women. (P-2)
416

Cameron, Ann. Julian's Glorious Summer. (2-4)
282, 411

Cameron, Ann. More Stories Julian Tells. (2-4)
592

Cameron, Ann. The Stories Julian Tells. (2-4)
267, 409, 588

Childress, Alice. A Hero Ain't Nothin' but a Sandwich. (6)
413

Clifton, Lucille. Everett Anderson's Friend. (P-2)
11

Clifton, Lucille. Everett Anderson's Goodbye. (P-2)
588

Clifton, Lucille. My Friend Jacob. (K-2)
271

Collier, James. Jump Ship to Freedom. (5-6)
588

Collier, James. War Comes to Willy Freeman. (4-6)
768

Fitzhugh, Louise. Nobody's Family Is Going to Change. (5-6)
411

Flournoy, Valerie. Patchwork Quilt. (K-3)
265, 271

Fox, Paula. The Slave Dancer. (6)
2, 227, 269, 573, 939, 1023

Greene, Bette. Phillip Hall Like Me, I Reckon Maybe. (4-6)
68, 534, 890

Greenfield, Eloise. Grandmama's Joy. (1-3)
588

Hamilton, Virginia. House of Dies Drear. (5-6)
675, 1025

Hamilton, Virginia. M. C. Higgins the Great. (6)
269

Hamilton, Virginia. Zeely. (4-6)
694

Keats, Ezra Jack. Hi Cat! (P-2)
255

Keats, Ezra Jack. Peter's Chair. (P-1)
254, 258, 587

Keats, Ezra Jack. Snowy Day (P-2)
1, 12, 18, 128, 265, 269, 407, 654, 804, 998, 1057

Keats, Ezra Jack. Whistle for Willie. (P-2)
95, 267, 665, 1003

Konigsburg, Elaine. Jennifer, Hecate, Macbeth, William McKinley and Me, Elizabeth. (4-6)
234, 411, 526

Lexau, Joan M. I Should Have Stayed in Bed. (1-3)
587

Mathis, Sharon Bell. The Hundred Penny Box. (4-6)
471, 641, 719

Mathis, Sharon Bell. Sidewalk Story. (3-5)
411

Mayer, Mercer. Liza Lou and the Yeller Belly Swamp. (1-3)
255

Mendez, Phil. The Black Snowman. (1-3)
588

Monjo, F. N. Drinking Gourd. (1-3)
32, 417

Neufeld, John. Edgar Allen. (5-6)
342

San Souci, Robert D. The Boy and the Ghost. (1-4)
588

Schroeder, Alan. Ragtime Tumpie. (1-3)
588

Sebestyen, Ouida. Words by Heart. (5-6)
414, 953

Steptoe, John. Stevie. (K-3)
13, 267, 973

Stolz, Mary. Storm in the Night. (K-3)
587

Taylor, Mildred. The Friendship. (4-6)
417, 1023

Taylor, Mildred. The Gold Cadillac. (4-6)
417, 588

Taylor, Mildred. Let the Circle Be Unbroken. (4-6)
413

Taylor, Mildred. Roll of Thunder, Hear My Cry. (5-6)
2, 17, 74, 224, 269, 398, 411, 413, 539, 611, 685,
962, 1020

Taylor, Mildred. Song of the Trees. (4-6)
411, 891

Taylor, Theodore. The Cay. (5-6)
16, 82, 197, 277, 340, 413, 582, 904, 1015, 1046

Udry, Janice. What Mary Jo Shared. (K-2)
12, 407

Wagner, Jane. J. T. (3-6)
34, 298, 472, 856

Williams, Vera B. Cherries and Cherry Pits. (1-3)
409

Yarbrough, Camille. Cornrows. (3-5)
588

AFRO – AMERICANS – FOLKLORE
Hamilton, Virginia. The People Could Fly: American
Black Folktales. (4-6)
588, 594

Harris, Joel Chandler. Jump Again! More Adventures
of Brer Rabbit. (3-4)
588

Keats, Ezra Jack. John Henry. (1-4)
416, 587

Lester, Julius. The Tales of Uncle Remus. (4-5)
588

AFRO – AMERICANS – POETRY
Adoff, Arnold. My Black Me. (5-6)
588

Greenfield, Eloise. Honey, I Love and Other Love
Poems. (2-4)
588

Hughes, Langston. The Dream Keeper and Other
Poems. (4-6)
595

AGRICULTURE – UNITED STATES
Ancona, George. The American Family Farm. (4-6)
588

AIR PILOTS
Provenson, Alice. The Glorious Flight. (K-3)
1, 269, 271, 415

Tessendorf, K. C. Barnstormers and Daredevils. (4-6)
587

AIRPLANES
Berliner, Don. Airplanes of the Future. (4-6)
588

Mayers, Florence Cassin. The National Air Space
Museum ABC. (2-6)
588

Provenson, Alice. The Glorious Flight. (K-3)
1, 269, 271, 415

AIRPLANES – FICTION
Yep, Lawrence. Dragonwings. (5-6)
247, 411, 556, 910

AIRPLANES – POETRY
Livingston, Myra Cohn. Up in the Air. (2-4)
588

AIRPORTS
Barton, Byron. Airports. (P-2)
588

ALAMO (SAN ANTONIO, TEXAS)
Fisher, Leonard Everett. The Alamo. (A)
588

ALAMO (SAN ANTONIO, TEXAS) – BIOGRAPHY
Jakes, John. Susanna of the Alamo. (3-5)
417, 588

ALCOTT, LOUISA MAY
Meigs, Cornelia. Invincible Louisa. (6)
269

ALEXANDER THE GREAT
Wepman, Dennis. Alexander the Great. (6)
595

ALLIGATORS – FICTION
Carter, David A. Surprise Party. (P-2)
412

Mayer, Mercer. There's an Alligator Under My Bed.
(P-1)
587, 1004

McPhail, David. Alligators Are Awful. (P-2)
419

ALPHABET
Anno. Anno's Alphabet. (P-2)
267

Azarian, Mary. A Farmer's Alphabet. (P-1)
11

Balian, Lorna. Humbug Potion: An ABC Cipher.
(P-2)
410

Banks, Kate. Alphabet Soup. (P-2)
18

Baskin, Leonard. Hosie's Alphabet. (A)
11, 587

Bayer, Jane. A My Name Is Alice. (P-1)
410, 588

Brown, Marcia. All Butterflies. (P-1)
587

Crowther, Robert. The Most Amazing Hide and Seek
Alphabet Book. (P-1)
589

Demi. Find the Animal ABC. (P-1)
271

Duke, Kate. Guinea Pig ABC. (K-2)
11, 590

Ehlert, Lois. Eating the Alphabet. (P-1)
412

Elting, Mary. Q Is for Duck: An Alphabet Guessing
Game. (K-3)
1056

Emberly, Ed. Ed Emberly's ABC. (P-1)
11

Feelings, Muriel L. Jambo Means Hello: A Swahili Alphabet Book. (P-1)
412, 416

Gag, Wanda. ABC Bunny. (P-1)
587

Geisert, Arthur. Pigs from A to Z. (1-3)
587

Hague, Kathleen. Alphabears: An ABC Book. (P-1)
587

Hoban, Tana. A B See. (P-2)
11, 407

Hoguet, Susan Ramsey. I Unpacked Grandmother's Trunk. (K-3)
410, 590

Isadora. Rachel. City Seen from A to Z. (P-1)
588

Lobel, Anita. On Market Street. (P-1)
11, 410

McDonald, Suse. Alphabetics. (P-1)
587

Martin, Bill. Chicka Chicka Boom Boom. (P-1)
412, 1054

Mayers, Florence Cassin. The National Air Space Museum ABC. (2-6)
588

Musgrove, Margaret. Ashanti to Zulu. (3-6)
269, 621, 1026

Obligado, Lillian. Faint Frogs Feeling Feverish. (1-3)
257, 266

Seely, Laura L. The Book of Shadowboxes. (P-2)
412

Ungerer, Tomi. Crictor. (K-2)
408, 590

Van Allsburg, Chris. The Z Was Zapped. (P-2)
587

AMERICA—EXPLORATION AND DISCOVERY

D'Aulaire, Ingri. Columbus. (2-4)
407

Fritz, Jean. Where Do You Think You're Going, Christopher Columbus? (3-6)
864

ANATOMY, HUMAN

Cole, Jo Anna. The Magic School Bus Inside the Human Body. (2-5)
1057

ANIMAL FACES

Asch, Frank. I Can Blink. (P-1)
412

ANIMAL FEET

Parnall, Peter. Feet. (P-2)
587

ANIMAL SOUNDS—FICTION

Forrester, Victoria. The Magnificent Moo. (P-2)
271

Ginsburg, Mirra. Good Morning, Chick. (P-2)
254

Tafuri, Nancy. Do Not Disturb. (P-1)
587

ANIMAL TAILS—FICTION

Carle, Eric. Do You Want to Be My Friend? (P-K)
587, 1005

ANIMALS—FICTION

See also Circus Animals, Desert Animals, Farm Animals, Pets, Zoos, and names of specific animals, e.g., Badgers.

Aardema, Verna. Why Mosquitoes Buzz In People's Ears. (1-3)
1, 14, 145, 255, 269, 407, 666, 712, 1010, 1045

Aesop. Aesop's Fables. Illustrated by Michael Hague. (2-4)
591

Allen, Pamela. Who Sank the Boat? (P-2)
415, 1056

Barrett, Judi. Animals Should Definitely Not Wear Clothing. (P-1)
271

Bayer, Jane. A, My Name Is Alice. (P-1)
410, 588

Brett, Jan. Annie and the Wild Animals. (K-3)
255, 587

Brown, Marc. Arthur's Christmas. (K-2)
271

Brown, Marc. Arthur's Eyes. (K-2)
97, 410

Brown, Marc. Arthur's Halloween. (K-2)
271

Brown, Marc. Arthur's Nose. (K-2)
271, 1006

Brown, Marc. Arthur's Thanksgiving. (K-2)
271

Brown, Marc. Arthur's Tooth. (P-2)
273

Brown, Marc. The Bionic Bunny Show. (K-3)
415

Brown, Marcia. Once a Mouse. (1-3)
1, 267, 269, 271, 648

Brown, Margaret Wise. Wait til the Moon Is Full. (P-2)
587

Campbell, Rod. Dear Zoo. (P-1)
1028, 1057

Campbell, Rod. The Pop-Up Pet Shop. (P-2)
1028

Caple, Kathy. The Biggest Nose. (P-2)
272

Carle, Eric. Do You Want to Be My Friend? (P-K)
587, 1005

Cazet, Denys. Frosted Glass. (P-2)
410

Demi. Find the Animal ABC. (P-1)
271

De Regniers, Beatrice Schenk. May I Bring a Friend? (P-2)
1, 12, 269, 407, 710, 800, 1004

de Paola, Tomie. The Hunter and the Animals. (K-1)
587

Elting, Mary. Q Is for Duck: An Alphabet Guessing Game. (K-3)
1056

Ernst, Kathryn. Owl's New Cards. (P-2)
408

Fatio, Louise. The Happy Lion. (P-2)
5
Flack, Marjorie. Ask Mr. Bear. (P-1)
12, 254, 587, 1005
Fox, Mem. Hattie and the Fox. (P-2)
410
Galdone, Paul. The Little Red Hen. (P-2)
1033
Gannett, Ruth Stiles. My Father's Dragon. (3-5)
259
Grahame, Kenneth. The Wind in the Willows. (4-6)
196, 383, 548, 587, 616
Grimm, Jacob. The Breman Town Musicians. (2-4)
252
Heine, Helme. Friends. (P-1)
1039
Hoban, Tana. One Crow. (P-2)
587
Howe, Deborah. Bunnicula. (3-6)
149, 256, 311, 407, 418, 509, 587, 672, 718, 868
Howe, James. The Celery Stalks at Midnight. (4-6)
411
Jonas, Ann. The Trek. (P-2)
587
Kellogg, Steven. Chicken Little. (K-3)
409, 587, 589
Krauss, Ruth. The Happy Day. (P-2)
254
Langstaff, John. Over in the Meadow. (P-1)
744, 1006
Leedy, Loreen. The Furry News: How to Make a Newspaper. (1-3)
412
Lester, Helen. It Wasn't My Fault. (P-2)
271
Lindbergh, Reeve. The Midnight Farm. (P-K)
1056
The Little Red Hen. (P-2)
10, 251, 708, 999
Lloyd, David. Hello, Goodbye. (P-2)
587
Lobel, Arnold. Fables. (3-6)
1, 269, 271, 407, 587, 591, 636, 1002
Marshall, James. Willis. (1-3)
272
Mendoza, Joyce. Need a House? Call Ms. Mouse. (P-2)
410, 588
Milne, A. A. Winnie the Pooh. (1-4)
13, 192, 407, 414, 998
Milne, A. A. The World of Pooh: The Complete Winnie the Pooh and House at Pooh Corner. (1-4)
587
Obligado, Lillian. Faint Frogs Feeling Feverish. (1-3)
257, 266
Ormerod, Jan. The Story of Chicken Licken. (P-1)
587
Payne, Emmy. Katy No-Pocket. (K-2)
18, 587, 736

Petersham, Maud. The Box with Red Wheels. (P-2)
587
Rylant, Cynthia. Night in the Country. (P-2)
416
Sewall, Marcia. Animal Song. (P-2)
587
Sharmat, Marjorie. One Terrific Thanksgiving. (P-3)
271
Steig, William. The Real Thief. (2-4)
988
Tafuri, Nancy. Do Not Disturb. (P-1)
587
Tafuri, Nancy. Have You Seen My Duckling. (P-1)
587
Tafuri, Nancy. Junglewalk. (P-1)
587
Tafuri, Nancy. Rabbit's Morning. (P-2)
254
Tompert, Ann. Nothing Sticks Like a Shadow. (K-2)
742
Waber, Bernard. Dear Hildegarde. (P-2)
408
Waber, Bernard. You Look Ridiculous Said the Rhinoceros to the Hippopotamus. (P-2)
419
Wildsmith, Brian. Wild Animals. (P-2)
587
Williams, Barbara. A Valentine for Cousin Archie. (K-3)
271
Zemach, Margot. The Little Red Hen. (P-2)
587

ANIMALS—AUSTRALIA—FICTION
Trinca, Rod. One Woolly Wombat. (P-1)
1056
ANIMALS—DRAWING
Arnosky, Jim. Sketching Outdoors in Autumn. (A)
587
ANIMALS—FOLKLORE
Aesop. Aesop's Fables. Illustrated by Michael Hague. (2-4)
591
Brown, Marcia. Once a Mouse. (1-3)
1, 267, 269, 271, 648
The Gingerbread Boy. (P-2)
10, 251, 705, 999
Harris, Joel Chandler. Jump Again! More Adventures of Brer Rabbit. (3-4)
588
Lester, Julius. The Tales of Uncle Remus. (4-5)
588
Schmidt, Karen Lee. The Gingerbread Man. (P-2)
18
Tresselt, Alvin. The Mitten. (P-2)
254, 410, 801
ANIMALS—HABITS AND BEHAVIORS
Hader, Berta. Animal Habits and Behavior (K-2)
1

Zolotow, Charlotte. The Sleepy Book. (P-2)
587

ANIMALS, IMAGINARY – FICTION

Blassingame, Wyatt. Pecos Bill Catches a Hidebehind. (1-4)
271

Lofting, Hugh. The Voyages of Doctor Doolittle. (5-6)
269

Peet, Bill. No Such Things. (1-3)
271

Peet, Bill. The Pinkish Purplish Bluish Egg. (K-3)
271

Peet, Bill. The Whingdingdilly. (1-3)
271, 408, 1007

Peet, Bill. The Wump World. (K-3)
419, 1017, 1048

Seuss, Dr. If I Ran the Zoo. (P-3)
996

ANIMALS – MISCELLANEOUS

Pope, Joyce. Do Animals Dream? (4-6)
1026

Simon, Seymour. Animal Fact/Animal Fable. (2-4)
1055

ANIMALS, MYTHICAL – FICTION

Gannett, Ruth Stiles. My Father's Dragon. (3-5)
259

Garrison, Christian. The Dream Eater.
271

Grahame, Kenneth. The Reluctant Dragon. (3-5)
1015

Hodges, Margaret. Saint George and the Dragon. (2-5)
1, 257, 269

Hunter, Mollie. The Kelpie's Pearls. (5-6)
414

Hunter, Mollie. A Stranger Came Ashore. (6)
942

Kellogg, Steven. The Mysterious Tadpole. (K-3)
255, 273

Korschunow, Irina. Adam Draws Himself a Dragon. (2-4)
259

McKinley, Robin. The Hero and the Crown. (6)
2, 269, 411, 1027

Munsch, Robert. The Paper Bag Princess. (1-3)
843

Phillips, Louis. The Brothers Wrong and Wrong Again. (1-3)
271

Sargent, Sarah. Weird Henry Berg. (3-5)
1027

Williams, Jay. Everyone Knows What a Dragon Looks Like. (1-3)
257

Wilson, Sarah. Beware the Dragons. (K-2)
1036

ANIMALS, NOCTURNAL

Cole, Joanna. Large as Life Nighttime Animals. (2-5)
410

ANIMALS, PREHISTORIC – FICTION

Brett, Jan. The First Dog. (1-3)
587

ANIMALS – TREATMENT

Arnold, Caroline. Pets Without Homes. (1-4)
588

ANIMALS – TREATMENT – FICTION

Baylor, Byrd. Hawk, I'm Your Brother. (2-4)
733

Brinckloe, Julie. Fireflies. (P-2)
730

Keats, Ezra Jack. Jennie's Hat. (P-2)
587

Locker, Thomas. Mare on the Hill. (P-2)
587

London, Jack. Call of the Wild. (5-6)
81, 207, 406, 581, 1022

McNulty, Faith. The Lady and the Spider. (P-2)
738

McPhail, David. The Bear's Toothache. (K-2)
782

Morey, Walt. Gentle Ben. (5-6)
198, 516, 887

Rogers, Jean. The Secret Moose. (3-5)
259

Stolz, Mary. Cat Walk. (3-6)
164

ANTS – FICTION

Van Allsburg, Chris. Two Bad Ants. (1-3)
1005

ANTS – FOLKLORE

Aesop. The Ants and the Grasshopper. (K-3)
1002

APARTMENT HOUSES – FICTION

Baker, Leslie. The Third Story Cat. (P-2)
267

Guthrie, Donna. The Witch Who Lives Down the Hall. (1-3)
272, 419

Hurwitz, Johanna. Busybody Nora. (2-4)
279

Levy, Elizabeth. Frankenstein Moved in on the Fourth Floor. (3-5)
152

APPEARANCE – FICTION

Freeman, Don. Dandelion. (K-1)
13, 633, 997

Salus, Naomi Panush. My Daddy's Mustache. (P-2)
408

Small, David. Imogene's Antlers. (P-2)
265, 271, 410, 713

APPLES

Aliki. The Story of Johnny Appleseed. (2-4)
407, 805

Gibbons, Gail. The Seasons of Arnold's Apple Tree. (P-2)
1029, 1057

Kellogg, Steven. Johnny Appleseed. (1-3)
18, 272, 588, 1034

LeSueur, Meridel. Little Brother of the Wilderness: The Story of Johnny Appleseed. (4-6)
417, 588

York, Carol Beach. Johnny Appleseed. (2-4)
11

ANTARCTIC
Bonners, Susan. A Penguin Year. (1-4)
1042

APRIL FOOL'S DAY
Kelley, Emily. April Fool's Day. (3-5)
588

APRIL FOOL'S DAY — FICTION
Jacobs, Leland B. April Fool! (P-2)
271

ARABIA
Balit, Christina. An Arabian Home. (4-6)
588

ARABIA — FICTION
Alexander, Sue. Nadia the Willful. (K-3)
419

ARBOR DAY
Burns, Diane. Arbor Day. (3-5)
588

ARCHEOLOGY
Gibbons, Gail. Sunken Treasure. (4-6)
587

ARCTIC REGIONS — FICTION
Paulsen, Gary. Dogsong. (6)
413, 908

ARMENIA — FOLKLORE
Hogrogian, Nonny. One Fine Day. (K-3)
1, 267, 269, 408, 435, 589, 649

ART
Baylor, Byrd. When Clay Sings. (1-3)
412, 588

ART — FICTION
Bulla, Clyde Robert. The Chalk Box Kid. (2-4)
291, 833

Estes, Eleanor. The Hundred Dresses. (3-5)
61, 297, 411, 520, 855, 1015

Johnson, Crockett. Harold and the Purple Crown. (P-1)
254, 408, 1003

Konigsburg, Elaine. From the Mixed-Up Files of Mrs. Basil E. Frankweiler. (4-6)
2, 16, 60, 211, 269, 345, 405, 414, 515, 595, 674, 721, 912, 1017

Schwartz, Amy. Begin at the Beginning. (K-2)
271

Trevino, Elizabeth Borton de. I, Juan de Pareja. (6)
269

Walsh, Ellen Stoll. Mouse Paint. (P-2)
1005

Testa, Fulvio. If You Take a Pencil. (1-3)
117

ARTIFICIAL SATELLITES
Branley, Franklin. Rockets and Satellites. (1-4)
597

ARTISTS — FRANCE
Raboff, Ernest Lloyd. Pierre Auguste Renoir. (4-6)
595

ASTRONAUTS
Barton, Byron. I Want to Be an Astronaut. (P-2)
588, 1057

Ride, Sally. To Space and Back with Sally Ride. (3-5)
597

AUSTRALIA — FICTION
Baker, Jeannie. Where the Forest Meets the Sea. (P-2)
587

Factor, June. Summer. (P-2)
588

Thiele, Colin. Farmer Schulz's Ducks. (K-3)
587

Trinca, Rod. One Woolly Wombat. (P-1)
1056

AUTHORS, AMERICAN — BIOGRAPHY
Bulla, Clyde Robert. A Grain of Wheat: A Writer Begins. (3-5)
587

Cleary, Beverly. Girl from Yamhill. (5-6)
587

Fritz, Jean. Homesick, My Own Story. (4-6)
373, 411, 587, 758

Meigs, Cornelia. Invincible Louisa. (6)
269

Peet, Bill. Bill Peet: An Autobiography. (4-6)
587

Quackenbush, Robert. Mark Twain? What Kind of Name is That? A Story of Samuel Langhorn Clemens. (6)
587

Stevenson, James. Higher on the Door. (3-4)
587

Stevenson, James. When I Was Nine. (3-4)
587

Yates, Elizabeth. My Diary, My Life. (6)
413

AUTHORS, CANADIAN — BIOGRAPHY
Little, Jean. Little by Little: A Writer's Childhood. (5-6)
587

AUTHORS, ENGLISH — BIOGRAPHY
Collins, David R. The Country Artist: A Story about Beatrix Potter. (4-6)
587

Collins, David R. To the Point: A Story about E. B. White. (4-6)
587

Kamen, Gloria. Storyteller of East and West: Rudyard Kipling. (6)
587

AUTOMOBILES
Parker, Nancy Winslow. The President's Car. (4-6)
588

AUTOMOBILES — FICTION
Burningham, John. Mr. Gumpy's Motorcar. (K-3)
415

Peet, Bill. Jennifer and Josephine. (1-3)
155

Pinkwater, Daniel. Tooth Gnasher Superflash. (P-2)
408

Scarry, Richard. Richard Scarry's Cars and Trucks and Things That Go. (P-2)
588, 1030

Spurr, Elizabeth. Mrs. Minetta's Car Pool. (K-2)
271, 419

AUTOMOBILES—INDUSTRY AND TRADE
Mitchell, Barbara. We'll Race You, Henry. (4-6)
588

AUTUMN
Arnosky, Jim. Sketching Outdoors in Autumn. (A)
587

BABIES. See Infants

BABOONS—FICTION
Lobel, Arnold. Fables. "The Baboon Dances." (3-6)
1002

BABYSITTERS—FICTION
Aruego, Jose. Rockabye Crocodile. (P-2)
587

Coombs, Patricia. Dorrie and the Goblin. (1-3)
271

Day, Alexander. Carl Goes Shopping. (P-1)
1005

Rayner, Mary. Mr. and Mrs. Pig's Evening Out. (K-2)
11, 255

BACTERIA
Berger, Melvin. Germs Make Me Sick. (K-3)
1057

BADGERS—FICTION
Eckert, Allan W. Incident at Hawk's Hill. (6)
561, 918

Grahame, Kenneth. The Wind in the Willows. (4-6)
196, 383, 548, 587, 616

Hoban, Russell. A Baby Sister for Frances. (P-1)
590

Hoban, Russell. A Bargain for Frances. (P-1)
272, 424, 590, 810

Hoban, Russell. Bedtime for Frances. (P-1)
11, 96, 590, 622, 695, 1007

Hoban, Russell. Best Friends for Frances. (P-1)
590

Hoban, Russell. Bread and Jam for Frances. (P-1)
13, 18, 94, 124, 255, 625, 711, 1003

BAHAMAS—FICTION
Greenfield, Eloise. Under the Sunday Tree. (2-6)
588

BAKERS AND BAKERIES—FICTION
Forest, Heather. The Baker's Dozen: A Colonial American Tale. (4-5)
588

BALLOONS—FICTION
Adams, Adrienne. The Great Valentine's Day Balloon Race. (K-3)
271

Calhoun, Mary. Hot Air Henry. (K-2)
11, 1057

Coerr, Eleanor. The Big Balloon Race. (K-3)
415

Du Bose, William Pene. The Twenty-One Balloons. (4-6)
269, 362, 895, 1021

Inkpen, Mike. The Blue Balloon. (1-3)
412

Mari, Isla. The Little Red Balloon. (P-1)
408

BANANAS
Ancona, George. Bananas: From Manolo to Margie. (3-5)
407, 588

BASEBALL
Robbins, Ken. At the Ballpark. (2-5)
587

Sullivan, George. All About Baseball. (4-6)
587

BASEBALL—FICTION
Blassingame, Wyatt. John Henry and Paul Bunyan Play Baseball. (1-4)
271

Cohen, Barbara. Thank You, Jackie Robinson. (4-6)
414

Isadora, Rachel. Max. (1-3)
121, 255

Lord, Bette Bao. In the Year of the Boar and Jackie Robinson. (3-6)
14, 98, 268, 348, 411, 677, 719, 774, 917, 1020

Park, Barbara. Skinnybones. (4-6)
859, 1055

Slote, Alfred. Hang Tough, Paul Mather. (4-6)
276

BASEBALL—POETRY
Thayer, Ernest Laurence. Casey at the Bat. (2-6)
594, 1018

Thayer, Ernest Laurence. Casey at the Bat. Illus. by Paul Frame. (2-6)
587

Thayer, Ernest Laurence. Casey at the Bat. Illus. by Patricia Pollaco. (2-6)
587

BASKETBALL
Aaseng, Nate. Basketball: You Are the Coach. (4-6)
413

Anderson, Dave. The Story of Basketball. (4-6)
413

BATHS—FICTION
Wood, Audrey. King Bidgood's in the Bath. (P-2)
587, 591

BEACHES—FICTION
Kimmelman, Leslie. Frannie's Fruits.
588

BEARS—FICTION
See also Teddy Bears
Alexander, Martha. Blackboard Bear. (K-2)
113

Asch, Frank. Bear Shadow. (P-2)
271, 781, 1057

Asch, Frank. Goodbye House. (P-1)
588

Asch, Frank. Happy Birthday Moon. (P-2)
18

Asch, Frank. Mooncake. (K-1)
597

Berenstain, Stan. Bears on Wheels. (P-2)
1056

Berenstain, Stan. Berenstain Bears' Trouble with
Money. (P-3)
272

Bond, Michael. A Bear Called Paddington. (2-5)
190, 451, 593

Brett, Jan. Goldilocks and the Three Bears. (P-2)
18

Bunting, Eve. The Valentine Bears. (P-2)
271, 1001

Butler, Jan. Too Many Eggs: A Counting Book.
(P-1)
412

Degen, Bruce. Jamberry. (P-2)
698

Eisen, Armand. Goldilocks and the Three Bears.
(P-2)
1031

Galdone, Paul. The Three Bears. (P-2)
265, 587

Grimm, Jacob. Show White and Rose Red. (1-4)
264

Kjelgaard, Jim. Big Red. (6)
552

Mack, Stan. Ten Bears in My Bed. (P-2)
1056

Marshall, James. Goldilocks and the Three Bears. (P-2)
588

Marshall, James. What's the Matter with Carruthers?
(P-2)
587

Mayer, Mercer. East O' the Sun and West O' the Moon.
267

McCloskey, Robert. Blueberries for Sal. (P-2)
11, 12, 255, 265, 271, 587, 624, 784, 998

McPhail, David. The Bear's Toothache. (K-2)
782

Martin, Bill. Brown Bear, Brown Bear, What Do You
See? (P-2)
12, 94, 258, 412, 708, 997, 1056

Milne, A. A. Winnie the Pooh. (1-4)
13, 192, 407, 414, 998

Milne, A. A. The World of Pooh: The Complete
Winnie the Pooh and House at Pooh Corner. (1-4)
587

Minarik, Else Holmelund. Father Bear Comes Home.
(P-2)
591

Minarik, Else Holmelund. Kiss for Little Bear. (P-2)
591

Minarik, Else Holmelund. Little Bear. (P-1)
12, 591

Minarik, Else Holmelund. Little Bear's Friend. (P-2)
591

Minarik, Else Holmelund. Little Bear's Visit. (P-2)
114, 591

Murphy, Jill. What's Next Baby Bear? (K-2)
808

Peet, Bill. Big Bad Bruce. (1-3)
97, 255, 271, 714, 998

Polushkin, Maria. Bubba and Bubba. (K-3)
271

Rupprecht, Siegfried P. The Tale of the Vanishing
Rainbow. (P-2)
588

Sharmat, Marjorie. I'm Terrific. (K-2)
255, 271, 408

Tashlin, Frank. The Bear That Wasn't. (P-1)
983

The Three Bears. (P-1)
251, 706, 999

Turkle, Brinton. Deep in the Forest. (P-2)
104, 267, 1006

Ward, Lynd. The Biggest Bear. (1-3)
1, 13, 142, 255, 269, 271, 623, 812, 1003

Wildsmith, Brian. The Lazy Bear. (P-2)
254

Winter, Paula. The Bear and the Fly. (P-1)
105

BEAVERS—FICTION

Minarik, Else Holmelund. Percy and the Five Houses.
(P-2)
587

BEDTIME—FICTION

Bourgeois, Paulette. Franklin in the Dark. (P-1)
790, 1054

Bowers, Kathleen Rice. At This Very Minute. (P-2)
410

Brown, Margaret Wise. Goodnight Moon. (P-1)
254, 705, 997

Crowe, Robert L. Clyde Monster. (P-1)
410

Hoban, Russell. Bedtime for Frances. (P-1)
11, 96, 590, 622, 695, 1007

Jonas, Ann. The Quilt. (P-2)
587

Kitamura, Satoshi. When Sheep Cannot Sleep. (P-1)
1056

Lindbergh, Reeve. The Midnight Farm. (P-K)
1056

Mack, Stan. Ten Bears in My Bed. (P-2)
1056

Marshall, James. What's the Matter with Carruthers?
(P-2)
587

Mayer, Mercer. There's a Nightmare in My Closet. (P-1)
11, 94, 108, 254, 267, 408, 445, 659, 703, 1003

Mayer, Mercer. There's an Alligator Under My Bed.
(P-1)
587, 1004

Murphy, Jill. What's Next Baby Bear? (K-2)
808

Ormerod, Jan. Moonlight. (P-1)
992

Rees, Mary. Ten in a Bed. (P-2)
587

Shepperson, Rob. The Sandman. (P-2)
272

BEDOUINS

Balit, Christina. An Arabian Home. (4-6)
588

BURIED TREASURE – FICTION

Mowat, Farley. Lost in the Barrens. (5-6)
184

Stevenson, Robert Louis. Treasure Island. (5-6)
91, 401, 414, 577, 614, 964

BUTCHERS – FICTION

Yorinks, Arthur. Louis the Fish. (K-3)
598

BUTTERFLIES – FICTION

See also Caterpillars

Carle, Eric. The Very Hungry Caterpillar. (P-2)
11, 12, 18, 94, 123, 254, 265, 407, 589, 705, 998, 1035, 1056, 1057

Brown, Marcia. All Butterflies. (P-1)
587

Brown, Ruth. If at First You Do Not See. (K-3)
1057

Grifalconi, Ann. Darkness and the Butterfly. (P-2)
410

Kent, Jack. The Caterpillar and the Polliwog. (P-2)
726, 786

CALDECOTT MEDAL AWARD

Aardema, Verna. Why Mosquitoes Buzz in People's Ears. (1-3)
1, 14, 145, 255, 269, 407, 666, 712, 1010, 1045

Ackerman, Karen. The Song and Dance Man. (K-2)
269, 587, 1011

Bemelmans, Ludwig. Madeline's Rescue. (P-2)
1, 11, 138, 269, 271, 590

Brown, Margaret Wise. The Little Island. (1-3)
1, 269, 711, 739

Brown, Marcia. Once a Mouse. (1-3)
1, 267, 269, 271, 648

Burton, Virginia. The Little House. (K-2)
1, 13, 95, 269, 407, 588, 643, 797, 1004

Cendrars, Blaise. Shadow. (1-3)
1, 269, 415

Cooney, Barbara. Chanticleer and the Fox. (2-6)
1, 269

D'Aulaire, Ingri. Abraham Lincoln. (2-4)
1, 11, 269, 591

De Regniers, Beatrice Schenk. May I Bring a Friend? (P-2)
1, 12, 269, 407, 710, 800, 1004

Emberley, Barbara. Drummer Hoff. (P-1)
1, 254, 269, 587

Ets, Marie Hall. Nine Days to Christmas. (1-3)
1, 269, 588

Goble, Paul. The Girl Who Loved Wild Horses. (1-4)
1, 137, 255, 267, 269, 271

Hader, Berta. The Big Snow. (K-2)
1, 269

Haley, Gail. A Story, A Story. (K-3)
1, 269, 409, 592, 1045

Hall, Donald. Ox-Cart Man. (K-3)
1, 269, 271, 416, 588, 714

Handforth, Thomas. Mei Li. (1-3)
1, 269

Hodges, Margaret. Saint George and the Dragon. (2-5)
1, 257, 269

Hogrogian, Nonny. One Fine Day. (K-3)
1, 267, 269, 408, 435, 589, 649

Keats, Ezra Jack. Snow Day. (P-2)
1, 12, 18, 128, 265, 269, 407, 654, 804, 998, 1057

Lathrop, Dorothy P. Animals of the Bible. (3-6)
1, 269

Lawson, Robert. They Were Strong and Good. (4-6)
1, 269

Lobel, Arnold. Fables. (3-6)
1, 269, 271, 407, 587, 591, 636

McCloskey, Robert. Make Way for Ducklings. (P-1)
1, 12, 95, 269, 271, 272, 407, 415, 430, 646, 799, 1008

McCloskey, Robert. Time of Wonder. (A)
1, 269

McDermott, Gerald. Arrow to the Sun. (1-4)
1, 269, 587, 1041

Milhous, Katherine. The Egg Tree. (K-3)
1, 269

Musgrove, Margaret. Ashanti to Zulu. (3-6)
1, 269, 621, 1026

Ness, Evaline. Sam, Bangs and Moonshine. (K-3)
1, 41, 160, 269, 271, 489, 587, 715, 825

Nic Leodhas, Sorche. Always Room for One More. (K-2)
1, 269

Perrault, Charles. Cinderella or the Little Glass Slipper. Pictures by Marcia Brown. (P-2)
1, 269

Petersham, Maud. The Rooster Crows. (K-2)
1, 269

Politi, Leo. Song of the Swallows. (K-3)
1, 269, 407

Provenson, Alice. The Glorious Flight. (K-3)
1, 269, 271, 415

Ransome, Arthur. The Fool of the World and the Flying Ship. (2-5)
1, 269, 407

Robbins, Ruth. Baboushka and the Three Kings. (2-4)
1, 269, 588

Sendak, Maurice. Where the Wild Things Are. (P-3)
1, 12, 18, 27, 95, 118, 255, 265, 269, 271, 407, 449, 664, 704, 708, 1009

Spier, Peter. Noah's Ark. (P-2)
1, 269

Steig, William. Sylvester and the Magic Pebble. (K-2)
1, 13, 97, 144, 255, 265, 269, 271, 272, 444, 587, 590, 658, 708, 806, 1009

Thurber, James. Many Moons. (2-4)
1, 269, 587, 987

Tresselt, Alvin. White Snow, Bright Snow. (P-2)
1, 269

Udry, Janice May. A Tree Is Nice. (K-2)
1, 12, 269, 415, 1057

Van Allsburg, Chris. Jumanji. (K-6)
1, 15, 265, 269, 271, 411, 1055

Van Allsburg, Chris. The Polar Express. (A)
1, 269, 271, 438, 591, 1016

Ward, Lynd. Biggest Bear. (1-3)
1, 13, 142, 255, 269, 271, 623, 812, 1003

Will. Finders Keepers. (K-2)
1, 269

Yolen, Jane. Owl Moon. (P-3)
1, 18, 265, 269, 587, 1015

Yorinks, Arthur. Hey, Al. (1-3)
1, 269, 271, 587

Zemach, Harve. Duffy and the Devil. (1-4)
1, 269, 587

CAMELS—FICTION
Lobel, Arnold. Fables. "The Camel Dances." (3-6)
1002

CAMPING—FICTION
Cleary, Beverly. Runaway Ralph. (3-5)
173, 487

Delton, Judy. Camp Ghost-Away. (2-4)
274

McPhail, David. Pig Pig Goes to Camp. (P-2)
271

Parish, Peggy. Amelia Bedelia Goes Camping. (1-3)
135

Smith, Robert Kimmel. Jelly Belly. (4-6)
525

Stork, Catherine. Sophie's Knapsack. (P-2)
588

Tafuri, Nancy. Do Not Disturb. (P-1)
587

CANADA—FICTION
Andrews, Jan. Very Last First Time. (K-3)
415, 588

Paulsen, Gary. Hatchet. (5-6)
85, 249, 371, 413, 558, 1055

CANADA—BRITISH COLUMBIA—FICTION
Blades, Ann. Mary of Mile 18. (1-3)
587

CANADA—KLONDIKE GOLD FIELDS—FICTION
London, Jack. Call of the Wild. (5-6)
81, 207, 406, 581, 1022

CANADA—NORTHWEST—FICTION
Mowat, Farley. Lost in the Barrens. (5-6)
184

CANADA—ONTARIO—FICTION
Burnford, Sheila. The Incredible Journey. (5-6)
7, 86, 181, 347, 418, 562, 603, 919, 957

CANADA—PRINCE EDWARD ISLAND—FICTION
Montgomery, Lucy M. Anne of Green Gables. (4-6)
201, 368, 413

CANADA—SASKATCHEWAN—FICTION
Eckert, Allan W. Incident at Hawk's Hill. (6)
561, 918

Mowat, Farley. Owls in the Family. (4-6)
172, 413, 481, 592, 878

CANADA—YUKON VALLEY—FICTION
London, Jack. Call of the Wild. (5-6)
81, 207, 406, 581, 1022

CANADA—YUKON VALLEY—POETRY
Service, Robert F. The Cremation of Sam McGee. (5-6)
594

CAR POOLS—FICTION
Spurr, Elizabeth. Mrs. Minetta's Car Pool. (K-2)
271, 419

CARIBBEAN AREA—FICTION
Taylor, Theodore. The Cay. (5-6)
16, 82, 197, 277, 340, 413, 582, 904, 1015, 1046

CARVER, GEORGE WASHINGTON
Aliki. A Weed is a Flower: The Life of George Washington Carver. (3-5)
588

CASTLES—FICTION
Winthrop, Elizabeth. Castle in the Attic. (4-6)
419, 587, 1027

CATERPILLARS—FICTION
See also Butterflies
Brown, Ruth. If at First You Do Not See. (K-3)
1057

Carle, Eric. The Very Hungry Caterpillar. (P-2)
11, 12, 18, 94, 123, 254, 265, 407, 589, 705, 998, 1035, 1056, 1057

Kent, Jack. The Caterpillar and the Polliwog. (P-2)
726, 786

CATS
Patterson, Dr. Francine. Koko's Kitten. (3-5)
15, 737

CATS—FICTION
Babbitt, Natalie. Nellie, a Cat on Her Own. (K-2)
1006

Baker, Leslie. The Third Story Cat. (P-2)
267

Balian, Lorna. Leprechauns Never Lie. (K-3)
271, 1001

Brett, Jan. Annie and the Wild Animals. (K-3)
255, 587

Brandenberg, Franz. Aunt Nina and Her Nieces and Nephews. (P-2)
588

Burnford, Sheila. The Incredible Journey. (5-6)
7, 86, 181, 347, 418, 562, 603, 919, 957

Calhoun, Mary. Cross Country Cat. (1-3)
587

Calhoun, Mary. Hot Air Henry. (K-2)
11, 1057

Calhoun, Mary. Wobble the Witch Cat. (K-2)
11

Cleary, Beverly. Socks. (3-4)
261, 330, 592

Coatsworth, Elizabeth. The Cat Who Went to Heaven. (3-5)
269

Flack, Marjorie. Angus and the Cats. (P-1)
11

Fox, Paula. The One-Eyed Cat. (5-6)
243, 376, 419, 531, 682, 928

Gag, Wanda. Millions of Cats. (P-2)
254, 265, 587, 997

Hazen, Barbara. Shook Tight Times. (K-2)
265, 588

Holmes, Efner Tudor. The Christmas Cat. (K-2)
271

Hooks, William H. Pioneer Cat. (3-4)
417, 588

Keats, Ezra Jack. Hi Cat! (P-2)
255

LeGuin, Ursula. A Visit from Dr. Katz. (P-2)
587

Ness, Evaline. Sam, Bangs and Moonshine. (K-3)
1, 41, 160, 269, 271, 489, 587, 715, 825

Neville, Emily Cheney. It's Like This, Cat. (5-6)
218, 269, 524

Peet, Bill. Jennifer and Josephine. (1-3)
155

Selden, George. Cricket in Times Square. (3-6)
57, 239, 314, 414, 461, 587, 869

Seuss, Dr. Cat in the Hat. (P-2)
590

Smith, Miriam. Annie and Moon. (P-2)
588

Smyth, Glenda. A Pet for Mrs. Arbuckle. (P-2)
419

Stolz, Mary. Cat Walk. (3-6)
164

Titus, Eve. Anatole and the Cat. (1-3)
11

Turkle, Brinton. Do Not Open. (K-2)
255

Viorst, Judith. Tenth Good Thing About Barney. (K-3)
11, 13, 45, 265, 497, 974, 1009, 1054

Wagner, Jane. J. T. (3-6)
34, 298, 472, 856

CATS – POETRY
Lobel, Arnold. The Rose in My Garden. (K-3)
1056

Lobel, Arnold. Whiskers and Rhymes. (K-3)
591

CHAIRS
Williams, Vera. A Chair for My Mother. (P-3)
22, 255, 265, 271, 588, 628, 713, 787, 814

CHAPMAN, JOHN
Aliki. The Story of Johnny Appleseed. (2-4)
407, 805

Kellogg, Steven. Johnny Appleseed. (1-3)
18, 272, 588, 1034

LeSueur, Meridel. Little Brother of the Wilderness: The Story of Johnny Appleseed.
417, 588

York, Carol Beach. Johnny Appleseed. (2-4)
11

CHARACTERISTICS – ACCEPTING RESPONSIBILITY – FICTION
Bauer, Marion Dane. On My Honor. (6)
270, 353, 405, 411, 413, 927, 1015

Bulla, Clyde Robert. Shoeshine Girl. (3-5)
329, 414, 418, 1016

Cleary, Beverly. Henry and the Clubhouse. (3-5)
261, 470

Cleary, Beverly. Mouse and the Motorcycle. (2-5)
37, 169, 259, 418, 479, 587, 875

Gramatky, Hardie. Little Toot. (P-1)
997

CHARACTERISTICS – AMBITION – FICTION
Peet, Bill. Chester the Worldly Pig. (1-3)
13, 271, 409, 1006

CHARACTERISTICS – BEING DIFFERENT
White, E. B. Stuart Little. (3-6)
8, 43, 161, 256, 494, 712, 1013

CHARACTERISTICS – CLEVERNESS – FICTION
Babbitt, Natalie. The Search for Delicious. (4-6)
1027

Boden, Alice. The Field of Buttercups. (P-2)
408

Cole, Joanna. Doctor Change. (1-3)
410

Dahl, Roald. Danny, the Champion of the World. (4-6)
1016

Dahl, Roald. Fantastic Mr. Fox. (4-6)
317, 465, 637, 465

Grahame, Kenneth. The Reluctant Dragon. (3-5)
1015

Kellogg, Steven. Much Bigger Than Martin. (K-2)
1056

Lionni, Leo. Inch By Inch. (P-1)
258, 407, 1056

Lobel, Arnold. Mouse Soup. (K-2)
840

Marshall, Edward. Troll Country. (K-2)
828

Munsch, Robert. The Paper Bag Princess. (1-3)
843

Norton, Mary. The Borrowers. (3-6)
54, 193, 414, 506, 587, 593, 900

O'Brien, Robert C. Mrs. Frisby and the Rats of NIMH. (4-6)
2, 16, 66, 99, 213, 268, 269, 374, 414, 568, 681, 776, 925, 1021

Rayner, Mary. Mr. and Mrs. Pig's Evening Out. (K-2)
11, 255

Rockwell, Anne. The Bump in the Night. (P-2)
408

Small, David. Paper John. (P-2)
410

Steig, William. Doctor DeSoto. (P-3)
271, 634, 729, 817

Turkle, Brinton. Do Not Open. (L-2)
255

Wood, Audrey. Heckedy Peg. (K-3)
265, 266

CHARACTERISTICS – CLEVERNESS – FOLKLORE
Aesop. The Crow and the Pitcher. (2-4)
1002

Bang, Molly. Wiley and the Hairy Man. (1-3)
419

Brown, Marcia. Stone Soup. (K-3)
13, 96, 255, 271, 440, 655, 712, 1009

Galdone, Paul. The Monkey and the Crocodile. (1-3)
1004

Galdone, Paul. The Three Little Pigs. (P-2)
18

The Three Little Pigs. (P-2)
10, 251, 999

Zemach, Margot. The Three Little Pigs. (P-2)
588

CHARACTERISTICS – COURAGE – FICTION

Andersen, Hans Christian. The Snow Queen. (1-4)
263

Avi. Wolf Rider. (7)
1025

Bunting, Eve. How Many Days to America? (1-3)
266, 588

Burnford, Sheila. The Incredible Journey. (5-6)
7, 86, 181, 347, 418, 562, 603, 919, 957

Christopher, John. The White Mountains. (5-6)
189, 382, 595

Collier, James. War Comes to Willy Freeman. (4-6)
768

Collodi, Carlo. The Adventures of Pinnochio. (3-6)
999, 1017

Collodi, Carlo. The Adventures of Pinnochio. Illus. by Roberto Innocenti. (3-6)
587

Dalgliesh, Alice. The Courage of Sarah Noble. (3-5)
417, 460, 631, 772

Edmonds, Walter D. Matchlock Gun. (2-4)
269

Farley, Walter. The Black Stallion. (4-6)
504, 867, 1019, 1055

Forbes, Esther. Johnny Tremain. (4-6)
220, 256, 269, 392, 417, 564, 605, 760, 959, 1023, 1052

Fox, Paula. The Slave Dancer. (6)
2, 227, 269, 573, 939, 1023

Garfield, James B. Follow My Leader. (4-6)
370, 411

George, Jean Craighead. Julie of the Wolves. (6)
2, 88, 221, 269, 277, 393, 405, 406, 565, 606, 775, 923

George, Jean Craighead. My Side of the Mountain. (5-6)
236, 268, 352, 570, 609, 777, 877, 1020

Gramatky, Hardie. Little Toot. (P-1)
997

Green, Norma. The Hole in the Dike. (P-2)
587

Hort, Lenny. Boy Who Held Back the Sea. (K-3)
588

Karl, Jean. Beloved Benjamin is Waiting. (5-6)
587

Knight, Eric. Lassie Come Home. (4-6)
1021

Lowery, Lois. Number the Stars. (4-6)
2, 6, 269, 277, 375, 529, 764

Mayer, Mercer. Liza Lou and the Yeller Belly Swamp. (1-3)
255

McSwigan, M. Snow Treasure. (5-6)
174, 380, 492, 940, 1023

Mowat, Farley. Lost in the Barrens. (5-6)
184

Naidoo, Beverly. Journey to Jo'Burg. (5-6)
321, 761

Nixon, Joan Lowery. The Stalker. (6)
1025

O'Brien, Robert C. Mrs. Frisby and the Rats of NIMH. (4-6)
2, 16, 66, 99, 213, 268, 269, 374, 414, 568, 681, 776, 925, 1021

O'Dell, Scott. Island of the Blue Dolphins. (5-6)
2, 17, 63, 99, 212, 268, 269, 349, 405, 523, 594, 604, 718, 921, 958, 1019

O'Dell, Scott. Sarah Bishop. (5-6)
6, 417, 933

O'Dell, Scott. Sing Down the Moon. (5-6)
245, 358, 411, 542, 767, 937, 1023

Paulsen, Gary. Hatchet. (5-6)
85, 249, 371, 413, 558, 1055

Piper, Watty. The Little Engine That Could. (P-1)
94, 587, 997

Slote, Alfred. Hang Tough, Paul Mather. (4-6)
276

Sperry, Armstrong. Call It Courage. (5-6)
2, 5, 17, 56, 226, 269, 339, 405, 554, 594, 601, 721, 901, 1014

Steig, William. Abel's Island. (3-5)
47, 587, 668

Steig, William. Brave Irene. (K-3)
271

Titus, Eve. Anatole and the Cat. (1-3)
11

Tolkien, J. R. R. The Hobbit. (4-6)
391, 559, 1022

Ullman, James Ramsey. Banner in the Sky. (4-6)
898

Voigt, Cynthia. The Homecoming. (5-6)
411, 560, 915

Williams, Linda. The Little Old Woman Who Was Not Afraid of Anything. (P-2)
1054

Winthrop, Elizabeth. Castle in the Attic. (4-6)
419, 587, 1027

Wojciechowska, Maia. Shadow of a Bull. (6)
2, 269, 571, 935

CHARACTERISTICS – CURIOSITY – FICTION

Allen, Jeffrey. Nosey Mrs. Rat. (K-2)
271

Flack, Marjorie. Angus and the Cat. (P-1)
11

Flack, Marjorie. Angus and the Ducks. (P-1)
587

Kipling, Rudyard. The Elephant's Child. (1-3)
14, 267, 419, 587

Lionni, Leo. Tillie and the Wall. (P-2)
587

Rey, H. A. Curious George. (P-2)
12, 95, 122, 272, 426, 590

Rey, H. A. Curious George Takes a Job. (P-2)
255

Rey, Margaret. Curious George Flies a Kite. (P-2)
815

Twain, Mark. The Prince and the Pauper. (6)
1022

CHARACTERISTICS – DETERMINATION – FICTION

George, Jean Craighead. My Side of the Mountain. (5-6)
236, 268, 352, 570, 609, 777, 877, 1020

Seuss, Dr. Horton Hears a Who. (P-3)
13, 590

Slate, Joseph. How Little Porcupine Played Christmas. (P-2)
272

Spear, Elizabeth George. The Witch of Blackbird Pond. (5-6)
2, 79, 230, 269, 384, 406, 417, 579, 594, 617, 896, 950, 1021

Spier, Peter. People. (A)
416

Wojciechowska, Maia. Shadow of a Bull. (6)
2, 269, 571, 935

Yashima, Taro. Crow Boy. (1-3)
13, 31, 96, 255, 407, 587, 632, 979

CHARACTERISTICS – KINDNESS – FICTION

Aruego, Jose. Rockabye Crocodile. (P-2)
587

Bang, Molly. The Paper Crane. (K-3)
267, 271, 410

Clements, Andrew. Big Al. (P-2)
587

Fleischman, Paul. The Scarebird. (P-2)
587

Peet, Bill. Kermit, the Hermit. (K-2)
96, 1055

Steig, William. Amos and Boris. (1-3)
11, 407, 409

Steptoe, John. Mufaro's Beautiful Daughters. (K-3)
257, 416, 1049

Ungerer, Tomi. Zarelda's Ogre. (P-2)
11

Wagner, Jane. J. T. (3-6)
34, 298, 472, 856

Wildsmith, Brian. Hunter and His Dog. (P-2)
419

Williams, Jay. Everone Knows What a Dragon Looks Like. (1-3)
257

CHARACTERISTICS – KINDNESS – FOLKLORE

Aesop. The Bee and the Dove. (2-4)
1002

Aesop. The Lion and the Mouse. (2-4)
250, 1002

Grimm, Jacob. The Elves and the Cobbler. (1-4)
264

Grimm, Jacob. Snow White and Rose Red. (1-4)
264

Polacco, Patricia. Rechenka's Eggs. (2-4)
588

Yagawa, Sumiko. The Crane Wife. (K-3)
419

CHARACTERISTICS – LAZINESS – FICTION

Jeffers, Susan. The Wild Robin. (P-2)
587

Polushkin, Maria. Bubba and Babba. (K-3)
271

Wildsmith, Brian. The Lazy Bear. (P-2)
254

CHARACTERISTICS – LAZINESS – FOLKLORE

Aesop. The Ants and the Grasshopper. (K-3)
1002

Galdone, Paul. The Three Little Pigs. (P-2)
18

The Little Red Hen. (P-2)
10, 251, 708, 999

The Three Little Pigs. (P-2)
10, 251, 999

Zemach, Margot. The Little Red Hen. (P-2)
587

Zemach, Margot. The Three Little Pigs. (P-2)
588

CHARACTERISTICS – LOYALTY – FICTION

Aliki. The Two of Them. (P-2)
588

Burton, Virginia. Mike Mulligan and His Steam Shovel. (K-2)
11, 12, 431, 709, 741, 998, 1010, 1057

Butterworth, Oliver. The Enormous Egg. (3-6)
59, 316, 414, 463, 886, 1016

Collodi, Carlo. The Adventures of Pinnochio. (3-6)
999, 1017

Collodi, Carlo. The Adventures of Pinnochio. Illus. by Robert Innocenti. (3-6)
587

Knight, Eric. Lassie Come Home. (4-6)
1021

Lewis, C. S. The Lion, the Witch and the Wardrobe. (4-6)
16, 65, 199, 277, 322, 414, 474, 587, 595, 607, 717, 874, 1020

Nixon, Joan Lowery. The Stalker. (6)
1025

Richter, Conrad. Light in the Forest. (6)
194, 394, 406, 567, 763

Tolkien, J. R. R. The Hobbit. (4-6)
391, 559, 1022

Viorst, Judith. Rosie and Michael. (K-2)
271

CHARACTERISTICS – PERSEVERANCE – FICTION

Andersen, H. C. The Steadfast Tin Soldier. (1-4)
14

Burton, Virginia. Katy and the Big Snow. (P-2)
255, 699, 1003

Byars, Betsy. Trouble River. (4-6)
256, 334, 414, 894

Heyward, Dubose. The Country Bunny and the Little Gold Shoes. (P-2)
271, 1001

Piper, Watty. The Little Engine That Could. (P-1)
94, 587, 997

Seuss, Dr. Horton Hatches the Egg. (P-3)
18, 407, 419

CHARACTERISTICS – PERSEVERANCE – FOLKLORE

Aesop. The Rabbit and the Tortoise. (2-4)
250, 1002

CHARACTERISTICS – PRIDE – FICTION
Duvoisin, Roger. Petunia. (K-2)
11, 12, 407, 587, 1006
Rockwell, Thomas. How to Eat Fried Worms. (4-6)
99, 259, 296, 414, 418, 519, 676, 836, 1014, 1055
Steptoe, John. Mufaro's Beautiful Daughters. (K-3)
257, 416, 1049
Taylor, Mildred. The Friendship. (4-6)
417, 1023

CHARACTERISTICS – PRIDE – FUTURE
Aesop. The Proud Turtle. (2-4)
1002

CHARACTERISTICS – PROCRASTINATION – FICTION
Allard, Harry. I Will Not Go to the Market Today. (P-2)
271
Schwartz, Amy. Begin at the Beginning. (K-2)
271

CHARACTERISTICS – PROCRASTINATION – FOLKLORE
Aesop. The Ants and the Grasshopper. (K-3)
1002

CHARACTERISTICS – RESOURCEFULNESS – FICTION
Cleaver, Vera. Where the Lilies Bloom. (5-6)
769, 948
Garfield, Leon. Young Nick and Jubilee. (4-6)
6
George, Jean Craighead. My Side of the Mountain. (5-6)
236, 268, 352, 570, 609, 777, 877, 1020
Giff, Patricia Reilly. Fourth Grade Celebrity. (4-6)
467
O'Dell, Scott. Island of the Blue Dolphin. (5-6)
2, 17, 63, 99, 212, 268, 269, 349, 405, 523, 594, 604, 718, 921, 958, 1019
Peterson, John. The Littles. (4-6)
267, 300, 477
Sperry, Armstrong. Call It Courage. (5-6)
2, 5, 17, 56, 226, 269, 339, 405, 554, 594, 601, 721, 901, 1014
Wilder, Laura Ingalls. The Long Winter. (3-6)
262, 417, 478, 608

CHARACTERISTICS – SELFISHNESS – FICTION
Lionni, Leo. It's Mine. (K-3)
415
Mueller, Virginia. A Playhouse for Monster. (P-1)
588
Seuss, Dr. How the Grinch Stole Christmas. (P-3)
266

CHARACTERISTICS – SHARING – FICTION
Brown, Marcia. Stone Soup. (K-3)
13, 96, 255, 271, 440, 655, 712, 1009
Hutchins, Pat. The Doorbell Rang. (P-2)
410, 1056

CHARACTERISTICS – VANITY – FICTION
Andersen, Hans Christian. The Emperor's New Clothes. (1-4)
253, 263, 635, 1007

Sharmat, Marjorie. I'm Terrific. (K-2)
255, 271, 408
Stevens, Janet. The Emperor's New Clothes. (1-4)
419

CHARACTERISTICS – VANITY – FOLKLORE
Brown, Marcia. Once a Mouse. (1-3)
1, 267, 269, 271, 648
Grimm, Jacob. Snow White and the Seven Dwarfs. (P-2)
252, 264, 999

CHARACTERISTICS – VEGITARIANISM – FICTION
Hurwitz, Johanna. Aldo Applesauce. (4-6)
147

CHICKENS – FICTION
Allard, Harry. I Will Not Go To Market Today. (P-2)
271
Coerr, Eleanor. The Josefina Quilt Story. (1-3)
259, 588
Fox, Mem. Hattie and the Fox. (P-2)
410
Hutchins, Pat. Rosie's Walk. (P-1)
12, 18, 112, 254, 409, 589, 653, 709
Kasza, Keiko. The Wolf's Chicken Stew. (P-1)
1056
Kellogg, Steven. Chicken Little. (K-3)
409, 587, 589
Lionni, Leo. Inch by Inch. (P-1)
258, 407, 1056
Pinkwater, Daniel Manus. The Hoboken Chicken Emergency. (3-5)
168

CHICKENS – FOLKLORE
Cooney, Barbara. Chanticleer and the Fox. (2-6)
1, 269
Galdone, Paul. The Little Red Hen. (P-2)
1033
Galdone, Paul. Henny Penny. (P-2)
587
Ginsburg, Mirra. Good Morning, Chick. (P-2)
254
Henny Penny. (P-2)
10, 251
The Little Red Hen. (P-2)
10, 251, 708, 999
Ormerod, Jan. The Story of Chicken Licken. (P-1)
587
Zemach, Margot. The Little Red Hen. (P-2)
587

CHILD ABUSE – FICTION
Byars, Betsy. The Pinballs. (4-6)
69, 98, 270, 355, 418, 535, 683, 929
Greene, Bette. The Summer of My German Soldier. (6)
400, 576, 963
Hahn, Mary Downing. Daphne's Book. (4-6)
341
Hunt, Irene. The Lottery Rose. (6)
924
Karl, Jean. Beloved Benjamin is Waiting. (5-6)
587

CHILDREN – EMPLOYMENT – FICTION
Beatty, Patricia. Turn Homeward, Hannalee
417, 588
CHILDREN – EMPLOYMENT – BIOGRAPHY
Bethell, Jean. Three Cheers for Mother Jones. (P-2)
11
CHILDREN AS AUTHORS
Baskin, Leonard. Hosie's Zoo. (A)
587
Baskin, Leonard. Hosie's Alphabet. (A)
11, 587
CHILDREN OF PRISONERS – FICTION
Armstrong, William H. Sounder. (5-6)
90, 99, 225, 269, 399, 405, 406, 419, 574, 612, 688,
722, 892, 941
Burch, Robert. Queenie Peavy. (5-6)
684
CHINA – FICTION
DeJong, Meindert. The House of Sixty Fathers. (4-6)
417, 588
Flack, Marjorie. The Story About Ping. (P-1)
272, 589, 997
Fritz, Jean. Homesick: My Own Story. (4-6)
373, 411, 587, 758
Handforth, Thomas. Mei Li. (1-3)
1, 269
Jensen, Helen Zane. When Panda Came to Our House.
(P-2)
410
Lewis, Elizabeth. Young Fu of the Upper Yangtze. (6)
269
Lobel, Arnold. Ming Lo Moves the Mountain. (K-2)
265
Williams, Jay. Everyone Knows What a Dragon Looks
Like. (1-3)
257
CHINA – FOLKLORE
Chrisman, Arthur Bowie. Shen of the Sea. (5-6)
269
Louie, Al-Ling. Yeh-Shen: A Cinderella Story from
China. (P-3)
15, 257, 591
Mosel, Arlene. Tikki Tikki Tembo. (P-2)
255, 271, 447, 660, 1010
CHINESE AMERICANS – FICTION
Coerr, Eleanor. Chang's Paper Pony. (2-3)
588
Lord, Bette Bao. In the Year of the Boar and Jackie
Robinson. (3-6)
14, 98, 268, 348, 411, 677, 719, 774, 917, 1020
Yep, Lawrence. Dragonwings. (5-6)
247, 411, 556, 910
**CHINESE AMERICANS – SOCIAL LIFE AND
CUSTOMS**
Behrens, June. Gung Hay Fat Choy. (3-5)
407
Brown, Tricia. Chinese New Year. (3-5)
588
CHINESE NEW YEAR
Behrens, June. Gung Hay Fat Choy. (3-5)
407

Brown, Tricia. Chinese New Year. (3-5)
588
CHINESE NEW YEAR – FICTION
Handforth, Thomas. Mei Li. (1-3)
1, 269
CHIPMUNKS – FICTION
Ryder, Joanne. Chipmunk Song. (K-3)
415
CHOCOLATE – FICTION
Catling, Patrick. The Chocolate Touch. (3-5)
259, 292, 459, 834
Dahl, Roald. Charlie and the Chocolate Factory. (4-6)
98, 180, 312, 456, 721, 852
Smith, Robert Kimmel. Chocolate Fever. (3-6)
458, 1012
CHRISTMAS
de Paola, Tomie. The Family Christmas Tree Book.
(3-5)
588
Gibbons, Gail. Christmas Time. (P-2)
588
Kelley, Emily. Christmas Around the World. (3-5)
588
CHRISTMAS – FICTION
Andersen, Hans Christian. The Fir Tree. (1-4)
263
Balian, Lorna. Bah! Humbug? (P-2)
271
Bemelmans, Ludwig. Madeline's Christmas. (P-2)
271
Brown, Marc. Arthur's Christmas. (K-2)
271
Carlson, Natalie Savage. The Family Under the Bridge.
(3-5)
270
Cazet, Denys. December 24th. (P-2)
588
Chaneles, Sol. Santa Makes a Change. (P-2)
408
Climo, Shirley. The Cobweb Christmas. (K-2)
271
Dickens, Charles. A Christmas Carol. (4-6)
414, 587
Ets, Marie Hall. Nine Days to Christmas. (1-3)
1, 269, 588
Factor, June. Summer. (P-2)
588
Forest, Heather. The Baker's Dozen: A Colonial Tale.
(4-5)
588
Hoban, Lillian. Arthur's Christmas Cookies. (1-3)
265
Holmes, Efner Tudor. The Christmas Cat. (K-2)
271
Jacobs, Howard, ed. The Cajun Night Before
Christmas. (1-3)
587
Mendez, Phil. The Black Snowman. (1-3)
588
Moore, Clement. The Night Before Christmas. Illus. by
Tomie de Paola. (A)
587

Rockwell, Anne. Hugo at the Window. (P-2)
587

Selden, George. Cricket in Times Square. (3-6)
57, 239, 314, 414, 461, 587, 869

CLEANLINESS — FICTION

de Paola, Tomie. Marianna May and Nursey. (P-2)
410

Hautzig, Deborah. Little Witch's Big Night. (P-2)
1001

Hutchins, Pat. Where's The Baby? (P-2)
587

Zion, Gene. Harry, the Dirty Dog. (P-2)
12, 254, 998

CLEARY, BEVERLY

Cleary, Beverly. Girl from Yamhill. (5-6)
587

CLOTHING — FICTION

See also names of specific types of clothing, e.g., Hats

Andersen, H. C. Emperor's New Clothes. (K-3)
253, 263, 635, 1007

Barrett, Judi. Animals Should Definitely Not Wear Clothing. (P-1)
271

Estes, Eleanor. The Hundred Dresses. (3-5)
61, 297, 411, 520, 855, 1015

Geringer, Laura. A Three Hat Day. (P-2)
410

Heyward, Dubose. The Country Bunny and the Little Gold Shoes. (P-2)
271, 1001

Hutchins, Pat. You'll Soon Grow into Them, Titch. (P-2)
588

Keats, Ezra Jack. Jennie's Hat. (P-2)
587

Kellogg, Steven. The Mystery of the Missing Mitten. (P-1)
254, 258

Lear, Edward. Quangle Wangle Hat. Illus. by Helen Oxenbury. (1-4)
587

Lear, Edward. Quangle Wangle Hat. Illus. by Janet Stevens. (1-4)
587

Lobel, Anita. The Seamstress of Salzburg. (P-2)
408

Matsuno, Masako. A Pair of Red Clogs. (P-K)
255

Miller, Margaret. Whose Hat? (P-1)
588

Morris, Ann. Hats, Hats, Hats. (K-2)
588

Riddell, Chris. Bird's New Shoes. (P-2)
410

Rogers, Jean. Runaway Mittens. (P-2)
588

Seuss, Dr. 500 Hats of Bartholomew Cubbins. (P-6)
255

Slobodkina, Esphyr. Caps for Sale. (P-2)
12, 18, 254, 587, 627, 696, 710, 785, 997, 1011

Stevens, Janet, illus. The Emperor's New Clothes. (K-3)
419

Tresselt, Alvin. The Mitten. (P-2)
254, 410, 801

Winthrop, Elizabeth. Shoes. (P-2)
587

Ziefert, Harriet. A New Coat for Anna. (P-2)
267, 972

Zion, Gene. No Roses for Harry. (P-2)
134

CLOUDS

de Paola, Tomie. The Cloud Book. (P-3)
409, 1038

CLOUDS — FICTION

Shaw, Charles G. It Looked Like Spilt Milk. (P-2)
18, 254, 587

Spier, Peter. Dreams. (P-2)
587

COALS AND COAL MINING

Hendershot, Judith. In Coal Country. (1-3)
416, 588

CODES

Mango, Karen. Codes, Ciphers and Other Secrets. (4-6)
587

COINS — FICTION

Mathis, Sharon Bell. The Hundred Penny Box. (4-6)
471, 641, 719

COLLECTORS AND COLLECTING

Gans, Roma. Rock Collecting. (1-3)
587

Hobson, Burton. Stamp Collecting As a Hobby. (5-6)
587

COLLECTORS AND COLLECTING — FICTION

Fox, Paula. Maurice's Room. (2-4)
301, 839

Geringer, Laura. A Three Hat Day. (P-2)
410

COLORS — FICTION

Carle, Eric. The Mixed-Up Chameleon. (P-2)
1005

Charlip, Remy. Harlequin and the Gift of Many Colors. (P-2)
408

Crews, Donald. Freight Train. (P-K)
12, 254, 588, 697, 705

Freeman, Don. A Rainbow of My Own. (P-1)
587, 1057

Johnson, Crockett. Harold and the Purple Crayon. (P-1)
254, 408, 1003

Lionni, Leo. A Color of His Own. (P-2)
408

Lionni, Leo. Little Blue and Little Yellow. (P-2)
254

McMillan, Bruce. Growing Colors. (P-2)
587

Pinkwater, Daniel. The Big Orange Splot. (K-2)
271, 588

Serfozo, Mary. Who Said Red? (K-2)
412

Sharmat, Marjorie Weinman. Nate the Great. (1-3)
96

Spier, Peter. Oh, Were They Ever Happy! (K-2)
255

Zolotow, Charlotte. Mr. Rabbit and the Lovely Present.
(P-2)
12, 407, 1004

COLORS – POETRY
O'Neill, Mary. Hailstones and Halibut Bones. (P-6)
11, 587, 1018

COLUMBUS, CHRISTOPHER
D'Aulaire, Ingri. Columbus. (2-4)
407

Fritz, Jean. Where Do You Think You're Going,
Christopher Columbus? (3-6)
864

COMMUNICATION
Hoban, Tana. I Read Signs. (P-2)
588

COMMUNITY HELPERS
Gibbons, Gail. The Post Office Book. (P-3)
272, 407, 588

Linn, Margot. A Trip to the Dentist. (P-2)
588

Linn, Margot. A Trip to the Doctor. (P-2)
588

Rogers, Fred. Going to the Doctor. (P-1)
272

COMPUTERS
Simon, Seymour. Meet the Computer. (3-5)
1057

COMPUTERS – FICTION
Granowsky, Alvin. Chicken Salad Soup. (P-2)
271

Pinkwater, Daniel M. Jolly Roger: A Dog of Hoboken.
(P-2)
587

CONSERVATION OF NATURAL RESOURCES
See also Environmental Protection, Litter, Pollution
Earth Works Group. 50 Simple Things Kids Can Do to
Save the Earth. (4-6)
1026, 1048

**CONSERVATION OF NATURAL RESOURCES –
BIOGRAPHY**
Quackenbush, Robert. Don't You Dare Shoot That
Bear. (6)
588

**CONSERVATION OF NATURAL RESOURCES –
FICTION**
Cherry, Lynne. The Great Kapok Tree. (K-3)
416, 1011, 1037

Seuss, Dr. The Lorax. (P-3)
419, 590, 1006

COOKERY
de Paola, Tomie. The Popcorn Book. (2-4)
18, 271, 407, 587

Cauley, Lorinda Bryan. Things to Make and Do for
Thanksgiving. (2-5)
271

Plotkin, Gregory. Cooking the Russian Way. (4-6)
588

Weston, Reiko. Cooking the Japanese Way. (2-4)
588

COOKERY – FICTION
Butler, M. Christian. Too Many Eggs. (P-K)
412

Granowsky, Alvin. Chicken Salad Soup. (P-2)
271

Mahy, Margaret. Jam. (P-3)
271

Rice, Eve. Benny Bakes a Cake. (P-2)
254

Ungerer, Tomi. Zarelda's Ogre. (P-2)
11

COOKIES – FICTION
Hutchins, Pat. The Doorbell Rang. (P-2)
410, 1056

CORN
Aliki. Corn is Maize: The Gift of the Indians. (1-4)
728

COSTUMES – FICTION
Balian, Lorna. Humbug Witch. (P-1)
271

COUNTRY LIFE – FICTION
Burch, Robert. Ida Early Comes Over the Mountain.
(5-6)
414

Burton, Virginia. The Little House. (K-2)
1, 13, 95, 269, 407, 588, 643, 797, 1004

Enright, Elizabeth. Gone Away Lake. (4-6)
411

Johnston, Tony. Yonder. (K-3)
588

McCloskey, Robert. Homer Price. (3-6)
411, 518, 854, 1012

Mowat, Farley. Owls in the Family. (4-6)
172, 413, 481, 592, 878

North, Sterling. Rascal. (4-6)
72, 537, 932

Montgomery, Lucy M. Anne of Green Gables. (4-6)
201, 368, 413

Paterson, Katherine. Bridge to Terabithia. (5-6)
2, 17, 55, 208, 256, 268, 269, 336, 405, 507, 587,
594, 671, 719, 884, 1019, 1058

Peck, Robert Newton. Soup. (4-6)
276, 575, 689

Provenson, Alice. Town and Country. (1-2)
11, 416

Rawls, Wilson. Where the Red Fern Grows. (5-6)
7, 92, 98, 204, 403, 405, 578, 615, 692, 949, 965, 1019,
1060

Rylant, Cynthia. Night in the Country. (P-2)
416

COUNTRY LIFE – FOLKLORE
Aesop. The Town Mouse and the Country Mouse.
Illus. by Lorinda Bryan Cauley. (1-3)
591, 1033

COUNTRY MUSIC – FICTION
Paterson, Katherine. Come Sing, Jimmy Jo. (5-6)
388

COWBOYS
Freedman, Russell. Cowboys of the Wild West. (4-6)
588

COWBOYS—FICTION
Erickson, John. Hank, the Cowdog. (4-6)
166
Martin, Bill. White Dynamite and the Curly Kid. (K-3)
271
COWBOYS—FOLKLORE
Blassingame, Wyatt. Pecos Bill Catches a Hidebehind. (1-4)
271
Kellogg, Steven. Pecos Bill. (2-6)
587, 588
COWS—FICTION
See also Bulls
Forrester, Victoria. The Magnificent Moo. (P-2)
271
CRABS—FICTION
Kipling, Rudyard. Crab That Played with the Sea: A Just So Story (1-4)
1046
Peet, Bill. Kermit, the Hermit. (K-2)
96, 1055
CRANE WIFE ADAPTATIONS
Bang, Molly. Dawn. (1-3)
587
CRANES—FICTION
Bang, Molly. The Paper Crane. (K-3)
267, 271, 410
Byars, Betsy. House of Wings. (5-6)
414
Lobel, Arnold. Fables. "The Pelican and the Crane." (3-6)
1002
CRANES—FOLKLORE
Yagawa, Sumiko. The Crane Wife. (K-3)
419
CRAZY HORSE
Meadowcroft, Enid LaMonte. Crazy Horse: Sioux Warrior. (2-4)
11
CRICKETS—FICTION
Caudill, Rebecca. A Pocketful of Cricket. (K-3)
587, 590
Howe, James. I Wish I Were a Butterfly. (K-3)
588, 1011, 1054
Selden, George. Cricket in Times Square. (3-6)
57, 239, 314, 414, 461, 587, 869
CRIMINALS—FICTION
See also Detectives, Robbers and Outlaws
Adler, David A. Cam Jansen and the Mystery of the Circus Clown. (2-4)
97
CROCKETT, DAVY
Quackenbush, Robert. Quit Pulling My Leg! A Story of Davy Crockett. (5-6)
588
CROCOCILES—FICTION
Aruego, Jose. Rockabye Crocodile. (P-2)
587
Hoban, Russell. Dinner at Alberta's. (K-3)
587, 816

Kipling, Rudyard. The Elephant's Child. (1-3)
14, 267, 419, 587
Kipling, Rudyard. The Elephant's Child. Illus. by Lorinda Bryan Cauley. (1-3)
587
Kunhardt, Edith. Trick or Treat, Danny. (P-2)
588
Waber, Bernard. The House on East Eighty-Eighth Street. (K-2)
590
Waber, Bernard. Loveable Lyle. (K-2)
590, 798
Waber, Bernard. Lyle and the Birthday Party. (K-2)
590
Waber, Bernard. Lyle Finds His Mother. (K-2)
274, 590
Waber, Bernard. Lyle, Lyle Crocodile. (P-2)
429, 590, 997
CROCODILES—FOLKLORE
Galdone, Paul. The Monkey and the Crocodile. (1-3)
1004
CROSS COUNTRY SKIING—FICTION
Calhoun, Mary. Cross Country Cat. (1-3)
587
CROWS—FICTION
Aesop. The Crow and the Pitcher. (2-4)
1002
CUMULATIVE TALES
Aardema, Verna. Bringing the Rain to Kapiti Plain. (1-3)
588, 626, 715, 725, 1056
Asbjornsen, P. C. The Three Billy Goats Gruff. (1-4)
252, 707, 807
Asbjornsen, P. C. The Three Billy Goats Gruff. Illus. by Janet Stevens. (P-2)
587
Cauley, Lorinda Bryan. The Pancake Boy. (P-2)
587
Cherry, Lynne. The Great Kapok Tree. (K-3)
416, 1011, 1037
Emberley, Barbara. Drummer Hoff. (P-1)
1, 254, 269, 587
Flack, Marjorie. Ask Mr. Bear. (P-1)
12, 254, 587, 1005
Forrester, Victoria. The Magnificent Moo. (P-2)
271
Fox, Mem. Hattie and the Fox. (P-2)
410
Gag, Wanda. Millions of Cats. (P-2)
254, 265, 587, 997
Galdone, Paul. Henny Penny. (P-2)
587
Galdone, Paul. The Little Red Hen. (P-2)
1033
The Gingerbread Boy. (P-2)
10, 251, 705, 999
Henny Penny. (P-2)
10, 251
Hogrogian, Nonny. One Fine Day. (K-3)
1, 267, 269, 408, 435, 589, 649

Most, Bernard. Whatever Happened to the Dinosaurs? (K-3)
596

Simon, Seymour. The Smallest Dinosaurs. (K-3)
596

DINOSAURS—FICTION

Adler, David. Cam Jansen and the Mystery of the Dinosaur Bones. (2-4)
290, 831

Brown, Laurene. Dinosaur's Divorce. (P-2)
588

Brown, Laurene. Dinosaur's Travel. (1-5)
588

Butterworth, Oliver. The Enormous Egg. (3-6)
59, 316, 414, 463, 886, 1016

Carrick, Carol. Patrick's Dinosaurs. (K-2)
265, 596, 802, 1057

Carrick, Carol. What Happened to Patrick's Dinosaurs? (K-2)
748, 1036

Hilton, Lisa. If Dinosaurs Were Alive Today. (P-2)
412

Giff, Patricia Reilly. In the Dinosaur's Paw. (2-4)
274, 281

Hoff, Syd. Danny and the Dinosaur. (K-2)
13, 127, 427, 1005

Most, Bernard. If the Dinosaurs Came Back. (P-2)
408

Sharmat, Marjorie Weinman. Nate the Great and the Sticky Case. (1-3)
38, 434

DINOSAURS—POETRY

Prelutsky, Jack. Tyrannosaurus Was a Beast. (K-5)
596

DIVORCE

Brown, Laurene. Dinosaur's Divorce. (P-2)
588

DIVORCE—FICTION

Adler, C. S. Silver Coach. (5-6)
357

Cleary, Beverly. Dear Mr. Henshaw. (4-6)
2, 17, 58, 210, 261, 269, 315, 405, 415, 513, 587, 594, 673, 720, 773, 906, 1013

Blume, Judy. It's Not the End of the World. (4-6)
260, 405

Byars, Betsy. The Cybil War. (4-6)
150, 413, 414

Hurwitz, Johanna. DeDe Takes Charge. (4-6)
405

Paulsen, Gary. Hatchet. (5-6)
85, 249, 371, 413, 558, 1055

Roy, Ron. Breakfast with My Father. (P-2)
588

Sachs, Marilyn. The Bear's House. (4-5)
270, 405

DOCTORS

Linn, Margot. A Trip to the Doctor. (P-2)
588

Rogers, Fred. Going to the Doctor. (P-1)
272

DOGS

Kuklin, Susan. Taking My Dog to the Vet. (K-2)
587

DOGS—FICTION

Armstrong, William H. Sounder. (5-6)
90, 99, 225, 269, 399, 405, 406, 419, 574, 612, 688, 722, 892, 941

Arnosky, Jim. Gray Boy. (5-6)
414

Bemelmans, Ludwig. Madeline's Rescue. (P-2)
1, 11, 138, 269, 271, 590

Brett, Jan. The First Dog. (1-3)
587

Bridwell, Norman. Clifford at the Circus. (P-2)
273

Bridwell, Norman. Clifford, the Big Red Dog. (P-2)
18, 107

Bridwell, Norman. Clifford's Birthday Party. (P-2)
998

Burnford, Sheila. The Incredible Journey. (5-6)
7, 86, 181, 347, 418, 562, 603, 919, 957

Carlson, Nancy. Harriet's Halloween Candy. (P-2)
271, 1056

Cazet, Denys. Frosted Glass. (P-2)
410

Cleary, Beverly. Henry Huggins. (3-5)
154

Cleary, Beverly. Ribsy. (3-5)
261

Cuyler, Marjorie. Freckles and Willie. (P-2)
271

Day, Alexander. Carl Goes Shopping. (P-1)
1005

Erickson, John. Hank, the Cowdog. (4-6)
166

Estes, Eleanor. Ginger Pye. (5-6)
269

Flack, Marjorie. Angus and the Cats. (P-1)
11

Flack, Marjorie. Angus and the Ducks. (P-1)
587

Gardiner, John Reynolds. Stone Fox. (3-6)
7, 15, 42, 270, 331, 411, 414, 417, 493, 587, 860, 1012, 1055

Gipson, Fred. Old Yeller. (4-6)
203, 530, 610, 961

Gipson, Fred. Savage Sam. (4-6)
7

Gray, Elizabeth Janet. Adam of the Road. (6)
269, 1053

Hill, Eric. Spot Goes to the Circus. (P-1)
1028

Hill, Eric. Spot Goes to the Farm. (P-1)
1004

Hoban, Lillian. The Laziest Robot in Zone One. (1-3)
409

Jukes, Mavis. No One Is Going to Nashville. (2-5)
842

Keats, Ezra Jack. Whistle for Willie. (P-2)
94, 267, 665, 1003

DOVES—FICTION

Peet, Bill. The Pinkish Purplish Bluish Egg. (K-3)
271

Wolff, Ashley. The Bells of London. (P-2)
587

DOVES—FOLKLORE

Aesop. The Bee and the Dove. (2-4)
1002

DRAGONFLIES—FICTION

Howe, James. I Wish I Were a Butterfly. (K-3)
588, 1011, 1054

DRAGONS—FICTION

Gannett, Ruth Stiles. My Father's Dragon. (3-5)
259

Garrison, Christian. The Dream Eater. (K-3)
271

Grahame, Kenneth. The Reluctant Dragon. (3-5)
1015

Hodges, Margaret. Saint George and the Dragon. (2-5)
1, 257, 269

Korschunow, Irina. Adam Draws Himself a Dragon. (2-4)
259

McKinley, Robin. The Hero and the Crown. (6)
2, 269, 411, 1027

Munsch, Robert. The Paper Bag Princess. (1-3)
843

Phillips, Louis. The Brothers Wrong and the Wrong Again. (1-3)
271

Sargent, Sarah. Weird Henry Berg. (3-5)
1027

Williams, Jay. Everyone Knows What a Dragon Looks Like. (1-3)
257

Wilson, Sarah. Beware the Dragons. (K-2)
1036

DRAWING

Ames, Lee. Draw 50 Vehicles. (4-6)
588

Arnosky, Jim. Sketching Outdoors in Autumn. (A)
587

DRAWING—FICTION

Bulla, Clyde Robert. The Chalk Box Kid. (2-4)
291, 833

Isadora, Rachel. The Pirates of Bedford Street. (P-2)
587

Johnson, Crockett. Harold and the Purple Crayon. (P-1)
254, 408, 1003

Schwartz, Amy. Begin at the Beginning. (K-2)
271

Testa, Fulvio. If You Take a Pencil. (1-3)
117

Williams, Vera B. Cherries and Cherry Pits. (1-3)
409

DREAMS—FICTION

Briggs, Raymond. The Snowman. (P-1)
102, 587, 994

Garrison, Christian. The Dream Eater. (K-3)
271

Jonas, Ann. The Quilt. (P-2)
587

Shulevitz, Uri. The Treasure. (2-4)
257

Spier, Peter. Dreams. (P-1)
587

Tafuri, Nancy. Junglewalk. (P-1)
587

DROUGHTS—FOLKLORE

Aardema, Verna. Bringing the Rain to Kapiti Plain. (1-3)
588, 626, 715, 725, 1056

DRUG ABUSE—FICTION

Childress, Alice. A Hero Ain't Nothin' but a Sandwich. (6)
413

DUCKS—FICTION

Bunting, Eve. Happy Birthday Dear Duck. (P-2)
1044

Flack, Marjorie. Angus and the Ducks. (P-1)
587

Flack, Marjorie. The Story About Ping. (P-1)
272, 589, 997

McCloskey, Robert. Make Way for Ducklings. (P-1)
1, 12, 95, 269, 271, 272, 407, 415, 430, 646, 799, 1008

Tafuri, Nancy. Have You Seen My Duckling? (P-1)
587

Thiele, Colin. Farmer Schulz's Ducks. (K-3)
587

EARTH

Cole, Jo Anna. The Magic School Bus Inside the Earth. (2-5)
1043, 1055, 1057

McNulty, Faith. How to Dig a Hole to the Other Side of the World. (2-4)
734, 1043

EARTH—ROTATION

Branley, Franklin. What Makes Day and Night. (K-3)
597

EARTHQUAKES—FICTION

Hodges, Margaret. The Wave. (4-6)
5, 402

EASTER—FICTION

Friedrich, Priscilla. The Easter Bunny That Overslept. (P-2)
587

Heyward, Dubose. The Country Bunny and the Little Gold Shoe. (P-2)
271, 1001

McClenathan, Louise. The Easter Pig. (1-3)
271

Milhous, Katherine. Egg Tree. (K-3)
1, 269

Stevenson, James. The Great Big Especially Beautiful Easter Egg. (K-3)
271

Zolotow, Charlotte. Mr. Rabbit and the Lovely Present. (P-2)
12, 407, 1004

Bate, Lucy. Little Rabbit's Loose Tooth. (K-2)
13, 18, 254, 272, 407, 706, 1004

Grimm, Jacob. Three Spinning Fairies. (1-4)
264

Karlin, Barbara. Cinderella. (P-2)
18

Mayer, Bernice. Sidney Rella and the Glass Sneakers. (1-4)
271

Perrault, Charles. Cinderella. (P-2)
716, 999

Perrault, Charles. Cinderella or the Little Glass Slipper. Pictures by Marcia Brown. (P-2)
1, 269

Perrault, Charles. The Sleeping Beauty. (P-2)
999

Tompert, Ann. Grandfather Tang's Story. (1-4)
1056

FAIRY TALES

Ahlberg, Janet. The Jolly Postman. (A)
271, 410, 412, 1005, 1011

Andersen, Hans Christian. Emperor's New Clothes. (K-3)
253, 263, 635, 1007

Andersen, Hans Christian. The Fir Tree. (1-4)
263

Andersen, Hans Christian. The Little Match Girl. (1-4)
263

Andersen, Hans Christian. The Little Match Girl. Illus. by Rachel Isadora. (1-4)
587

Andersen, Hans Christian. The Little Mermaid. (1-4)
263

Andersen, Hans Christian. Michael Hague's Favorite Hans Christian Andersen Fairy Tales. (2-5)
593

Andersen, Hans Christian. The Princess and the Pea. (1-4)
253, 263, 408

Andersen, Hans Christian. The Snow Queen. (1-4)
263

Andersen, Hans Christian. The Steadfast Tin Soldier. (1-4)
14

Andersen, Hans Christian. Thumbelina. (1-4)
263

Andersen, Hans Christian. The Ugly Duckling. (1-4)
253, 263, 448, 661

Andersen, Hans Christian. The Wild Swans. (1-4)
263

Babbitt, Natalie. The Search for Delicious. (4-6)
1027

Bang, Molly. Dawn. (1-3)
587

Bang, Molly. The Paper Crane. (K-3)
267, 271, 410

Banks, Lynne Reid. The Fairy Rebel. (4-6)
464

Barrie, J. M. Peter Pan. (3-5)
587, 593

Berson, Harold. The Thief Who Hugged a Moonbeam. (P-2)
271

Brett, Jan. Goldilocks and the Three Bears. (P-2)
18

Cole, Brock. The Winter Wren. (K-3)
257

Cole, Joanna. Doctor Change. (1-3)
410

Collodi, Carlo. The Adventures of Pinnochio. (3-6)
999, 1017

Collodi, Carlo. The Adventures of Pinnochio. Illus. by Robert Innocenti. (3-6)
587

Dahl, Roald. The BFG. (4-6)
8

de Paola, Tomie. Helga's Dowery. (1-3)
587

De Regniers, Beatrice Schenk. Red Riding Hood: Retold in Verse for Boys and Girls to Read Themselves. (P-2)
408

Galdone, Paul. The Three Sillies. (P-4)
271

Gannett, Ruth Stiles. My Father's Dragon. (3-5)
259

Grahame, Kenneth. The Reluctant Dragon. (3-5)
1015

Grass, Ruth. Hansel and Gretel. (P-1)
587

Grimm, Jacob. Ashputtel (Cinderella). (1-4)
264

Grimm, Jacob. The Breman Town Musicians. (2-4)
252

Grimm, Jacob. Elves and the Shoemaker. (1-4)
264

Grimm, Jacob. Fisherman and His Wife. (1-4)
264

Grimm, Jacob. The Frog Prince. (1-4)
264

Grimm, Jacob. Golden Goose. (1-4)
264

Grimm, Jacob. Hansel and Gretel. (P-2)
252, 264, 999

Grimm, Jacob. Little Red Riding Hood. (P-2)
252, 264, 999

Grimm, Jacob. Rapunzel. (1-4)
264, 408

Grimm, Jacob. Rapunzel. Illus. by Barbara Rogasky. (1-4)
587

Grimm, Jacob. Rumplestiltskin. (1-4)
252

Grimm, Jacob. Sleeping Beauty. (1-4)
264

Grimm, Jacob. Snow White and Rose Red. (1-4)
264

Grimm, Jacob. Show White and the Seven Dwarfs. (P-2)
252, 264, 999

Grimm, Jacob. Three Spinning Fairies. (1-4)
264

Grimm, Jacob. The Water of Life. Illus. by Barbara Rogasky. (4-6)
414, 587

Haley, Gail. A Story, A Story. (K-3)
1, 269, 409, 592, 1045

Hardendorff, Jeanne B. The Bed Just So. (P-2)
408

Haviland, Virginia. Favorite Fairy Tales Told Around the World. (2-5)
592

Jeffers, Susan. The Wild Robin. (P-2)
587

Louie, Al-Ling. Yeh-Shen: A Cinderella Story from China. (P-3)
15, 257, 591

Marshall, James. Goldilocks and the Three Bears. (P-2)
588

Mayer, Mercer. East O' the Sun and West O' the Moon. (4-6)
267

Mayer, Mercer. The Twelve Dancing Princesses. (1-4)
587

Mayer, Bernice. Sidney Rella and the Glass Sneakers. (1-4)
271

Random House Book of Fairy Tales for Children. (P-6)
591

Rockwell, Anne. The Three Bears and 15 Other Stories. (K-3)
589, 590

Saint Exupery, Antoine De. The Little Prince. (4-6)
395, 645, 1016

Stevens, Janet, illus. The Emperor's New Clothes. (1-4)
419

Stockton, Frank R. The Beeman of Orn. (5-6)
984

Thurber, James. Many Moons. (2-4)
1, 269, 587, 987

Turkle, Brinton. Deep in the Forest. (P-2)
104, 267, 1006

Wilson, Sarah. Beware the Dragons! (K-2)
1036

Wood, Audrey. Heckedy Peg. (K-3)
265, 266

FAMILY LIFE—FICTION

Alcott, Louisa May. Little Women. (5-6)
414, 1022

Armstrong, William H. Sounder. (5-6)
90, 99, 225, 269, 399, 405, 406, 419, 574, 612, 688, 722, 892, 941

Atwater, Richard Tupper. Mr. Popper's Penguins. (3-5)
242, 324, 414, 527, 876, 1042

Bauer, Carolyn Feller. My Mom Travels a Lot. (K-2)
115

Blaine, Marge. The Terrible Thing That Happened at Our House. (K-3)
265, 274, 588, 975

Blume, Judy. The One in the Middle Is the Green Kangaroo. (K-3)
97, 260, 265, 267, 480, 823

Blume, Judy. The Pain and the Great One. (K-3)
141, 260, 265, 824

Blume, Judy. Starring Sally J. Freedman. (5-6)
260

Byars, Betsy. Animal, Vegetable and John D. Jones. (5-6)
414

Byars, Betsy. The Blossoms Meet the Vulture Lady. (4-6)
414

Cameron, Ann. More Stories Julian Tells. (2-4)
592

Campbell, Wayne. What a Catastrophe. (P-2)
410

Carlson, Natalie Savage. Family under the Bridge. (3-5)
270

Cleary, Beverly. Ramona and Her Father. (3-6)
71, 256, 261, 267, 414

Cleary, Beverly. Ramona Quimby, Age 8. (3-5)
11, 40, 237, 274, 486, 652, 846

Cleary, Beverly. Ramona the Brave. (3-5)
304, 484

Cooney, Barbara. Island Boy. (1-3)
588

Drescher, Joan. My Mother Is Getting Married. (K-2)
971

Drescher, Joan. Your Family, My Family. (P-2)
588

Estes, Eleanor. Ginger Pye. (5-6)
269

Fisher, Iris. Katie Bo. (P-2)
588

Fitzhugh, Louise. Nobody's Family Is Going to Change. (5-6)
411

Flournoy, Valerie. Patchwork Quilt. (K-3)
265, 271

Fox, Paula. The One-Eyed Cat. (5-6)
243, 376, 419, 531, 682, 928

Friedman, Ina R. How My Parents Learned to Eat. (1-3)
968

Hall, Donald. Ox-Cart Man. (K-3)
1, 269, 271, 416, 588, 714

Hamilton, Virginia. M. C. Higgins the Great. (6)
269

Hoban, Russell. A Baby Sister for Frances. (P-1)
590

Hughes, Shirley. Moving Molly. (P-2)
265

Hughes, Shirley. Out and About. (P-2)
587

Hunt, Irene. Across Five Aprils. (5-6)
48, 246, 413, 417, 549, 599, 749, 954

Hurwitz, Johanna. Busybody Nora. (2-4)
279

Hurwitz, Johanna. Rip Roaring Russell. (2-4)
286

FAMILY LIFE—AUNTS—FICTION
 Brandenburg, Franz. Aunt Nina and Her Nieces and
  Nephews. (P-2)
  588
 Cassedy, Sylvia. Behind the Attic Wall. (5-6)
  162
 Cooney, Barbara. Miss Rumphius. (K-3)
  36, 265, 266, 271, 407, 410, 416, 419, 433, 711, 1008
 Dahl, Roald. James and the Giant Peach. (4-6)
  14, 64, 99, 183, 256, 268, 320, 473, 680, 717, 922,
  1012
 Hunt, Irene. Up a Road Slowly. (6)
  269
 Mathis, Sharon Bell. The Hundred Penny Box. (4-6)
  471, 641, 719
FAMILY LIFE—AUNTS AND UNCLES—FICTION
 Byars, Betsy. Midnight Fox. (4-6)
  414
 MacLachlan, Patricia. Arthur for the Very First Time.
  (4-6)
  882
 MacLachlan, Patricia. Seven Kisses in a Row. (2-4)
  287, 587
FAMILY LIFE—BROTHERS—FICTION
 Bauer, Marion Dane. Rain of Fire. (5-6)
  417
 Blume, Judy. Tales of a Fourth Grade Nothing. (2-5)
  44, 98, 176, 256, 260, 275, 333, 418, 496, 592, 862
 Blume, Judy. Superfudge. (2-5)
  175, 260, 332, 418, 495, 861
 Cameron, Ann. The Stories Julian Tells. (2-4)
  267, 409, 588
 Carrick, Carol. Patrick's Dinosaurs. (K-2)
  265, 596, 802, 1057
 Collier, James. My Brother Sam Is Dead. (5-6)
  248, 396, 406, 419, 569, 926
 Fitzgerald, John D. The Great Brain. (4-6)
  165, 318, 517, 872, 1015
 Hunt, Irene. No Promises in the Wind. (5-6)
  405, 960
 Kellogg, Steven. Much Bigger Than Martin. (K-2)
  1056
 Lawrence, James. Binky Brothers, Detectives. (1-3)
  409
 McDonald, Joyce. Mail Order Kid. (3-5)
  414, 587
 Mazer, Harry. Cave Under the City. (5-6)
  417
 Titherington, Jeanne. A Place for Ben. (P-2)
  587
FAMILY LIFE—BROTHERS—FOLKLORE
 Mosel, Arlene. Tikki Tikki Tembo. (P-2)
  255, 271, 447, 660, 1010
**FAMILY LIFE—BROTHERS AND SISTERS—
FICTION**
 Alexander, Sue. Nadia the Willful. (K-3)
  419
 Blume, Judy. Pain and the Great One. (K-3)
  141, 260, 265, 824
 Blume, Judy. The One in the Middle Is the Green
  Kangaroo. (K-3)
  97, 260, 265, 267, 480, 823

Byars, Betsy. The Night Swimmers. (4-6)
  270
Byars, Betsy. The Summer of the Swans. (5-6)
  2, 9, 17, 99, 228, 269, 360, 414, 544, 587, 721,
  944, 1017
Carlson, Nancy. Louanne Pig in the Perfect Family.
  (P-2)
  271
Cleaver, Vera. Where the Lilies Bloom. (5-6)
  769, 948
Clymer, Eleanor. My Brother Stevie. (3-5)
  325
Cole, Brock. The Winter Wren. (K-3)
  257
Fleischman, Sid. Chancy and the Grand Rascal. (4-6)
  753
Garfield, Leon. Young Nick and Jubilee. (4-6)
  6
Graham, Bob. Crusher is Coming! (K-2)
  587
Grimm, Jacob. Hansel and Gretel. (P-2)
  252, 264, 999
Hoban, Lillian. Arthur's Honey Bear. (1-3)
  125, 423
Hutchins, Pat. You'll Soon Grow into Them, Titch.
  (P-2)
  588
Gilbreath, Frank B. Cheaper by the Dozen. (6)
  202, 583, 905
Jeffers, Susan. The Wild Robin. (P-2)
  587
Konigsburg, Elaine. From the Mixed-Up Files of Mrs.
  Basil E. Frankweiler. (4-6)
  2, 16, 60, 211, 269, 345, 405, 414, 515, 595, 674,
  721, 912, 1017
L'Engle, Madeline. A Wrinkle in Time. (4-6)
  2, 9, 17, 80, 231, 256, 268, 269, 270, 404, 414, 580,
  595, 693, 722, 897, 1021, 1061
Lesser, Rika. Hansel and Gretel. (P-2)
  18, 587
Mayer, Mercer. The New Baby. (P-1)
  1030
Nelson, Theresa. And One for All. (5-6)
  417
Nixon, Joan Lowery. A Family Apart. (5-6)
  405, 417, 588, 756
Robinson, Barbara. The Best Christmas Pageant Ever.
  (4-6)
  163, 454, 669, 850
Shyer, Marlene Fanta. Welcome Home, Jellybean. (5-6)
  364
Voigt, Cynthia. Dicey's Song. (5-6)
  2, 84, 216, 269, 390, 584, 907, 956
Warner, Gertrude. Boxcar Children. (2-4)
  29
FAMILY LIFE—EXTENDED FAMILY—FICTION
 Levinson, Riki. I Go with My Family to Grandmothers.
  (P-2)
  588
FAMILY LIFE—FATHERS—FICTION
 Baker, Betty. My Sister Says. (1-3)
  416

Blaustein, Muriel. Play Ball, Zachary! (P-2)
588

Hendershot, Judith. In Coal Country. (1-3)
416, 588

Mahy, Margaret. Jam. (P-3)
271

Minarik, Else Holmelund. Father Bear Comes Home.
(P-2)
591

Schwartz, Amy. Bea and Mr. Jones. (K-2)
265, 271, 419, 967

Sorenson, Virginia. Miracles on Maple Hill. (4-6)
269

Udry, Janice. What Mary Jo Shared. (K-2)
12, 407

**FAMILY LIFE—FATHERS AND DAUGHTERS—
FICTION**

Boyd, Candy Dawson. Charlie Pippin. (5-6)
417, 588

Goffstein, M. B. Our Snowman. (P-2)
410

Martin, Bill. White Dynamite and the Curly Kid. (K-3)
271

Sebestyen, Ouida. Words by Heart. (5-6)
414, 953

Yolen, Jane. Owl Moon. (P-3)
1, 18, 265, 269, 587, 1015

FAMILY LIFE—FATHERS AND SONS—FICTION

Avi. The Fighting Ground. (6)
343, 588, 1052

Clifton, Lucille. Everett Anderson's Goodbye. (P-2)
588

Dahl, Roald. Danny, the Champion of the World. (4-6)
1016

McDermott, Gerald. Arrow to the Sun. (1-4)
1, 269, 587, 1041

Rogasky, Barbara. The Water of Life. (4-6)
414, 587

Yep, Lawrence. Dragonwings. (5-6)
247, 411, 556, 910

FAMILY LIFE—GRANDFATHERS—FICTION

Ackerman, Karen. The Song and Dance Man. (K-2)
269, 587, 1011

Aliki. The Two of Them. (P-2)
588

Burningham, John. Grandpa. (P-2)
416

Byars, Betsy. The Blossoms Meet the Vulture Lady.
(4-6)
414

Byars, Betsy. House of Wings. (5-6)
414

Cazet, Denys. December 24th. (P-2)
588

Dahl, Roald. Charlie and the Chocolate Factory. (4-6)
98, 180, 312, 456, 721, 852

de Paola, Tomie. Now One Foot, Now the Other. (K-3)
588, 1005, 1054

Douglass, Barbara. Good As New. (P-K)
1031

Flora, James. Grandpa's Farm. (K-3)
271

Gardiner, John Reynolds. Stone Fox. (3-6)
7, 15, 42, 270, 331, 411, 417, 493, 587, 860, 1012, 1055

Locker, Thomas. Mare on the Hill. (P-2)
587

MacLachlan, Patricia. Through Grandpa's Eyes. (1-3)
271, 588, 747

Martin, Bill. Knots on a Counting Rope. (1-3)
257

Radin, Ruth Yaffe. High in the Mountains. (K-3)
587

Smith, Robert Kimmel. The War with Grandpa. (4-6)
363, 418, 546, 691, 722, 946

Stevens, Carla. Anna, Grandpa and the Big Storm. (P-2)
588

Stevenson, James. The Great Big Especially Beautiful
Easter Egg. (K-3)
271

Stevenson, James. That Dreadful Day. (K-2)
271

Stevenson, James. There's Nothing to Do. (K-3)
271

Stevenson, James. What's Under My Bed. (K-3)
11, 271

Stolz, Mary. Storm in the Night. (K-3)
587

Tompert, Ann. Grandfather Tang's Story. (1-4)
1056

Zolotow, Charlotte. My Grandson, Lew. (K-2)
13, 255, 709, 1054

FAMILY LIFE—GRANDMOTHERS—FICTION

Adler, C. S. Silver Coach. (5-6)
357

Babbitt, Natalie. The Eyes of the Amaryllis. (5-6)
5

Bunting, Eve. The Wednesday Surprise. (P-2)
416

Clymer, Eleanor. Get Away Car. (4-6)
414

Clifford, Eth. The Remembering Box. (3-5)
270

Clymer, Eleanor. My Brother Stevie. (3-5)
325

Daly, Nicki. Not So Fast, Songolo. (K-3)
588

de Paola, Tomie. Nana Upstairs and Nana Downstairs.
(K-3)
94, 267, 997

De Regniers, Beatrice Schenk. Red Riding Hood: Retold
in Verse for Boys and Girls To Read Themselves.
(P-2)
408

Flournoy, Valerie. Patchwork Quilt. (K-3)
265, 271

Greenfield, Eloise. Grandmama's Joy. (P-2)
588

Grimm, Jacob. Little Red Riding Hood. (P-2)
252, 264, 999

Henriod, Lorraine. Grandma's Wheelchair. (K-2)
588

Jukes, M. Blackberries in the Dark. (1-4)
28, 414, 592, 829

Slote, Alfred. Moving In. (5-6)
414, 587
FAMILY LIFE – PARENTS – SINGLE – FICTION
Bunting, Eve. Is Anybody There? (5-6)
587
Byars, Betsy. After the Goat Man. (5-6)
414
Byars, Betsy. The Night Swimmers. (4-6)
270
Dahl, Roald. Danny, the Champion of the World. (4-6)
1016
Hurwitz, Johanna. DeDe Takes Charge. (4-6)
405
Sachs, Marilyn. The Bear's House. (4-5)
270, 405
Williams, Vera. Chair for My Mother. (P-3)
22, 255, 265, 271, 588, 628, 713, 787, 814
FAMILY LIFE – POETRY
Adoff, Arnold. All the Colors of the Race. (4-6)
587
Lewis, Claudia. Long Ago in Oregon. (3-6)
588
FAMILY LIFE – SIBLING RIVALRY – FICTION
Baker, Betty. My Sister Says. (1-3)
416
Blume, Judy. The Pain and the Great One. (K-3)
141, 260, 265, 824
Blume, Judy. Superfudge. (2-5)
175, 260, 332, 418, 495, 861
Blume, Judy. Tales of a Fourth Grade Nothing. (2-5)
44, 98, 176, 256, 260, 275, 333, 418, 496, 592, 862
Carlson, Nancy. Louanne Pig in the Perfect Family. (P-2)
271
Cleary, Beverly. Beezus and Ramona. (2-4)
96, 148, 452
Cleary, Beverly. Ramona the Pest. (3-5)
14, 158, 271, 418, 485, 587, 592, 1012
Fitzgerald, John D. The Great Brain. (4-6)
165, 318, 517, 872, 1015
Giff, Patricia Reilly. Fourth Grade Celebrity. (4-6)
467
Hahn, Mary Downing. Wait til Helen Comes: Ghost Story. (4-6)
276
Henriod, Lorraine. Grandma's Wheelchair. (K-2)
588
Hoban, Russell. A Baby Sister for Frances. (P-1)
590
Hutchins, Pat. The Very Worst Monster. (P-2)
11
Hurwitz, Johanna. Rip Roaring Russell. (2-4)
286
Keats, Ezra Jack. Peter's Chair. (P-1)
254, 258, 587
Lobel, Anita. The Seamstress of Salzburg. (P-2)
408
Lowery, Lois. Anastasia Krupnik. (4-6)
49, 270, 309, 717, 866
Mayer, Mercer. The New Baby. (P-1)
1030

McCully, Emily Arnold. The New Baby. (P-1)
588
Paterson, Katherine. Jacob Have I Loved. (6)
2, 87, 219, 269, 406, 563
Scott, Ann Herbert. On Mother's Lap. (P-2)
254
Smith, Janice Lee. The Monster in the Third Dresser Drawer: And Other Stories about Adam Joshua. (2-4)
283
Titherington, Jeanne. A Place for Ben. (P-2)
587
FAMILY LIFE – SIBLING RIVALRY – FOLKLORE
Karlin, Barbara. Cinderella. (P-2)
18
Perrault, Charles. Cinderella. (P-2)
716, 999
Perrault, Charles. Cinderella or the Little Glass Slipper. Pictures by Marcia Brown. (P-2)
1, 269
FAMILY LIFE – SISTERS – FICTION
Cleary, Beverly. Beezus and Ramona. (2-4)
96, 148, 452
Cleary, Beverly. Ramona Quimby, Age 8. (3-5)
11, 40, 237, 275, 486, 652, 846
Cleary, Beverly. Ramona the Brave. (3-5)
304, 484
Wright, Betty Ren. The Dollhouse Murders. (3-6)
885
FAMILY LIFE – STEPCHILDREN – FICTION
Hahn, Mary Downing. Wait til Helen Comes: Ghost Story. (4-6)
276
FAMILY LIFE – STEPMOTHERS – FICTION
Gates, Doris. Blue Willow. (3-5)
53, 670, 722
Jukes, Mavis. No One Is Going to Nashville. (2-5)
842
MacLachlan, Patricia. Sarah, Plain and Tall. (3-5)
2, 17, 75, 99, 214, 256, 268, 269, 270, 328, 405, 414, 490, 588, 592, 686, 717, 779, 847, 1013
FAMILY LIFE – STEPMOTHERS – FOLKLORE
Grass, Ruth. Hansel and Gretel. (P-2)
587
Grimm, Jacob. Hansel and Gretel. (P-2)
252, 264, 999
Karlin, Barbara. Cinderella. (P-2)
18
Lesser, Rika. Hansel and Gretel. (P-2)
18, 587
Perrault, Charles. Cinderella. (P-2)
716, 999
Perrault, Charles. Cinderella or the Little Glass Slipper. Pictures by Marcia Brown. (P-2)
1, 269
FAMILY LIFE – TWINS – FICTION
Lawrence, James. Binky Brothers, Detectives. (1-3)
409
Paterson, Katherine. Jacob Have I Loved. (6)
2, 87, 219, 269, 406, 563
Stolz, Mary. Noonday Friends. (4-6)
405

FAMILY LIFE—UNCLES—FICTION
Stolz, Mary. A Dog on Barkham Street. (4-6)
414, 587
FAMILY PROBLEMS
Clymer, E. Luke Was There. (4-6)
351
Hazen, Barbara Shook. Tight Times. (K-2)
265, 588
Sachs, Marilyn. The Bear's House. (4-5)
270, 405
FANTASY
Alexander, Lloyd. The High King. (6)
2, 269, 372
Alice's Adventures in Wonderland: The Ultimate Adventure. (K-2)
272
Babbitt, Natalie. The Search for Delicious. (4-6)
1027
Babbitt, Natalie. Tuck Everlasting. (4-6)
78, 188, 270, 276, 361, 414, 545, 690, 945, 1020
Banks, Lynne Reid. The Fairy Rebel. (4-6)
464
Banks, Lynne Reid. I, Houdini: The Autobiography of a Self-Educated Hamster. (4-6)
521
Banks, Lynne Reid. Indian in the Cupboard. (4-6)
62, 98, 182, 256, 270, 319, 411, 413, 522, 678, 718, 920, 1019
Banks, Lynne Reid. Return of the Indian. (4-6)
73, 276, 538
Banks, Lynne Reid. Secret of the Indian. (4-6)
541
Barrie, J. M. Peter Pan. (3-5)
587, 593
Baum, L. Frank. Wonderful Wizard of Oz. (3-6)
275, 414, 587, 593, 951
Bond, Michael. A Bear Called Paddington. (2-5)
190, 451, 593
Butterworth, Oliver. The Enormous Egg. (3-6)
59, 316, 414, 463, 886, 1016
Carrol, Lewis. Alice's Adventures in Wonderland. (4-6)
414, 587, 999
Cassedy, Sylvia. Behind the Attic Wall. (5-6)
162
Cleary, Beverly. Mouse and the Motorcycle. (2-5)
37, 169, 259, 418, 479, 587, 875
Cleary, Beverly. Ralph S. Mouse. (3-5)
261, 483
Cleary, Beverly. Runaway Ralph. (3-5)
173, 487
Cooper, Susan. The Dark Is Rising. (5-6)
389
Cooper, Susan. The Grey King. (6)
2, 269, 413
Cooper, Susan. Over Sea, Under Stone. (5-6)
595
Dahl, Roald. Charlie and the Chocolate Factory. (4-6)
98, 180, 312, 456, 721, 852
Dahl, Roald. Fantastic Mr. Fox. (4-6)
317, 465, 637

Dahl, Roald. James and the Giant Peach. (4-6)
14, 64, 99, 183, 256, 268, 320, 473, 680, 717, 922, 1012
Dillon, Barbara. The Teddy Bear Tree. (3-5)
256
Eager, Edward. Knight's Castle. (4-6)
411
Field, Rachel. Hitty: Her First Hundred Years. (4-6)
269
Fleischman, Sid. The Whipping Boy. (4-6)
2, 215, 256, 269, 365, 414, 502, 780, 865, 1014
Garner, Alan. The Owl Service. (5-6)
413
Gormley, Beatrice. Mail Order Wings. (4-6)
411
Grahame, Kenneth. The Reluctant Dragon. (3-5)
1015
Grahame, Kenneth. The Wind in the Willows. (4-6)
196, 383, 548, 587, 616
Horwitz, Elinor. When the Sky Is Like Lace. (P-2)
11
Howe, Deborah. Bunnicula. (3-6)
149, 256, 311, 407, 418, 509, 587, 672, 718, 868
Hunter, Mollie. The Kelpie's Pearls. (5-6)
414
Hunter, Mollie. A Stranger Came Ashore. (6)
942
Juster, Norton. The Phantom Tollbooth. (5-6)
67, 185, 276, 354, 533, 587, 778, 879
Kellogg, Steven. The Mysterious Tadpole. (K-3)
255, 273
Kendall, Carol. The Gammage Cup. (5-6)
587
Key, Alexander. The Forgotten Door. (6)
466
King-Smith, Dick. Babe, the Gallant Pig. (2-5)
503, 719
Langton, Jane. The Fledgling. (4-6)
587
Lawson, Ben. Ben and Me. (4-6)
52, 179, 289, 417, 453, 883, 1055
Lawson, Robert. Mr. Revere and I. (5-6)
417, 528
Lawson, Robert. Rabbit Hill. (4-6)
70, 223, 269, 414, 536
Lewis, C. S. The Lion, the Witch and the Wardrobe. (4-6)
16, 65, 199, 277, 322, 414, 474, 587, 595, 607, 717, 874, 1020
L'Engle, Madeline. A Wrinkle in Time. (4-6)
2, 9, 17, 80, 231, 256, 268, 269, 270, 404, 414, 580, 595, 693, 722, 897, 1021, 1061
Lindgren, Astrid. Pippi Longstocking. (3-5)
8, 39, 157, 326, 482, 593, 651, 844
Lofting, Hughes. The Voyages of Doctor Doolittle. (5-6)
269
McKinley, Robin. The Hero and the Crown. (6)
2, 269, 411, 1027
Norton, Mary. The Borrowers. (3-6)
54, 193, 414, 506, 587, 593, 900

O'Brien, Robert C. Mrs. Frisby and the Rats of NIMH. (4-6)
2, 16, 66, 99, 213, 268, 269, 374, 414, 568, 681, 776, 925, 1021

Peterson, John. The Littles. (4-6)
267, 300, 477

Pinkwater, Daniel Manus. The Hoboken Chicken Emergency. (3-5)
168

Richler, Mordecai. Jacob Two-Two Meets the Hooded Fang. (4-6)
414

Rodgers, Mary. Freaky Friday. (5-6)
16, 153, 344, 468, 871

Sachar, Louis. Sideways Stories from Wayside School. (3-6)
98

Saint Exupery, Antoine De. The Little Prince. (4-6)
395, 645, 1016

Sargent, Sarah. Weird Henry Berg. (3-5)
1027

Selden, George. Cricket in Times Square. (3-6)
57, 239, 314, 414, 461, 587, 869

Sendak, Maurice. Where the Wild Things Are. (P-3)
1, 12, 18, 27, 95, 118, 255, 265, 269, 271, 407, 449, 664, 704, 708, 1009

Seymour, Peter. The Magic Toyshop. (P-2)
1006

Smith, Robert Kimmel. Chocolate Fever. (3-6)
458, 1012

Spurr, Elizabeth. Mrs. Minetta's Car Pool. (K-2)
271, 419

Steig, William. Abel's Island. (3-5)
47, 587, 668

Tolkien, J. R. R. The Hobbit. (4-6)
391, 559, 1022

Van Allsburg, Chris. The Garden of Abdul Gasazi. (1-3)
11, 257, 271

Van Allsburg, Chris. The Stranger. (4-6)
587

White, E. B. Charlotte's Web. (3-6)
8, 11, 15, 30, 97, 233, 268, 275, 313, 414, 457, 593, 602, 720, 853, 1012, 1050

White, E. B. Stuart Little. (3-6)
8, 43, 161, 256, 494, 712, 1013

White, E. B. Trumpet of the Swan. (3-6)
77, 187, 498

Williams, Margery. Velveteen Rabbit. (2-4)
14, 191, 268, 271, 335, 499, 662, 713, 1007

Winthrop, Elizabeth. Castle in the Attic. (4-6)
419, 587, 1027

Wright, Betty Ren. The Dollhouse Murders. (3-6)
885

Yorinks, Arthur. Hey, Al. (1-3)
1, 269, 271, 587

Yorinks, Arthur. Louis the Fish. (K-3)
598

FARM ANIMALS

Pearce, Q. L. Nature's Footprints: In the Barnyard. (P-2)
1028

Tafuri, Nancy. Spots, Feathers, and Curly Tails. (K-2)
587

FARM ANIMALS—FICTION

Aylesworth, Jim. One Crow: A Counting Rhyme. (P-2)
587

Forrester, Victoria. The Magnificent Moo. (P-2)
271

Petersham, Maud. The Box with Red Wheels. (P-2)
587

FARM LIFE

Ancona, George. The American Family Farm. (4-6)
588

FARM LIFE—FICTION

Aylesworth, Jim. Hannah's Hog. (1-3)
587

Azarian, Mary. A Farmer's Alphabet. (P-1)
11

Beatty, Patricia. Charley Skedaddle. (5-6)
417, 752, 1051

Bell, Frederic. Jenny's Corner. (4-6)
417

Byars, Betsy. Midnight Fox. (4-6)
414

Carle, Eric. The Very Busy Spider. (P-2)
18, 258, 410, 412, 415, 587, 1003

Caudill, Rebecca. A Pocketful of Cricket. (K-3)
587, 590

Cooney, Barbara. Chanticleer and the Fox. (2-6)
1, 269

Duvoisin, Roger. Petunia. (K-2)
11, 12, 407, 587, 1006

Enright, Elizabeth. Thimble Summer. (4-6)
269

Flack, Marjorie. Ask Mr. Bear. (P-1)
12, 254, 587, 1005

Fleischman, Paul. The Scarebird. (P-2)
587

Fleischman, Sid. McBroom and the Big Wind. (3-6)
271

Flora, James. Grandpa's Farm. (K-3)
271

Forrester, Victoria. The Magnificent Moo. (P-2)
271

Fox, Mem. Hattie and the Fox. (P-2)
410

Gage, Wilson. Mrs. Gaddy and the Fast Growing Vine. (1-3)
271

Ginsburg, Mirra. Good Morning, Chick. (P-2)
254

Hague, Kathleen. The Man Who Kept House. (K-3)
419

Hall, Donald. Ox-Cart Man. (K-3)
1, 269, 271, 416, 588, 714

Hamilton, Virginia. Zeely. (4-6)
694

Hill, Eric. Spot Goes to the Farm. (P-1)
1004

Howard, Ellen. Edith Herself. (4-6)
405

Hunt, Irene. Across Five Aprils. (5-6)
48, 246, 413, 417, 549, 599, 749, 954

Hutchins, Pat. Rosie's Walk. (P-1)
12, 18, 112, 254, 409, 589, 653, 709

Jackson, Louise A. Grandpa Had a Windmill: Grandma Had a Churn. (1-3)
416

King-Smith, Dick. Babe, the Gallant Pig. (2-5)
503, 719

Lenski, Lois. Strawberry Girl. (4-6)
269

Lindbergh, Reeve. The Midnight Farm. (P-K)
1056

Lobel, Arnold. Small Pig. (P-2)
419

Locker, Thomas. Family Farm. (K-3)
588

Locker, Thomas. Mare on the Hill. (P-2)
587

Lunn, Janet. The Root Cellar. (5-6)
417

MacLachlan, Patricia. Sarah, Plain and Tall. (3-5)
2, 17, 75, 99, 214, 256, 268, 269, 270, 328, 405, 414, 490, 588, 592, 686, 717, 779, 847, 1013

McCurdy, Michael. Hannah's Farm. (1-3)
588

Nixon, Joan Lowery. Caught in the Act. (4-6)
417

Nobel, Trinka Hakes. The Day Jimmy's Boa Ate the Wash. (K-2)
13

Paterson, Katherine. Park's Quest. (6)
377

Paulsen, Gary. The Winter Room. (6)
93

Pellowski, Anne. First Farm in the Valley: Anna's Story. (3-5)
417

Petersham, Maud. The Box with Red Wheels. (P-2)
587

Potter, Beatrix. The Tale of Benjamin Bunny. (P-1)
587

Potter, Beatrix. The Tale of Peter Rabbit. (P-2)
12, 18, 94, 258, 407, 589, 590, 1003, 1010

Provenson, Alice. The Year at Maple Hill Farm. (K-2)
1056, 1057

Rawls, Wilson. Summer of the Monkeys. (4-6)
418, 543, 943

Thiele, Colin. Farmer Schulz's Ducks. (K-3)
587

Tolstoy, Alexi. The Great Big Enormous Turnip. (P-2)
254

Turner, Ann. Dakota Dugout. (1-3)
588

Van Allsburg, Chris. The Stranger. (A)
587

Wallace, Bill. A Dog Called Kitty. (4-6)
414

White, E. B. Charlotte's Web. (3-6)
8, 11, 15, 30, 97, 233, 268, 275, 313, 414, 457, 593, 602, 720, 853, 1012, 1050

Wiggin, Kate Douglas Smith. Rebecca of Sunnybrook Farm. (5-6)
414

Wilder, Laura Ingalls. Farmer Boy. (3-6)
757

FARM LIFE—FOLKLORE

The Little Red Hen. (P-2)
10, 251, 708, 999

Zemach, Margot. The Little Red Hen. (P-2)
587

FEELINGS—ANGER—FICTION

Cleary, Beverly. Dear Mr. Henshaw. (4-6)
2, 17, 58, 210, 261, 269, 315, 405, 415, 513, 587, 594, 673, 720, 773, 906, 1013

Bulla, Clyde Robert. Shoeshine Girl. (3-5)
329, 414, 418, 1016

Mayer, Mercer. I Was So Mad. (P-2)
110

Taylor, Mildred. The Friendship. (4-6)
417, 1023

Zolotow, Charlotte. The Quarreling Book. (K-2)
1010

FEELINGS—BELONGING—FICTION

Brown, Margaret Wise. Home for a Bunny. (P-2)
1001

Freeman, Don. Corduroy. (P-2)
12, 23, 94, 254, 258, 273, 407, 408, 425, 587, 590, 630, 1008

Lord, Betty Bao. In the Year of the Boar and Jackie Robinson. (3-6)
14, 98, 268, 348, 411, 677, 719, 774, 917, 1020

Manes, Stephen. Be a Perfect Person in Just Three Days. (3-5)
288, 418, 450, 720, 770, 849, 1014, 1055

FEELINGS—BOREDOM—FICTION

Delton, Judy. My Mom Hates Me in January. (K-2)
271

Raskin, Ellen. Nothing Ever Happens on My Block. (K-2)
591

Stevenson, James. There's Nothing to Do. (K-3)
271

Van Allsburg, Chris. Jumanji. (K-6)
1, 15, 265, 269, 271, 411, 1055

FEELINGS—DISCONTENT—FICTION

Aesop. The City Mouse and the Country Mouse. (2-4)
250, 1002

Chaneles, Sol. Santa Makes a Change. (P-2)
408

Cleary, Beverly. Runaway Ralph. (3-5)
173, 487

Gage, Wilson. Mrs. Gaddy and the Fast Growing Vine. (1-3)
271

Kent, Jack. Joey Runs Away. (P-2)
11, 796

McDermott, Gerald. The Stonecutter. (1-4)
587

Minarik, Else Holmelund. Percy and the Five Houses. (P-2)
587

Peet, Bill. The Whingdingdilly. (1-3)
271, 408, 1007

Twain, Mark. The Prince and the Pauper. (6)
1022

Yeoman, John. The Wild Washerwomen. (K-4)
271

FEELINGS — FEAR — FICTION

Blume, Judy. Otherwise Known as Sheila the Great. (4-6)
171, 260

Bourgeois, Paulette. Franklin in the Dark. (P-1)
790, 1054

Byars, Betsy. The 18th Emergency. (4-6)
151, 870

Cameron, Ann. Julian's Glorious Summer. (2-4)
282, 411

Cleary, Beverly. Ramona the Brave. (3-5)
304, 484

Cohen, Miriam. Starring First Grade. (P-2)
1054

Crowe, Robert L. Clyde Monster. (P-1)
410

Gackenbach, Dick. Harry and the Terrible Whatzit. (K-1)
254, 271, 819

Gates, Doris. A Morgan for Melinda. (4-6)
414

Grifalconi, Ann. Darkness and the Butterfly. (P-2)
410

Holman, Felice. Slake's Limbo. (6)
186, 359, 938

Joose, Barbara M. Spiders in the Fruit Cellar. (P-1)
253

Mayer, Mercer. There's a Nightmare in My Closet. (P-1)
11, 94, 108, 254, 267, 408, 445, 659, 703, 1003

Mayer, Mercer. There's an Alligator under My Bed. (P-1)
587, 1004

Most, Bernard. Boo. (P-2)
410

Oppenheim, Joanne. Mrs. Peloki's Snake. (K-2)
271

Peet, Bill. Cowardly Clyde. (K-2)
1055

Smith, Janice Lee. The Monster in the Third Dresser Drawer: And Other Stories about Adam Joshua. (2-4)
283

Sperry, Armstrong. Call It Courage. (5-6)
2, 5, 17, 56, 226, 269, 339, 405, 554, 594, 601, 721, 901, 1014

Stevenson, James. What's under My Bed. (K-3)
11, 271

Stolz, Mary. Storm in the Night. (K-3)
587

Waber, Bernard. Ira Sleeps Over. (K-2)
11, 12, 18, 25, 94, 119, 254, 265, 407, 428, 642, 710, 820, 1007

Wallace, Bill. A Dog Called Kitty. (4-6)
414

FEELINGS — GRIEF — FICTION

Aardema, Verna. Why Mosquitoes Buzz in People's Ears. (1-3)
1, 14, 145, 255, 269, 407, 666, 712, 1010, 1045

Bauer, Marion Dane. On My Honor. (6)
270, 353, 405, 411, 413, 927, 1015

Buck, Pearl. The Big Wave. (4-6)
310, 405, 413, 553, 771, 851

de Paola, Tomie. Nana Upstairs and Nana Downstairs. (K-3)
95, 267, 997

Jukes, Mavis. Blackberries in the Dark. (1-4)
28, 414, 592, 829

Miles, Miska. Annie and the Old One. (3-5)
15, 21, 232, 271, 278, 587, 620, 714, 978, 1016, 1047, 1055

Paterson, Katherine. Bridge to Terabithia. (5-6)
2, 17, 55, 208, 256, 268, 269, 336, 405, 507, 587, 594, 671, 719, 884, 1019, 1058

Rawls, Wilson. Where the Red Fern Grows. (5-6)
7, 92, 98, 204, 403, 405, 578, 615, 692, 949, 1019, 1060

Smith, Doris Buchanan. A Taste of Blackberries. (4-6)
177, 306, 405, 411, 863, 1017, 1055

Viorst, Judith. Tenth Good Thing about Barney. (K-3)
11, 13, 45, 265, 497, 974, 1009, 1054

White, E. B. Charlotte's Web. (3-6)
8, 11, 15, 30, 97, 233, 268, 275, 313, 414, 457, 593, 602, 720, 853, 1012, 1050

Zolotow, Charlotte. My Grandson, Lew. (K-2)
13, 255, 709, 1054

FEELINGS — GUILT — FICTION

Aardema, Verna. Why Mosquitoes Buzz in People's Ears. (1-3)
1, 14, 145, 255, 269, 407, 666, 712, 1010, 1045

Bauer, Marion Dane. On My Honor. (6)
270, 353, 405, 411, 413, 927, 1015

Estes, Eleanor. The Hundred Dresses. (3-5)
61, 297, 411, 520, 831, 855, 1015

Fox, Paula. The One-Eyed Cat. (5-6)
243, 376, 419, 531, 682, 928

Greenwald, Sheila. Rosy Cole's Great American Guilt Club. (2-4)
587

Smith, Doris Buchanan. A Taste of Blackberries. (4-6)
177, 306, 405, 411, 863, 1017, 1055

FEELINGS — HATE — FICTION

Udry, Janice May. Let's Be Enemies. (P-1)
588

Zolotow, Charlotte. The Hating Book. (K-2)
271

FEELINGS — JEALOUSY — FICTION

Blume, Judy. The Pain and the Great One. (K-3)
141, 260, 265, 824

Blume, Judy. Tales of a Fourth Grade Nothing. (2-5)
44, 98, 176, 256, 260, 275, 333, 418, 496, 592, 862

Cleary, Beverly. Socks. (3-4)
261, 330, 592

Cohen, Miriam. Starring First Grade. (P-2)
1054

FERRET – FICTION
Wallace, Bill. Ferrets in the Bedroom, Lizards in the Fridge. (4-6)
270

FIGHTING – ARGUING
Byars, Betsy. The 18th Emergency. (4-6)
151, 870
Blume, Judy. It's Not the End of the World. (4-6)
260, 405
Carle, Eric. The Grouchy Ladybug. (P-2)
272, 415, 791, 1004, 1056
Gag, Wanda. Millions of Cats. (P-2)
254, 265, 587, 997
Grahame, Kenneth. The Reluctant Dragon. (3-5)
1015
Lionni, Leo. It's Mine. (K-3)
415
Merrill, Jean. The Pushcart War. (5-6)
378, 930
Polushkin, Maria. Bubba and Babba. (K-3)
271
Rupprecht, Siegfried P. The Tale of the Vanishing Rainbow. (P-2)
588
Udry, Janice May. Let's Be Enemies. (P-1)
588
Zolotow, Charlotte. The Quarreling Book. (K-2)
1010

FINANCE, PERSONAL – FICTION
Berenstain, Stan. Berenstain Bears' Trouble with Money. (P-3)
272
Viorst, Judith. Alexander, Who Used to Be Rich Last Sunday. (P-3)
257, 267, 588, 1056

FINGER PLAY
Brown, Marc. Play Rhymes. (P-2)
587

FIRE FIGHTERS
Maass, Robert. Firefighters. (P-2)
588

FIRE FIGHTERS – FICTION
Felton, Harold W. Big Mose: Hero Fireman. (1-4)
271

FIREARMS – FICTION
Edmonds, Walter D. The Matchlock Gun. (2-4)
269
Fox, Paula. The One-Eyed Cat. (5-6)
243, 376, 419, 531, 682, 928

FIREFLIES – FICTION
Brinckloe, Julie. Fireflies. (P-2)
730

FISH – FICTION
Clements, Andrew. Big Al. (P-2)
587
Lionni, Leo. Fish Is Fish. (P-2)
267
Lionni, Leo. Swimmy. (P-2)
11, 415, 443, 588, 598, 703, 1057
Yorinks, Arthur. Louis the Fish. (K-3)
598

FISH – FOLKLORE
Grimm, Jacob. The Fisherman and His Wife. (1-4)
264

FISHERMAN AND FISHING – FICTION
Asch, Frank. Bear Shadow. (P-2)
271, 871, 1057
Grimm, Jacob. The Fisherman and His Wife. (1-4)
264
Mayer, Mercer. A Boy, a Dog and a Frog. (P-1)
990
Wildsmith, Brian. Pelican. (P-2)
11, 271

FLEAS – FICTION
Wood, Audrey. The Napping House. (P-2)
94, 254, 258, 587, 710, 1054

FLIES (INSECTS) – FICTION
Winter, Paula. The Bear and the Fly. (P-1)
105

FLIGHT – FICTION
Gormley, Beatrice. Mail Order Wings. (4-6)
411
Langton, Jane. The Fledgling. (4-6)
587
Ransome, Arthur. The Fool of the World and the Flying Ship. (2-5)
1, 269, 407

FLIGHT – POETRY
Livingston, Myra Cohn. Up in the Air. (2-4)
588

FLOODS – FICTION
Green, Norma. The Hole in the Dike. (P-2)
587

FLOWERS – FICTION
See also Gardening, Plants, Seeds, Trees
Anno. The King's Flower. (1-3)
408
Cooney, Barbara. Miss Rumphius. (K-3)
36, 265, 266, 271, 407, 410, 416, 419, 433, 711, 1008
Lobel, Arnold. The Rose in My Garden. (K-3)
1056
Rockwell, Anne. My Spring Robin. (P-K)
1029

FLOWERS – FOLKLORE
de Paola, Tomie. Legend of the Bluebonnet. (2-4)
156, 419, 837, 1041
de Paola, Tomie. Legend of the Indian Paintbrush. (2-4)
588

FOG – FICTION
Tresselt, Alvin. Hide and Seek Fog. (P-2)
587

FOLK DANCING
Ancona, George. Dancing Is. (3-5)
588

FOLK SONGS – GREAT BRITAIN
Westcott, Nadine Bernard. I Know an Old Woman Who Swallowed a Fly. (P-3)
271

FOLK SONGS – UNITED STATES
Diane Goode Book of American Folk Tales and Songs. Comp. by Ann Durell. (2-5)
588

Seeger, Ruth Crawford. American Folk Songs for Children in Home, School and Nursery School. (A)
413

FOLKLORE
Asbjornsen, P. C. The Three Billy Goats Gruff. (1-4)
252, 707, 807
Brett, Jan. Goldilocks and the Three Bears. (P-2)
18
Brown, Marcia. Stone Soup. (K-3)
13, 96, 255, 271, 440, 655, 712, 1009
Cauley, Lorinda Bryan. The Pancake Boy. (P-2)
587
De Regniers, Beatrice Schenk. Red Riding Hood: Retold in Verse for Boys and Girls to Read Themselves. (P-2)
408
Eisen, Armand. Goldilocks and the Three Bears. (P-2)
1031
Galdone, Paul. Henny Penny. (P-2)
587
Galdone, Paul. The Little Red Hen. (P-2)
1033
Galdone, Paul. The Three Bears. (P-2)
265, 587
Galdone, Paul. The Three Little Pigs. (P-3)
18
The Gingerbread Boy. (P-2)
10, 251, 705, 999
Haviland, Virginia. Favorite Fairy Tales Told Around the World. (2-5)
592
Henny Penny. (P-2)
10, 251
Jack and the Beanstalk. (P-2)
252, 999
Kellogg, Steven. Chicken Little. (K-3)
409, 587, 589
Little Red Hen. (P-2)
10, 251, 708, 999
Marshall, James. Goldilocks and the Three Bears. (P-2)
588
Ormerod, Jan. The Story of Chicken Licken. (P-1)
587
Random House Book of Fairy Tales for Children. (P-6)
591
Rockwell, Anne. The Three Bears and 15 Other Stories. (K-3)
589, 590
Schmidt, Karen Lee. The Gingerbread Man. (P-2)
18
Schwartz, Alvin. Cross Your Fingers, Spit in Your Hat. (4-6)
588
Schwartz, Alvin. There's a Carrot in My Ear and Other Noodle Tales. (1-3)
593
Three Bears. (P-1)
251, 706, 999
The Three Little Pigs. (P-2)
10, 251, 999

Zemach, Margot. The Little Red Hen. (P-2)
587
Zemach, Margot. The Three Little Pigs. (P-2)
588

FOLKLORE — AFRICA
Aardema, Verna. Bringing the Rain to Kapiti Plain. (1-3)
588, 626, 715, 725, 1056
Aardema, Verna. Why Mosquitoes Buzz in People's Ears. (1-3)
1, 14, 145, 255, 269, 407, 666, 712, 1010, 1045
Cendrars, Blaise. Shadow. (1-3)
1, 269, 415
Haley, Gail. A Story, A Story. (K-3)
1, 269, 409, 592, 1045
McDermott, Gerald. Anansi the Spider. (1-3)
422

FOLKLORE — AFRICA — WEST
Aardema, Verna. Why Mosquitoes Buzz in People's Ears. (1-3)
1, 14, 145, 255, 269, 407, 666, 712, 1010, 1045
McDermott, Gerald. Anansi the Spider. (1-3)
422

FOLKLORE — AFRO-AMERICAN
Harris, Joel Chandler. Jump Again! More Adventures Brer Rabbit. (3-4)
588
Hamilton, Virginia. The People Could Fly: American Black Folktales. (4-6)
588, 594
Keats, Ezra Jack. John Henry. (1-4)
587
Lester, Julius. The Tales of Uncle Remus. (4-5)
588

FOLKLORE — ARMENIA
Hogrogian, Nonny. One Fine Day. (K-3)
1, 267, 269, 408, 435, 589, 649

FOLKLORE — CHINA
Louie, Al-Ling. Yeh-Shen: A Cinderella Story from China. (P-2)
15, 257, 591
Mosel, Arlene. Tikki Tikki Tembo. (P-2)
255, 271, 447, 660, 1010

FOLKLORE — FRANCE
Karlin, Barbara. Cinderella. (P-2)
18
Perrault, Charles. Cinderella. (P-2)
716, 999
Perrault, Charles. Cinderella or the Little Glass Slipper. Pictures by Marcia Brown. (P-2)
1, 269
Perrault, Charles. The Sleeping Beauty. (P-2)
999

FOLKLORE — GERMANY
De Regniers, Beatrice Schenk. Red Riding Hood: Retold in Verse for Boys and Girls to Read Themselves. (P-2)
408
Grass, Ruth. Hansel and Gretel. (P-2)
587
Grimm, Jacob. Ashputtel (Cinderella). 1-4)
264

FOLKLORE—UKRAINE

Tresselt, Alvin. The Mitten. (P-2)
254, 410, 801

FOLKLORE—UNITED STATES

Bang, Molly. Wiley and the Hairy Man. (1-3)
419

Blassingame, Wyatt. John Henry and Paul Bunyan Play Baseball. (1-4)
271

Blassingame, Wyatt. Pecos Bill Catches a Hidebehind. (1-4)
271

Diane Goode Book of Folk Tales and Songs. Comp. by Ann Durell. (2-5)
588

Emberley, Barbara. The Story of Paul Bunyan. (P-2)
11

Felton, Harold W. Big Mose: Hero Fireman. (1-4)
271

Forest, Heather. The Baker's Dozen: A Colonial American Tale. (4-5)
588

Galdone, Joanna. The Tailypo: A Ghost Story. (P-2)
413

Hamilton, Virginia. The People Could Fly: American Black Folktales. (4-6)
588, 594

Irving, Washington. Rip Van Winkle. (5-6)
587

Keats, Ezra Jack. John Henry. (1-4)
587

Kellogg, Steven. Paul Bunyan. (K-3)
588, 650

Kellogg, Steven. Pecos Bill. (2-6)
587, 588

Petersham, Maud. The Rooster Crows: A Book of American Rhymes and Jingles. (K-2)
1, 269

Schwartz, Alvin. Scary Stories to Tell in the Dark. (4-6)
593

Schwartz, Alvin. Unriddling. (2-6)
271

Schwartz, Alvin. Whoppers, Tall Tales and Other Lies. (2-6)
271

FOLKLORE—WALES

Alexander, Lloyd. The High King. (6)
2, 269, 372

FOOD

See also Cookery, Fruit, Vegetables, and names of specific foods, e.g., Cookies

Aliki. Corn is Maize: The Gift of the Indians. (1-4)
728

Ancona, George. Bananas: From Manolo to Margie. (3-5)
407, 588

de Paola, Tomie. The Popcorn Book. (2-4)
18, 271, 407, 587

Gibbons, Gail. The Seasons of Arnold's Apple Tree. (P-2)
1029, 1057

Horwitz, Joshua. Night Markets: Bringing Food to the City. (3-5)
588

Morris, Ann. Bread, Bread, Bread. (K-2)
588

Rogow, Zack. Oranges. (2-4)
588

FOOD—FICTION

Aesop. The Fox and the Grapes. (2-4)
250, 1002

Ahlberg, Janet. Each Peach, Pear, Plum. (K-2)
587, 789

Allard, Harry. I Will Not Go to the Market Today. (P-2)
271

Banks, Kate. Alphabet Soup. (P-2)
18

Barrett, Judi. Cloudy with a Chance of Meatballs. (K-3)
11, 18, 255, 266, 591, 629, 727, 1003, 1011, 1038

Berenstain, Stan. The Berenstain Bears and Too Much Junk Food. (P-2)
1054

Carle, Eric. The Very Hungry Caterpillar. (P-2)
11, 12, 18, 94, 123, 254, 265, 407, 589, 705, 998, 1035, 1056, 1057

Carlson, Nancy. Harriet's Halloween Candy. (P-2)
271, 1056

Catling, Patrick. The Chocolate Touch. (3-5)
259, 292, 459, 834

Cauley, Lorinda Bryan. The Pancake Boy. (P-2)
587

Dahl, Roald. Charlie and the Chocolate Factory. (4-6)
98, 180, 312, 456, 721, 852

Dahl, Roald. James and the Giant Peach. (4-6)
14, 64, 99, 183, 256, 268, 320, 473, 680, 717, 922, 1012

Degen, Bruce. Jamberry. (P-2)
698

de Paola, Tomie. Pancakes for Breakfast. (P-1)
18, 101, 254, 993

de Paola, Tomie. Strega Nona. (1-4)
11, 13, 18, 97, 255, 265, 271, 408, 442, 657, 714

de Paola, Tomie. Watch out for the Chicken Feet in Your Soup. (K-2)
588

Devlin, Wende. Cranberry Thanksgiving. (1-3)
271

Ehlert, Lois. Eating the Alphabet. (P-1)
412

Friedman, Ina R. How My Parents Learned to Eat. (1-3)
968

Gelman, Rita Goldin. The Biggest Sandwich Ever. (P-2)
408

The Gingerbread Boy. (P-2)
10, 251, 705, 999

Granowsky, Alvin. Chicken Salad Soup. (P-2)
271

Hoban, Lillian. Arthur's Christmas Cookies. (1-3)
265

Hoban, Russell. Bread and Jam for Frances. (P-1)
13, 18, 94, 124, 255, 625, 711, 1003

Hoban, Russell. Dinner at Alberta's. (K-3)
587, 816

Hutchins, Pat. Don't Forget the Bacon. (P-2)
271, 788

Hutchins, Pat. The Doorbell Rang. (P-2)
410, 1056

Jarrell, Randall. Gingerbread Rabbit. (P-2)
411

Kasza, Keiko. The Wolf's Chicken Stew. (P-1)
1056

Krauss, Ruth. The Carrot Seed. (P-2)
12, 407, 998, 1054

Kroll, Steven. The Biggest Pumpkin Ever. (K-2)
724, 783, 1001

Kroll, Steven. The Hokey-Pokey Man. (P-2)
417

Lord, John Vernon. The Giant Jam Sandwich. (K-3)
271, 1056

McCloskey, Robert. Blueberries for Sal. (P-2)
11, 12, 255, 265, 271, 587, 624, 784, 998

McMillan, Bruce. Growing Colors. (P-2)
587

Mahy, Margaret. Jam. (P-3)
271

Mayer, Mercer. Frog Goes to Dinner. (P-1)
100

Nixon, Joan Lowery. Beats Me, Claude. (1-3)
587

Parkes, Brenda. The Enormous Watermelon. (K-3)
412, 1057

Rice, Eve. Benny Bakes a Cake. (P-2)
254

Rockwell, Thomas. How to Eat Fried Worms. (4-6)
99, 259, 296, 414, 418, 519, 676, 836, 1014, 1055

Schmidt, Karen Lee. The Gingerbread Man. (P-2)
18

Sendak, Maurice. Chicken Soup with Rice. (P-1)
18, 109, 271, 995

Seuss, Dr. Green Eggs and Ham. (P-1)
267, 998

Sharmat, Marjorie Weinman. Nate the Great. (1-3)
96

Sharmat, Marjorie. One Terrific Thanksgiving. (P-3)
271

Sharmat, Mitchell. Gregory, the Terrible Eater. (P-3)
18, 271, 415, 639, 732

Smith, Robert Kimmel. Chocolate Fever. (3-6)
458, 1012

Spinelli, Eileen. Thanksgiving at the Tapleton's. (K-3)
271

Wood, Audrey. Heckedy Peg. (K-3)
265, 266

Zolotow, Charlotte. Mr. Rabbit and the Lovely Present. (P-2)
12, 407, 1004

FOOD — FOLKLORE

Aesop. The Fox and the Grapes. (2-4)
250, 1002

Brown, Marcia. Stone Soup. (K-3)
13, 96, 255, 271, 440, 655, 712, 1009

FOOD — POETRY

Poem Stew. (4-6)
1054

FOOTBALL — FICTION

Myers, Bernice. Sidney Rella and the Glass Sneakers. (1-4)
271

FORD, HENRY

Mitchell, Barbara. We'll Race You, Henry. (4-6)
588

FOREIGN LANGUAGES

Feelings, Muriel. Jambo Means Hello: A Swahili Alphabet Book. (1-3)
412, 416

Feelings, Muriel. Moja Means One: A Swahili Counting Book. (1-3)
11

Stanek, Muriel. I Speak English for My Mom. (1-3)
588

FOREIGN LANDS

See also names of specific countries, e.g., Great Britain

Allen, Thomas B. Where the Children Live. (P-2)
588

Anno, Mitsumasa. All in a Day. (3-5)
588

Handford, Martin. Where's Waldo? (A)
271, 1004

Kelley, Emily. Christmas Around the World. (3-5)
588

FOREST ANIMALS

de Paola, Tomie. The Hunter and the Animals. (K-1)
587

Miller, Edna. Mousekin's Woodland Sleepers. (P-2)
1057

Peet, Bill. Big Bad Bruce. (1-3)
97, 255, 271, 714, 998

Sharmat, Marjorie. The 329th Friend. (P-2)
271, 408

Ward, Lynd. The Biggest Bear. (1-3)
1, 13, 142, 255, 269, 271, 623, 812, 1003

FORESTS

Romanova, Natalia. Once There Was a Tree. (K-2)
743

FORESTS — FICTION

Baker, Jeannie. Where the Forest Meets the Sea. (P-2)
587

Hader, Berta. The Big Snow. (K-2)
1, 269

Marshall, Edward. Troll Country. (K-2)
828

Miller, Edna. Mousekin's Woodland Sleepers. (P-2)
1057

Peet, Bill. Big Bad Bruce. (1-3)
97, 255, 271, 714, 998

Taylor, Mildred. Song of the Trees. (4-6)
411, 891

Yolen, Jane. Owl Moon. (P-3)
1, 18, 265, 269, 587, 1015

FORESTS — POETRY

Frost, Robert. Stopping by the Woods on a Snowy Evening. Illus. by Susan Jeffers. (A)
587

Blume, Judy. Iggie's House. (4-6)
260, 275

Blume, Judy. Otherwise Known as Sheila the Great.
(4-6)
171, 260

Briggs, Raymond. The Snowman. (P-1)
102, 587, 994

Bulla, Clyde Robert. Shoeshine Girl. (3-5)
329, 414, 418, 1016

Burnett, Frances Hodgson. The Secret Garden. (4-6)
9, 200, 379, 413, 414, 540, 587, 718, 934, 1019

Byars, Betsy. The Cybil War. (4-6)
150, 413, 414

Byars, Betsy. The Pinballs. (4-6)
69, 98, 270, 355, 418, 535, 683, 929

Calhoun, Mary. Julie's Tree. (K-2)
587

Cameron, Ann. More Stories Julian Tells. (2-4)
592

Cleary, Beverly. Ellen Tebbits. (3-5)
261, 414

Cleary, Beverly. Mouse and the Motorcycle. (2-5)
37, 169, 259, 418, 479, 587, 875

Clifton, Lucille. Everett Anderson's Friend. (P-2)
37, 169, 259, 418, 479, 587, 875

Clifton, Lucille. Everett Anderson's Friend. (P-2)
11

Clifton, Lucille. My Friend Jacob. (K-2)
271

Cohen, Barbara. Thank You, Jackie Robinson. (4-6)
414

Cohen, Miriam. Will I Have a Friend? (P-2)
407

Cohen, Miriam. Starring First Grade. (P-2)
1054

Cool, Joyce. The Kidnapping of Courtney Van Allen
and What's Her Name. (5-6)
270

Cuyler, Marjorie. Freckles and Willie. (P-2)
271

Daugherty, James. Andy and the Lion. (1-3)
587

De Clements, Barthe. Nothing's Fair in the Fifth Grade.
(4-6)
170, 270, 418

De Regniers, Beatrice Schenk. May I Bring a Friend?
(P-2)
1, 12, 269, 407, 710, 800, 1004

Duvoisin, Roger. Petunia. (K-2)
11, 12, 407, 587, 1006

Ehrlich, Amy. Lee, Zack and Emmie. (1-3)
587

Enright, Elizabeth. Gone Away Lake. (4-6)
411

Erickson, Russell. A Toad for Tuesday. (1-3)
259

Estes, Eleanor. The Hundred Dresses. (3-5)
61, 297, 411, 520, 855, 1015

Fleischman, Paul. The Scarebird. (P-2)
587

Fox, Mem. Wilfred Gordon MacDonald Partridge.
(1-3) 257, 266

Freeman, Don. Dandelion. (K-1)
13, 633, 997

Garrigue, Sheila. Between Friends. (5-6)
405, 587

Gates, Doris. A Morgan for Melinda. (4-6)
414

Giff, Patricia Reilly. Fourth Grade Celebrity. (4-6)
467

Gilson, Jamie. Do Bananas Chew Gum? (4-6)
256

Graham, Bob. Crusher is Coming! (K-2)
587

Grahame, Kenneth. The Wind in the Willows. (4-6)
196, 383, 548, 587, 616

Greene, Bette. Phillip Hall Likes Me, I Reckon Maybe.
(4-6)
68, 534, 890

Greene, Bette. Summer of My German Soldier. (6)
400, 576, 963

Hamilton, Virginia. Zeely. (4-6)
694

Heine, Helme. Friends. (P-1)
1039

Henry, Marguerite. King of the Wind. (4-6)
2, 222, 269, 566, 889, 1013

Hoban, Russell. A Bargain for Frances. (P-1)
272, 424, 590, 810

Hoban, Russell. Best Friends for Frances. (P-1)
590

Hoff, Syd. Danny and the Dinosaur. (K-2)
13, 127, 427, 1005

Howe, James. I Wish I Were a Butterfly. (K-3)
588, 1011, 1054

Honeycutt, Natalie. The All New Jonah Twist. (3-5)
270

Hughes, Shirley. Moving Molly. (P-2)
265

Hurwitz, Johanna. The Adventures of Ali Baba
Bernstein. (3-4)
146, 274

Hurwitz, Johanna. Aldo Applesauce. (4-6)
147

Hutchins, Pat. The Doorbell Rang. (P-2)
410, 1056

Kellogg, Steven. Best Friends. (K-2)
271, 1039

Kline, Suzy. Horrible Harry in Room 2B. (1-3)
97

Konigsburg, Elaine. Jennifer, Hecate, Macbeth, William
McKinley and Me, Elizabeth. (4-6)
234, 526, 411

Krumgold, Joseph. Onion John. (5-6)
269

Levoy, Myron. Alan and Naomi. (6)
367

Lindgren, Astrid. Pippi Longstocking. (3-5)
8, 39, 157, 326, 482, 593, 651, 844

Lionni, Leo. Little Blue and Little Yellow. (P-2)
254

Lobel, Arnold. Days with Frog and Toad. (K-2)
4, 591

Lobel, Arnold. Fables. "The Baboon Dances." (3-6)
1002

Lobel, Arnold. Frog and Toad All Year. (K-2)
4, 446, 591

Lobel, Arnold. Frog and Toad Are Friends. (K-2)
4, 13, 24, 96, 446, 591, 638, 707, 1007, 1056

Lobel, Arnold. Frog and Toad Together. (K-2)
4, 255, 259, 274, 446, 591, 985, 1003

Lord, Bette Bao. In the Year of the Boar and Jackie Robinson. (3-6)
14, 98, 268, 348, 411, 677, 719, 774, 917, 1020

Lovelace, Maud Hart. Heavens to Betsy. (5-6)
413

MacLachlan, Patricia. The Facts and Fictions of Minna Pratt. (5-6)
911

Marshall, James. George and Martha. (P-2)
255, 259, 587, 1032

Marshall, James. What's the Matter with Carruthers? (P-2)
587

Marshall, James. Willis. (1-3)
272

Mathis, Sharon Bell. Sidewalk Story. (3-5)
411

Mayer, Mercer. A Boy, a Dog and a Frog. (P-1)
990

Minarik, Else Holmelund. Little Bear's Friend. (P-2)
591

Montgomery, Lucy M. Anne of Green Gables. (4-6)
201, 368, 413

Mowat, Farley. Lost in the Barrens. (5-6)
184

Mueller, Virginia. A Playhouse for Monster. (P-1)
588

Nelson, Theresa. And One for All. (5-6)
417

Novak, Matt. Claude and Sun. (P-1)
410

Paterson, Katherine. Bridge to Terabithia. (5-6)
2, 17, 55, 208, 256, 268, 269, 336, 405, 507, 587, 594, 671, 719, 884, 1019, 1050, 1058

Peck, Robert Newton. Soup. (4-6)
276, 575, 689

Rockwell, Thomas. How to Eat Fried Worms. (4-6)
99, 259, 296, 414, 418, 519, 676, 836, 1014, 1055

Rupprecht, Seigfried P. The Tale of the Vanishing Rainbow. (P-2)
588

Sanders, Scott Russell. Aurora Means Dawn. (1-3)
416, 588

Sawyer, Ruth. Roller Skates. (5-6)
269

Selden, George. Cricket in Times Square. (3-6)
57, 239, 314, 414, 461, 587, 869

Sharmat, Marjorie. The 329th Friend. (P-2)
271, 408

Shura, Mary Francis. Chester. (4-6)
587

Shura, Mary Francis. The Search for Grissi. (3-6)
880

Smith, Doris Buchanan. A Taste of Blackberries. (4-6)
177, 306, 405, 411, 863, 1017, 1055

Speare, Elizabeth George. Sign of the Beaver. (4-6)
6, 16, 98, 244, 356, 413, 414, 417, 419, 572, 588, 687, 936, 1013, 1059

Steptoe, John. Stevie. (K-3)
13, 267, 973

Twain, Mark. Adventures of Tom Sawyer. (5-6)
76, 205, 385, 550, 587

Udry, Janice May. Let's Be Enemies. (P-1)
588

Viorst, Judith. Rosie and Michael. (K-2)
271

Waber, Bernard. The House on East Eighty-Eighth Street. (K-2)
590

Waber, Bernard. Ira Sleeps Over. (K-2)
12, 18, 25, 94, 119, 254, 265, 271, 407, 428, 642, 710, 820, 1007

Waber, Bernard. Loveable Lyle. (K-2)
590, 798

Wallace, Bill. Ferrets in the Bedroom, Lizards in the Fridge. (4-6)
270

Weiss, Nicki. Maude and Sally. (P-2)
271

Wells, Rosemary. Timothy Goes to School. (P-1)
254, 1006

White, E. B. Charlotte's Web. (3-6)
8, 11, 15, 30, 97, 233, 268, 275, 313, 414, 457, 593, 602, 720, 853, 1012, 1050

Winthrop, Elizabeth. Katherine's Doll. (P-2)
587

Winthrop, Elizabeth. Lizzie and Harold. (P-2)
588

Winthrop, Elizabeth. The Best Friends Club. (P-2)
588

Wittman, Sally. The Boy Who Hated Valentine's Day. (P-2)
272

Zolotow, Charlotte. The Hating Book. (K-2)
271

Zolotow, Charlotte. I Know a Lady. (K-2)
271, 986

Zolotow, Charlotte. A Tiger Called Thomas. (P-2)
587

FRIENDSHIP – IMAGINARY

Alexander, Martha. Blackboard Bear. (K-2)
113

Blegvad, Lenore. Rainy Day Kate. (K-2)
588

St. George, Judith. The Halloween Pumpkin Smasher. (2-4)
271

Stevenson, Jocelyn. O'Diddy. (3-5)
303

FRITZ, JEAN

Fritz, Jean. Homesick: My Own Story. (4-6)
373, 411, 587, 758

FROGS—FICTION

Alexander, Martha. No Ducks in Our Bathtub. (K-2)
255

Campbell, Wayne. What a Catastrophe. (P-2)
410

Grimm, Jacob. The Frog Prince. (1-4)
264

Erickson, Russell. A Toad for Tuesday. (1-3)
259

Isele, Elizabeth. The Frog Princess. (K-3)
271

Kent, Jack. The Caterpillar and the Polliwog. (P-2)
726, 786

Lionni, Leo. Fish Is Fish. (P-2)
267

Lionni, Leo. It's Mine. (K-3)
415

Lobel, Arnold. Days with Frog and Toad. (K-2)
4, 591

Lobel, Arnold. Frog and Toad All Year. (K-2)
4, 446, 591

Lobel, Arnold. Frog and Toad Are Friends. (K-2)
4, 13, 24, 96, 446, 591, 638, 707, 1007, 1056

Lobel, Arnold. Frog and Toad Together. (K-2)
4, 255, 259, 274, 446, 591, 985, 1003

Mayer, Mercer. A Boy, a Dog and a Frog. (P-1)
990

Mayer, Mercer. Frog Goes to Dinner. (P-1)
100

Thaler, Mike. In the Middle of the Puddle. (P-2)
587

Winer, Yvonne. Never Snap at a Turtle. (K-2)
1040

FRONTIER AND PIONEER LIFE

Anderson, Joan. Pioneer Children of Appalachia. (4-6)
588

Freedman, Russell. Children of the Wild West. (4-6)
588

Freedman, Russell. Cowboys of the Wild West. (4-6)
588

FRONTIER AND PIONEER LIFE—BIOGRAPHY

Aliki. The Story of Johnny Appleseed. (2-4)
272, 407, 805

Daugherty, James. Daniel Boone. (2-4)
2, 269

Kellogg, Steven. Johnny Appleseed. (1-3)
18, 266, 588, 1034

Lawson, Robert. They Were Strong and Good. (4-6)
1, 269

LeSueur, Meridel. Little Brother of the Wilderness: The Story of Johnny Appleseed. (4-6)
417, 588

Quackenbush, Robert. Quit Pulling My Leg! A Story of Davy Crockett. (5-6)
588

York, Carol Beach. Johnny Appleseed. (2-4)
11

FRONTIER AND PIONEER LIFE—FICTION

Banks, Lynne Reid. Secret of the Indian. (4-6)
541

Blos, Joan W. A Gathering of Days. (6)
2, 269

Brenner, Barbara. Wagon Wheels. (2-4)
411, 417, 588

Brink, Carol Ryrie. Caddie Woodlawn. (4-6)
209, 269, 338, 417, 511, 594, 600, 1021

Byars, Betsy. Trouble River. (4-6)
256, 334, 414, 894

Coerr, Eleanor. The Josefina Story Quilt. (1-3)
259, 588

Dalgliesh, Alice. The Courage of Sarah Noble. (3-5)
417, 460, 631, 772

Fleischman, Sid. Chancy and the Grand Rascal. (4-6)
753

Fritz, Jean. The Cabin Faced West. (2-4)
337, 417, 510, 588

Gipson, Fred. Old Yeller. (4-6)
203, 530, 610, 961

Gipson, Fred. Savage Sam. (4-6)
7

Harvey, Brett. Cassie's Journey. (1-3)
588

Henry, Jo Anne Landers. Log Cabin in the Woods. (4-6)
588

Henry, Marguerite. San Domingo: The Medicine Hat Stallion. (5-6)
417

Hooks, William H. Pioneer Cat. (3-4)
417, 588

Lawlor, Laurie. Addie Across the Prairie. (2-4)
417, 588

MacLachlan, Patricia. Sarah, Plain and Tall. (3-5)
2, 17, 75, 99, 214, 256, 268, 269, 270, 328, 405, 414, 490, 588, 592, 686, 717, 779, 847, 1013

Nixon, Joan Lowery. Beats Me, Claude. (1-3)
587

Nixon, Joan Lowery. In the Face of Danger. (4-6)
417

Richter, Conrad. Light in the Forest. (6)
194, 394, 406, 567, 763

Sanders, Scott Russell. Aurora Means Dawn. (1-3)
416, 588

Sandin, Joan. Long Way Westward. (1-3)
588

Shub, Elizabeth. White Stallion. (1-3)
46

Spear, Elizabeth George. Sign of the Beaver. (4-6)
6, 16, 98, 244, 356, 413, 414, 417, 419, 572, 588, 687, 936, 1013, 1059

Stevens, Carla. Trouble for Lucy. (3-5)
417

Talbot, Charlene Joy. An Orphan for Nebraska. (4-6)
417

Turner, Ann. Dakota Dugout. (1-3)
588

Turner, Ann. Grasshopper Summer. (4-6)
417

Waddell, Martin. Going Home. (2-4)
419
Whelan, Gloria. Next Spring an Oriole. (2-4)
284
Wilder, Laura Ingalls. By the Shores of Silver Lake. (3-6)
262, 417
Wilder, Laura Ingalls. Little House in the Big Woods. (3-6)
35, 195, 259, 262, 407, 417, 475, 592, 644, 711
Wilder, Laura Ingalls. Little House on the Prairie. (3-6)
256, 262, 350, 414, 417, 476, 857, 1020
Wilder, Laura Ingalls. The Long Winter. (3-6)
262, 417, 478, 608
Wilder, Laura Ingalls. On the Banks of Plum Creek. (3-6)
262, 411, 417
Wilder, Laura Ingalls. These Happy Golden Years. (3-6)
262, 417

FRUIT
Ancona, George. Bananas: From Manolo to Margie. (3-5)
407, 588
Gibbons, Gail. The Seasons of Arnold's Apple Tree. (P-2)
1029, 1057
McMillan, Bruce. Growing Colors. (P-2)
587
Rogow, Zack. Oranges. (2-4)
588

FRUIT—FICTION
Ahlberg, Janet. Each Peach, Pear, Plum. (K-2)
587, 789
Dahl, Roald. James and the Giant Peach. (4-6)
14, 64, 99, 183, 256, 268, 320, 473, 680, 717, 922, 1012
Degen, Bruce. Jamberry. (P-2)
698
Devlin, Wende. Cranberry Thanksgiving. (1-3)
271
Kimmelman, Leslie. Frannie's Fruits. (1-3)
588
McCloskey, Robert. Blueberries for Sal. (P-2)
11, 12, 255, 265, 271, 587, 624, 784, 998
Mahy, Margaret. Jam. (P-3)
271
Parkes, Brenda. The Enormous Watermelon. (K-3)
412, 1057

FRUIT—FOLKLORE
Aesop. The Fox and the Grapes. (2-4)
250, 1002

FUTURE—FICTION
Christopher, John. The White Mountains. (5-6)
189, 382, 595

GALILEO
Brighton, Catherine. Five Secrets in a Box. (3-6)
412

GAMES
Ahlberg, Janet. Each Peach, Pear, Plum. (K-2)
789
Anno, Mitsumasa. Anno's Italy. (A)
587

Anno, Mitsumasa. Anno's Journey. (A)
587
Ernst, Kathryn. Owl's New Cards. (P-2)
408
Gryski, Camilla. Super String Games. (4-6)
587
Handford, Martin. Where's Waldo? (A)
271, 1004
Hayes, Sarah. Stamp Your Feet. (P-1)
587
Hoguet, Susan Ramsey. I Unpacked Grandmother's Trunk. (K-3)
410, 590
Jonas, Ann. The Trek. (P-2)
587
Ruben, Patricia. True or False? (P-2)
408
Shaw, Charles G. It Looked Like Spilt Milk. (P-2)
18, 254, 587
Van Allsburg, Chris. Jumanji. (K-6)
1, 15, 265, 269, 271, 411, 1055

GARAGE SALES
Rockwell, Anne. Our Garage Sale. (P-1)
272

GARDENING—FICTION
Burnett, Frances Hodgson. The Secret Garden. (4-6)
9, 200, 379, 413, 414, 540, 587, 718, 934, 1019
Himmelman, John. Amanda and the Witch Switch. (P-2)
271
Hunt, Irene. The Lottery Rose. (6)
924
Krauss, Ruth. The Carrot Seed. (P-2)
12, 407, 998, 1054
Kroll, Steven. The Biggest Pumpkin Ever. (K-2)
724, 783, 1001
Parish, Peggy. Amelia Bedelia Helps Out. (1-3)
3, 591
Rylant, Cynthia. This Year's Garden. (P-2)
588
Titherington, Jeanne. Pumpkin, Pumpkin. (P-2)
18, 272, 1057

GEESE—FICTION
Duvoisin, Roger. Petunia. (K-2)
11, 12, 407, 587, 1006
Langton, Jane. The Fledgling. (4-6)
587
Steig, William. The Real Thief. (2-4)
988

GEESE—FOLKLORE
Aesop. The Goose That Laid the Golden Egg. (K-3)
250, 1002
Grimm, Jacob. The Golden Goose. (1-4)
264
Polacco, Patricia. Rechenka's Eggs. (2-4)
588

GENEALOGY
Cooper, Kay. Where Did You Get Those Eyes? (4-6)
587

GENDER ROLES—FICTION

Alcott, Louisa May. Little Women. (5-6)
414, 1022

Bauer, Carolyn Feller. My Mom Travels a Lot. (K-2)
115

Berenstain, Stan. He Bear, She Bear. (P-2)
1054

Blaine, Marge. Terrible Thing That Happened at Our
House. (K-3)
265, 274, 588, 975

Brink, Carol Ryrie. Caddie Woodlawn. (4-6)
209, 269, 338, 417, 511, 594, 600, 1021

Burch, Robert. Queenie Peavy. (5-6)
684

Campbell, Lisa. Sam Johnson and the Blue Ribbon
Quilt. (P-2)
416

Cleary, Beverly. Ramona the Brave. (3-5)
304, 484

Cleaver, Vera. Where the Lilies Bloom. (5-6)
769, 948

Dalgliesh, Alice. The Courage of Sarah Noble. (3-5)
417, 460, 631, 772

de Paola, Tomie. Oliver Button Is a Sissy. (K-2)
1010

Fitzhugh, Louise. Harriet the Spy. (4-6)
167, 405, 888

Fitzhugh, Louise. Nobody's Family Is Going to Change.
(5-6)
411

Gauche, Patricia Lee. This Time, Tempe Wick? (3-5)
417

George, Jean Craighead. Julie of the Wolves. (6)
2, 88, 221, 269, 277, 393, 405, 406, 565, 606, 775, 923

Hague, Kathleen. The Man Who Kept House. (K-3)
419

Heyward, Dubose. The Country Bunny and the Little
Gold Shoes. (P-2)
271, 1001

Isadora, Rachel. Max. (1-3)
121, 255

Konigsburg, Elaine. From the Mixed-Up Files of Mrs.
Basil E. Frankweiler. (4-6)
2, 16, 60, 211, 269, 345, 405, 414, 515, 595, 674, 721,
912, 1017

L'Engle, Madeline. A Wrinkle in Time. (4-6)
2, 9, 17, 80, 231, 256, 268, 269, 270, 404, 414, 580,
595, 693, 722, 897, 1021, 1061

Lowery, Lois. Number the Stars. (4-6)
2, 6, 269, 277, 375, 529, 764

MacLachlan, Patricia. Arthur for the Very First Time.
(4-6)
882

Mathis, Sharon Bell. Sidewalk Story. (3-5)
411

Munsch, Robert. The Paper Bag Princess. (1-3)
267, 843

O'Dell, Scott. Island of the Blue Dolphins. (5-6)
2, 17, 63, 99, 212, 268, 269, 349, 405, 523, 594,
604, 718, 921, 958, 1019

O'Dell, Scott. Sarah Bishop. (5-6)
6, 417, 933

O'Dell, Scott. Sing Down the Moon. (5-6)
245, 358, 411, 542, 767, 937, 1023

Sorenson, Virginia. Plain Girl. (4-6)
765

Turkle, Brinton. Rachel and Obadiah. (K-3)
417

Voigt, Cynthia. Dicey's Song. (5-6)
2, 84, 216, 269, 390, 584, 907, 956

Voigt, Cynthia. The Homecoming. (5-6)
411, 560, 915

Waber, Bernard. Ira Sleeps Over. (K-2)
12, 18, 25, 94, 119, 254, 265, 271, 407, 428, 642, 710,
820, 1007

Winthrop, Elizabeth. Lizzie and Harold. (K-2)
588

Zolotow, Charlotte. William's Doll. (P-2)
12, 706, 976, 1009

GENERAL STORES

Field, Rachel. General Store. (P-3)
588

GEOLOGY

Cole, Jo Anna. The Magic School Bus Inside the Earth.
(2-5)
1043, 1055, 1057

McNulty, Faith. How to Dig a Hole to the Other Side of
the World. (2-4)
734, 1043

GEORGE III, KING OF GREAT BRITAIN

Fritz, Jean. Can't You Make Them Behave, King
George? (3-6)
455, 588

GEORGE, SAINT

Hodges, Margaret. Saint George and the Dragon. (2-5)
1, 257, 269

GERMANY—FICTION

Climo, Shirley. The Cobweb Christmas. (K-2)
271

GERMANY—FOLKLORE

Grass, Ruth. Hansel and Gretel. (P-1)
587

Grimm, Jacob. Ashputtel (Cinderella). (1-4)
264

Grimm, Jacob. The Breman Town Musicians. (2-4)
252

Grimm, Jacob. Elves and the Shoemaker. (1-4)
264

Grimm, Jacob. Fisherman and His Wife. (1-4)
264

Grimm, Jacob. The Frog Prince. (1-4)
264

Grimm, Jacob. Golden Goose. (1-4)
264

Grimm, Jacob. Hansel and Gretel. (P-2)
252, 264, 999

Grimm, Jacob. Little Red Riding Hood. (P-2)
252, 264, 999

Grimm, Jacob. Rapunzel. (1-4)
264, 408

Grimm, Jacob. Rapunzel. Illus. by Barbara Rogasky.
(2-4)
587

Grimm, Jacob. Rumplestiltskin. (1-4)
252

Grimm, Jacob. Sleeping Beauty. (1-4)
264

Grimm, Jacob. Snow White and Rose Red. (1-4)
264

Grimm, Jacob. Snow White and the Seven Dwarfs.
(P-2)
252, 264, 999

Grimm, Jacob. Three Spinning Fairies. (1-4)
264

Grimm, Jacob. The Water of Life. Illus. by Barbara
Rogasky. (4-6)
414, 587

Lesser, Rika. Hansel and Gretel. (P-2)
18, 587

Mayer, Marianna. The Twelve Dancing Princesses. (1-4)
587

Zelinsky, Paul. Rumplestiltskin. (P-3)
587

GHOSTS—FICTION

Brittain, Bill. Who Knew There'd Be Ghosts? (5-6)
414

Cassedy, Sylvia. Behind the Attic Wall. (5-6)
162

Dickens, Charles. A Christmas Carol. (4-6)
414, 587

Galdone, Paul. The Teeny Tiny Woman. (K-2)
271

Hahn, Mary Downing. Wait til Helen Comes: Ghost
Story. (4-6)
276

Hamilton, Virginia. House of Dies Drear. (5-6)
675, 1025

Hancock, Sibyl. Esteban and the Ghost. (K-3)
419

San Souci, Robert D. The Boy and the Ghost. (1-4)
588

Schwartz, Alvin. Scary Stories to Tell in the Dark. (4-6)
593

Wright, Betty Ren. The Dollhouse Murders. (3-6)
885

GIANTS—FICTION

Briggs, Raymond. Jim and the Beanstalk. (P-2)
11

Dahl, Roald. The BFG. (4-6)
8

Ungerer, Tomi. Zarelda's Ogre. (P-2)
11

GIANTS—FOLKLORE

Jack and the Beanstalk. (P-2)
252, 999

GIFTS

Hautzig, Esther. Make It Special: Cards, Decorations
and Party Favors for Holidays and Other
Celebrations. (4-6)
587

GIFTS—FICTION

Bunting, Eve. The Mother's Day Mice. (P-2)
587, 1001

Campbell, Rod. My Presents. (P-1)
1057

Hautzig, Esther. A Gift for Mama. (3-6)
294

Williams, Vera. Something Special for Me. (K-3)
969

GIFTS—FOLKLORE

Perrault, Charles. The Sleeping Beauty. (P-2)
999

GILBREATH, FRANK N.

Gilbreath, Frank B. Cheaper by the Dozen. (6)
202, 583, 905

GILBREATH, LILLIAN MOLLER

Gilbreath, Frank B. Cheaper by the Dozen. (6)
202, 583, 905

GINGERBREADMAN ADAPTATIONS

Jarrell, Randall. Gingerbread Rabbit. (P-8)
411

GIRAFFES

Sharmat, Marjorie. Helga High Up. (P-2)
271

GLASSES. See Eyeglasses

GLOBES

Knowlton, Jack. Maps and Globes. (2-5)
416

GOATS—FICTION

Mitchell, Sharmat. Gregory the Terrible Eater. (P-3)
18, 271, 415, 639, 732

GOATS—FOLKLORE

Asbjornsen, P. C. The Three Billy Goats Gruff. (1-4)
252, 707, 807

Stevens, Janet. The Three Billy Goats Gruff. (P-2)
587

Three Billy Goats Gruff. (1-4)
252, 707, 807

GOBLINS—POETRY

Coombs, Patricia. Dorrie and the Goblin. (1-3)
271

GOLD MINES AND GOLD MINING—FICTION

Coerr, Eleanor. Chang's Paper Pony. (2-3)
588

GOOD AND EVIL

Alexander, Lloyd. The High King. (6)
2, 269, 372

Cooper, Susan. The Dark Is Rising. (5-6)
389

Cooper, Susan. The Grey King. (6)
2, 269, 413

Cooper, Susan. Over Sea, Under Stone. (5-6)
595

Hunter, Mollie. A Stranger Came Ashore. (6)
942

L'Engle, Madeline. A Wrinkle in Time. (4-6)
2, 9, 17, 80, 231, 256, 268, 269, 270, 404, 414, 580,
595, 693, 722, 897, 1021, 1061

Lewis, C. S. The Lion, the Witch and the Wardrobe.
(4-6)
16, 65, 199, 277, 322, 414, 474, 587, 595, 607, 717,
874, 1020

GORILLAS
  Patterson, Dr. Francine. Koko's Mitten. (3-5)
  15, 737
GOSSIP — FICTION
  Allen, Jeffrey. Nosey Mrs. Rat. (K-2)
  271
GRASSHOPPERS — FOLKLORE
  Aesop, The Ants and the Grasshopper. (K-3)
  1002
  Turner, Ann. Grasshopper Summer. (4-6)
  417
GRASSLANDS
  Catchpole, Clive. Grasslands. (3-5)
  1057
GREAT BRITAIN — FICTION
  Bemelmans, Ludwig. Madeline in London. (P-2)
  590
  Bond, Michael. A Bear Called Paddington. (2-5)
  190, 451, 593
  Bulla, Clyde Robert. A Lion to Guard Us. (3-5)
  417
  Burnett, Frances Hodgson. The Secret Garden. (4-6)
  9, 200, 379, 413, 414, 540, 587, 718, 934, 1019
  Cooper, Susan. The Dark Is Rising. (5-6)
  389
  Cooper, Susan. Over Sea, Under Stone. (5-6)
  595
  Dahl, Roald. Danny, the Champion of the World. (4-6)
  1016
  Garfield, Leon. Young Nick and Jubilee. (4-6)
  6
  Grahame, Kenneth. The Reluctant Dragon. (3-5)
  1015
  Hughes, Shirley. Out and About. (P-2)
  587
  King-Smith, Dick. Babe, the Gallant Pig. (2-5)
  503, 719
  Knight, Eric. Lassie Come Home. (4-6)
  1021
  Newman, Robert. Case of the Baker Street Irregular. (6)
  413, 1025
  Twain, Mark. The Prince and the Pauper. (6)
  1022
  Wolff, Ashley. The Bells of London. (P-2)
  587
GREAT BRITAIN — FOLK SONGS
  Westcott, Nadine Bernard. I Know an Old Woman Who Swallowed a Fly. (P-3)
  271
GREAT BRITAIN — FOLKLORE
  Galdone, Paul. The Teeny Tiny Woman. (2-4)
  271
  Galdone, Paul. The Three Sillies. (P-4)
  271
  Hodges, Margaret. Saint George and the Dragon. (2-5)
  1, 257, 269
  McGovern, Ann. Robin Hood of Sherwood Forest. (4-6)
  1053

  Jack and the Beanstalk. (P-2)
  252, 999
  The Three Little Pigs. (P-2)
  10, 251, 999
  Zemach, Harve. Duffy and the Devil. (1-4)
  1, 269, 587
  Zemach, Margot. The Three Little Pigs. (P-2)
  588
GREAT BRITAIN HISTORY — 1154-1399 — FICTION
  Gray, Elizabeth Janet. Adam of the Road. (6)
  269, 1053
GREAT BRITAIN — HISTORY — EDWARD III — 1327-1377 — FICTION
  De Angeli, Marguerite. Door in the Wall. (4-6)
  2, 217, 269, 369, 514, 595, 754, 909, 1053
GREAT BRITAIN — HISTORY — GEORGE III — 1714-1837 — BIOGRAPHY
  Fritz, Jean. Can't You Make Them Behave, King George? (3-6)
  455, 588
GREECE — HISTORY — MACEDONIA EXPANSION 359-322 B.C.
  Wepman, Dennis. Alexander the Great. (6)
  595
GREECE — KINGS, QUEENS AND RULERS
  Wepman, Dennis. Alexander the Great. (6)
  595
GREEK MYTHOLOGY
  D'Aulaire, Ingri. D'Aulaire's Book of Greek Myths. (3-6)
  595
GROUNDHOGS — FICTION
  Cohen, Carol. Wake Up, Groundhog. (P-2)
  271
GROUNDHOGS DAY — FICTION
  Cohen, Carol. Wake Up Groundhog. (P-2)
  271
GROWTH — FICTION
  Hurwitz, Johanna. Russell Sprouts. (2-4)
  587
  Hutchins, Pat. You'll Soon Grow into Them, Titch. (P-2)
  588
  Krauss, Ruth. The Growing Story. (P-2)
  588
  Mayer, Mercer. When I Get Bigger. (P-2)
  588
  Rylant, Cynthia. Birthday Presents. (P-1)
  588, 1057
  Waddell, Martin. Once There Were Giants. (P-2)
  416
GUINEA PIGS — FICTION
  Duke, Kate. Guinea Pig ABC. (K-2)
  11, 590
GUNS. See Firearms
GYMNASTICS — FICTION
  Winthrop, Elizabeth. Castle in the Attic. (4-6)
  419, 587, 1027
GYPSIES — FICTION
  Bemelmans, Ludwig. Madeline and the Gypsies. (P-2)
  590

Cohen, Carol. Wake Up Groundhog. (P-2)
271

Marshall, James. What's the Matter with Carruthers? (P-2)
587

Miller, Edna. Mousekin's Woodland Sleepers. (P-2)
1057

Ryder, Joanne. Simon Underground. (K-3)
415

HICCUPS—FICTION

Mayer, Mercer. Hiccup. (P-1)
103

HIPPOPOTAMUSES—FICTION

Marshall, James. George and Martha. (P-2)
255, 259, 587, 1032

Mayer, Mercer. Hiccup. (P-1)
103

Thaler, Mike. A Hippopotamus Ate the Teacher. (K-2)
835

Waber, Bernard. You Look Ridiculous Said the Rhinoceros to the Hippopotamus. (P-2)
419

HISTORICAL FICTION

Alcott, Louisa May. Little Women. (5-6)
414, 1022

Avi. Encounters at Easton. (5-6)
417, 588

Avi. The Fighting Ground. (6)
343, 588, 1052

Avi. Night Journey. (5-6)
417, 588

Bauer, Marion Dane. Rain of Fire. (5-6)
417

Beatty, Patricia. Charley Skedaddle. (5-6)
417, 752, 1051

Beatty, Patricia. Eight Mules from Monterey. (5-6)
417

Beatty, Patricia. Turn Homeward, Hannalee. (5-6)
417, 588

Bell, Frederic. Jenny's Corner. (4-6)
417

Blume, Judy. Starring Sally J. Freedman. (5-6)
260

Blos, Joan W. A Gathering of Days. (6)
2, 269

Brenner, Barbara. Wagon Wheels. (2-4)
411, 417, 588

Bulla, Clyde Robert. Charlie's House. (3-6)
417

Bulla, Clyde Robert. A Lion to Guard Us. (3-5)
417

Burch, Robert. Queenie Peavy. (5-6)
684

Byars, Betsy. Trouble River. (4-6)
256, 334, 414, 894

Collier, James. My Brother Sam Is Dead. (5-6)
248, 396, 406, 419, 569, 926

Dalgliesh, Alice. The Courage of Sarah Noble. (3-5)
417, 460, 631, 772

DeJong, Meindert. The House of Sixty Fathers. (4-6)
417, 588

Eckert, Allan W. Incident at Hawk's Hill. (6)
561, 918

Edmonds, Walter D. Matchlock Gun. (2-4)
269

Forbes, Esther. Johnny Tremain. (4-6)
220, 256, 269, 392, 417, 564, 605, 760, 959, 1023, 1052

Fox, Paula. The Slave Dancer. (6)
2, 227, 269, 573, 939, 1023

Fritz, Jean. Early Thunder. (6)
417

Garfield, Leon. Young Nick and Jubilee. (4-6)
6

Gauche, Patricia Lee. This Time, Tempe Wick. (3-5)
417

Gipson, Fred. Old Yeller. (4-6)
203, 530, 610, 961

Harvey, Brett. Cassie's Journey. (1-3)
588

Henry, Jo Anne Landers. Log Cabin in the Woods. (4-6)
588

Henry, Marguerite. King of the Wind. (4-6)
2, 222, 269, 566, 889, 1013

Henry, Marguerite. San Domingo: The Medicine Hat Stallion. (5-6)
417

Hickman, Janet. Zoar Blue. (5-6)
417

Hooks, William H. Pioneer Cat. (3-4)
417, 588

Kroll, Steven. The Hokey-Pokey Man. (P-2)
417

Lawlor, Laurie. Addie Across the Prairie. (2-4)
417, 588

Levinson, Nancy Smiler. Clara and the Bookwagon. (1-3)
417, 588

Lewis, Elizabeth. Young Fu of the Upper Yangtze. (6)
269

Lewis, Thomas P. Hill of Fire. (1-3)
415, 640

Lord, Bette Bao. In the Year of the Boar and Jackie Robinson. (3-6)
14, 98, 268, 348, 411, 677, 719, 774, 917, 1020

Lovelace, Maud Hart. Heavens to Betsy. (5-6)
413

Lowery, Lois. Number the Stars. (4-6)
2, 6, 269, 277, 375, 529, 764

Lunn, Janet. The Root Cellar. (5-6)
417

Mazer, Harry. Cave Under the City. (5-6)
417

MacLachlan, Patricia. Sarah, Plain and Tall. (3-5)
2, 17, 75, 99, 214, 256, 268, 269, 270, 328, 405, 414, 490, 588, 592, 686, 717, 779, 847, 1013

McCurdy, Michael. Hannah's Farm. (1-3)
588

McKenna, Marita Conlon. Under the Hawthorn Tree. (4-6)
6

McSwigan, M. Snow Treasure. (5-6)
174, 380, 492, 940, 1023
Nixon, Joan Lowery. Caught in the Act. (4-6)
417
Nixon, Joan Lowery. A Family Apart. (5-6)
405, 417, 588, 756
Nixon, Joan Lowery. In the Face of Danger. (4-6)
417
O'Dell, Scott. Island of the Blue Dolphins. (5-6)
2, 17, 63, 99, 212, 268, 269, 349, 405, 523, 594, 604,
718, 921, 958, 1019
O'Dell, Scott. The King's Faith. (5-6)
413
O'Dell, Scott. Sing Down the Moon. (5-6)
245, 358, 411, 542, 767, 937, 1023
O'Dell, Scott. Zia. (6)
417
Paterson, Katherine. The Master Puppeteer. (6)
413
Peck, Robert Newton. Soup. (4-6)
276, 575, 689
Pellowski, Anne. First Farm in the Valley: Anna's Story.
(3-5)
417
Rawls, Wilson. Summer of the Monkeys. (4-6)
418, 543, 943
Richter, Conrad. Light in the Forest. (6)
194, 394, 406, 567, 763
Sanders, Scott Russell. Aurora Means Dawn. (1-3)
416, 588
Sandin, Joan. The Long Way to a New Land. (P-2)
588, 981
Sandin, Joan. Long Way Westward. (1-3)
588
Sawyer, Ruth. Roller Skates. (5-6)
269
Shub, Elizabeth. White Stallion. (1-3)
46
Speare, Elizabeth George. Sign of the Beaver. (4-6)
6, 16, 98, 244, 356, 413, 414, 417, 419, 572, 588, 687,
936, 1013, 1059
Speare, Elizabeth George. The Witch of Blackbird
Pond. (5-6)
2, 79, 230, 269, 384, 406, 417, 579, 594, 617, 896,
950, 1021
Stevenson, Robert Louis. Kidnapped. (6)
1022
Talbot, Charlene Joy. An Orphan for Nebraska. (4-6)
417
Taylor, Mildred. The Friendship. (4-6)
417, 1023
Taylor, Mildred. The Gold Cadillac. (4-6)
417, 588
Taylor, Mildred. Let the Circle Be Unbroken. (4-6)
413
Taylor, Mildred. Roll of Thunder, Hear My Cry. (5-6)
2, 17, 74, 224, 269, 398, 411, 413, 539, 611, 685,
962, 1020
Taylor, Theodore. The Cay. (5-6)
16, 82, 197, 277, 340, 413, 582, 904, 1015, 1046

Turkle, Brinton. Rachel and Obadiah. (K-3)
417
Turner, Ann. Dakota Dugout. (1-3)
588
Turner, Ann. Nettie's Trip South. (5-6)
417
Twain, Mark. Adventures of Tom Sawyer. (5-6)
76, 205, 385, 550, 587
Wilder, Laura Ingalls. By the Shores of Silver Lake.
(3-6)
262, 417
Wilder, Laura Ingalls. Farmer Boy. (3-6)
757
Wilder, Laura Ingalls. Little House in the Big Woods.
(3-6)
35, 195, 259, 262, 407, 417, 475, 592, 644, 711
Wilder, Laura Ingalls. Little House on the Prairie.
(3-6)
256, 262, 350, 414, 417, 476, 857, 1020
Wilder, Laura Ingalls. The Long Winter. (3-6)
262, 417, 478, 608
Wilder, Laura Ingalls. On the Banks of Plum Creek.
(3-6)
262, 411, 417
Wilder, Laura Ingalls. These Happy Golden Years.
(3-6)
262, 417
Wiggin, Kate Douglas Smith. Rebecca of Sunnybrook
Farm. (5-6)
414
Yep, Lawrence. Dragonwings. (5-6)
247, 411, 556, 910

HOLIDAYS. (See also names of specific holidays)
Livingston, Myra Cohn. Celebrations. (2-6)
587
Tudor, Tasha. A Time to Keep: The Tasha Tudor Book
of Holidays. (A)
266
Zolotow, Charlotte. Over and Over. (P-2)
588

HOLMES, SHERLOCK (FICTITIOUS CHARACTER)
Newman, Robert. Case of the Baker Street Irregular.
(6)
413, 1025

HOLOCAUST – JEWISH – 1939-1945 – BIOGRAPHY
Frank, Anne. Diary of a Young Girl. (6)
83, 206, 386, 406, 555, 1024

HOLOCAUST – JEWISH – 1939-1945 – FICTION
Levoy, Myron. Alan and Naomi. (6)
367

HOMELESS PERSONS – FICTION
Carlson, Natalie Savage. The Family under the Bridge.
(3-5)
270
Fleischman, Paul. The Scarebird. (P-2)
587
Garfield, Leon. Young Nick and Jubilee. (4-6)
6
Gates, Doris. Blue Willow. (3-5)
53, 670, 722

The Three Little Pigs. (P-2)
10, 251, 999
Zemach, Margot. The Three Little Pigs. (P-2)
588

HUMOROUS FICTION

Allard, Harry. Miss Nelson Is Missing. (1-3)
26, 96, 132, 265, 266, 271, 410, 432, 647, 715, 822,
1008
Atwater, Richard. Mr. Popper's Penguins. (3-5)
242, 324, 527, 1042
Blume, Judy. Superfudge. (2-5)
175, 260, 332, 418, 495, 861
Blume, Judy. Tales of a Fourth Grade Nothing. (2-5)
44, 98, 176, 256, 260, 275, 333, 418, 496, 592, 862
Burch, Robert. Ida Early Comes Over the Mountain.
(5-6)
414
Butterworth, Oliver. The Enormous Egg. (3-6)
59, 316, 414, 463, 886, 1016
Cleary, Beverly. Socks. (3-4)
261, 330, 592
Clifford, Eth. Help! I'm a Prisoner in the Library. (3-5)
1014
Cole, Joanna. Gooly Gump Swallowed a Fly. (P-2)
410
Dahl, Roald. Charlie and the Chocolate Factory. (4-6)
98, 180, 312, 456, 721, 852
Dahl, Roald. Matilda. (4-6)
8
de Paola, Tomie. Strega Nona. (1-4)
11, 13, 18, 97, 255, 265, 271, 408, 442, 657, 714
Du Bose, William Pene. The Twenty-One Balloons.
(4-6)
269, 362, 895, 1021
Fitzgerald, John D. The Great Brain. (4-6)
165, 318, 517, 852, 1015
Fleischman, Sid. Chancy and the Grand Rascal. (4-6)
753
Flora, James. The Great Green Turkey Creek Monster.
(1-3)
271
Gannett, Ruth Stiles. My Father's Dragon. (3-5)
259
Gardiner, John Reynolds. Top Secret. (3-5)
881
Gelman, Rita Goldin. The Biggest Sandwich Ever. (P-2)
408
Grahame, Kenneth. The Reluctant Dragon. (3-5)
1015
Greenwald, Sheila. The Mariah Delaney Lending
Library Disaster. (4-6)
419
Greenwald, Sheila. Rosy Cole's Great American Guilt
Club. (2-4)
587
Haas, Dorothy. To Catch a Crook. (2-4)
414, 587
Hall, Lynn. In Trouble Again, Zelda Hammersmith.
(3-5)
414
Hurwitz, Johanna. Aldo Applesauce. (4-6)
147

Hutchins, Pat. Don't Forget the Bacon. (P-2)
271, 788
Kasza, Keiko. The Wolf's Chicken Stew. (P-1)
1056
Kellogg, Steven. Pinkerton, Behave. (P-2)
116, 437
Kline, Suzy. Horrible Harry in Room 2B. (1-3)
97
Lawson, Robert. Mr. Revere and I. (5-6)
417, 528
Lexau, Joan M. I Should Have Stayed in Bed. (1-3)
587
Lindgren, Astrid. Pippi Longstocking. (3-5)
8, 39, 157, 326, 482, 593, 651, 844
MacLachlan, Patricia. Arthur for the Very First Time.
(4-6)
882
Lord, John Vernon. The Giant Jam Sandwich. (K-3)
271, 1056
Macauley, David. Why the Chicken Crossed the Road.
(1-3)
587
Manes, Stephen. Be a Perfect Person in Just Three
Days. (3-5)
288, 418, 450, 720, 770, 849, 1014, 1055
McCloskey, Robert. Homer Price. (3-6)
411, 518, 854, 1012
Noble, Trinka Hakes. The Day Jimmy's Boa Ate the
Wash. (K-2)
13, 18, 120, 266, 271, 588, 1054
Parish, Peggy. Amelia Bedelia. (1-3)
11, 20, 97, 255, 421, 591, 619, 712, 809, 1008, 1054,
1057
Parish, Peggy. Amelia Bedelia and the Baby. (1-3)
3, 591, 997
Parish, Peggy. Amelia Bedelia Goes Camping. (1-3)
135
Parish, Peggy. Amelia Bedelia Helps Out. (1-3)
3, 591
Park, Barbara. Skinnybones. (4-6)
859, 1055
Pinkwater, Daniel Manus. The Hoboken Chicken
Emergency. (3-5)
168
Rey, H. A. Curious George. (P-2)
12, 95, 122, 272, 426, 590
Rey, H. A. Curious George Takes a Job. (P-2)
255
Rey, Margaret. Curious George Flies a Kite. (P-2)
815
Rockwell, Thomas. How to Eat Fried Worms. (4-6)
99, 259, 296, 414, 418, 519, 676, 836, 1014, 1055
Sachar, Louis. Sideways Stories from Wayside School.
(3-6)
98
Seuss, Dr. And to Think that I Saw it on Mulberry
Street. (P-3)
587
Seuss, Dr. Butter Battle Book. (K-3)
419
Seuss, Dr. Cat in the Hat. (P-2)
590

Burningham, John. Would You Rather... (P-2)
408

Byars, Betsy. The 18th Emergency. (4-6)
151, 870

Carrick, Carol. What Happened to Patrick's Dinosaurs? (K-2)
748, 1036

Clifford, Eth. Help! I'm a Prisoner in the Library. (3-5)
1014

Ekker, Ernst A. What Is Beyond the Hill? (P-2)
587

Freeman, Don. A Rainbow of My Own. (P-1)
587, 1057

Gackenbach, Dick. Harry and the Terrible Whatzit. (K-1)
254, 271, 819

Hilton, Lisa. If Dinosaurs Came Back. (P-2)
412

Hutchins, Pat. Changes, Changes. (P-1)
106, 587, 588, 589, 888, 991

Johnson, Crockett. Harold and the Purple Crayon. (P-1)
254, 408, 1003

Jonas, Ann. The Trek. (P-2)
587

Keats, Ezra Jack. Regards to the Man in the Moon. (P-2)
136, 745

Khalsa, Dayal Kaur. I Want a Dog. (P-2)
410

Konigsburg, Elaine. Jennifer, Hecate, Macbeth, William McKinley and Me, Elizabeth. (4-6)
234, 411, 526

Korschunow, Irina. Adam Draws Himself a Dragon. (2-4)
259

Levy, Elizabeth. Frankenstein Moved in on the Fourth Floor. (3-5)
152

Lionni, Leo. Let's Make Rabbits. (P-2)
410

McPhail, David. Pig Pig Rides. (P-2)
588

Minarik, Else Holmelund. Father Bear Comes Home. (P-2)
591

Most, Bernard. If the Dinosaurs Came Back. (P-2)
408

Murphy, Jill. What's Next Baby Bear? (K-2)
808

Ness, Evaline. Sam, Bangs and Moonshine. (K-3)
1, 41, 160, 269, 271, 489, 587, 715, 825

Paterson, Katherine. Bridge to Terabithia. (5-6)
2, 17, 55, 208, 256, 268, 269, 336, 405, 507, 587, 594, 671, 719, 884, 1019, 1050, 1058

Pinkwater, Daniel. Tooth Gnasher Superflash. (P-2)
408

Prelutsky, Jack. The Baby Uggs Are Hatching. (1-3)
271, 590

Raskin, Ellen. Spectacles. (K-2)
415, 1057

Seuss, Dr. And to Think That I Saw It on Mulberry Street. (P-3)
587

Shaw, Charles G. It Looked Like Spilt Milk. (P-2)
18, 254, 587

Silverstein, Shel. Who Wants a Cheap Rhinoceros? (P-2)
410

Small, David. Imogene's Antlers. (P-2)
265, 271, 410, 713

Snyder, Zilpha Keatley. The Egypt Game. (5-6)
240, 411, 1025

Spier, Peter. Dreams. (P-1)
587

Tafuri, Nancy. Junglewalk. (P-1)
587

Van Allsburg, Chris. The Mysteries of Harris Burdick. (A)
587

Ward, Lynd. The Silver Pony. (4-6)
587

Willard, Nancy. A Visit to William Blake's Inn. (5-6)
2, 269

Williams, Vera B. Cherries and Cherry Pits. (1-3)
409

Yorinks, Arthur. Hey, Al. (1-3)
1, 269, 271, 587

Yorinks, Arthur. Louis the Fish. (K-3)
598

Young, Ruth. A Trip to Mars. (P-2)
412

IMMIGRANTS

Fisher, Leonard Everett. Ellis Island. (6)
588

IMMIGRANTS – FICTION

Bunting, Eve. How Many Days to America? A Thanksgiving Story. (1-3)
266, 588

Cohen, Barbara. Molly's Pilgrim. (2-4)
267, 417, 588, 592

Krumgold, Joseph. Onion John. (5-6)
269

Levinson, Riki. Watch the Stars Come Out. (K-2)
419, 588

Levoy, Myron. Witch of Fourth Street. (4-6)
307

Lord, Bette Bao. In the Year of the Boar and Jackie Robinson. (3-6)
14, 98, 268, 348, 411, 677, 719, 774, 917, 1020

Sandin, Joan. The Long Way to a New Land. (P-2)
588, 981

Sandin, Joan. Long Way Westward. (1-3)
588

Surat, Michele Marie. Angel Child, Dragon Child. (1-3)
977

Talbot, Charlene Joy. An Orphan for Nebraska. (4-6)
417

IMMORTALITY – FICTION

Babbitt, Natalie. Tuck Everlasting. (4-6)
78, 188, 270, 276, 361, 414, 545, 690, 945, 1020

IMPRESSIONISM (ART)
Raboff, Ernest Lloyd. Pierre Auguste Renoir. (4-6)
595

INDENTURED SERVANTS – FICTION
Avi. Encounter at Easton. (5-6)
417, 588
Avi. Night Journeys. (5-6)
417, 588
Bulla, Clyde Robert. Charlie's House. (3-6)
417

INDIA – FICTION
Mukerji, Dhan. Gay-Neck, the Story of a Pigeon. (6)
269

INDIA – FOLKLORE
Brown, Marcia. Once a Mouse. (1-3)
1, 267, 269, 271, 648
Galdone, Paul. The Monkey and the Crocodile. (1-3)
1004

INDIANS OF NORTH AMERICA – ANTIQUITIES
Baylor, Byrd. When Clay Sings. (1-3)
412, 588

INDIANS OF NORTH AMERICA – APACHE – CAPTIVITIES – FICTION
Gipson, Fred. Savage Sam. (4-6)
7

INDIANS OF NORTH AMERICA – BIOGRAPHY
Bulla, Clyde Robert. Squanto, Friend of the Pilgrims. (3-5)
417
Freedman, Russell. Indian Chief. (4-6)
588
Fritz, Jean. The Double Life of Pocahontas. (3-6)
755
Hunt, Bernice Kohn. Talking Leaves: The Story of Sequoyah. (3-5)
407
Kroeber, Theodore. Ishi, Last of His Tribe. (6)
679, 1024
Meadowcroft, Enid LaMonte. Crazy Horse: Sioux Warrior. (2-4)
11

INDIANS OF NORTH AMERICA – CHEROKEE – BIOGRAPHY
Hunt, Bernice Kohn. Talking Leaves: The Story of Sequoyah. (3-5)
407

INDIANS OF NORTH AMERICA – CHEYENNE – FICTION
Goble, Paul. Death of the Iron Horse. (K-3)
588

INDIANS OF NORTH AMERICA – COMANCHE – LEGENDS
de Paolo, Tomie. Legend of the Bluebonnet. (2-4)
156, 419, 837, 1041

INDIANS OF NORTH AMERICA – CREE – FICTION
Mowat, Farley. Lost in the Barrens. (5-6)
184

INDIANS OF NORTH AMERICA – DELAWARE – FICTION
Richter, Conrad. Light in the Forest. (6)
194, 394, 406, 567, 763

INDIANS OF NORTH AMERICA – ETHNIC IDENTITY
Ashabrenner, Brent. To Live in Two Worlds. (6)
588

INDIANS OF NORTH AMERICA – FICTION
Baylor, Byrd. Hawk, I'm Your Brother. (2-4)
733
Banks, Lynne Reid. Indian in the Cupboard. (4-6)
62, 98, 182, 256, 270, 319, 411, 413, 522, 678, 718, 920, 1019
Banks, Lynne Reid. Return of the Indian. (4-6)
73, 276, 538
Cohen, Carol Lee. The Mud Pony. (1-3)
587
Dalgliesh, Alice. The Courage of Sarah Noble. (3-5)
417, 460, 631, 772
Gardiner, John Reynolds. Stone Fox. (3-6)
7, 15, 42, 270, 331, 411, 414, 417, 493, 587, 860, 1012, 1055
Gipson, Fred. Savage Sam. (4-6)
7
Martin, Bill. Knots on a Counting Rope. (1-3)
257
Miles, Miska. Annie and the Old One. (3-5)
15, 21, 232, 271, 278, 587, 620, 714, 978, 1016, 1047, 1055
Mowat, Farley. Lost in the Barrens. (5-6)
184
O'Dell, Scott. Island of the Blue Dolphins. (5-6)
2, 17, 63, 99, 212, 268, 269, 349, 405, 523, 594, 604, 718, 921, 958, 1019
O'Dell, Scott. Sing Down the Moon. (5-6)
245, 358, 411, 542, 767, 937, 1023
O'Dell, Scott. Zia. (6)
417
Richter, Conrad. Light in the Forest. (6)
194, 394, 406, 567, 763
Spear, Elizabeth George. Sign of the Beaver. (4-6)
6, 16, 98, 244, 356, 413, 414, 417, 419, 572, 588, 687, 936, 1013
Whelan, Gloria. Next Spring an Oriole. (2-4)
284

INDIANS OF NORTH AMERICA – FOOD
Aliki. Corn Is Maize: The Gift of the Indians. (1-4)
728

INDIANS OF NORTH AMERICA – GREAT PLAINS – LEGENDS
Freedman, Russell. Buffalo Hunt. (4-6)
588
Goble, Paul. The Girl Who Loved Wild Horses. (1-4)
1, 137, 255, 267, 269, 271

INDIANS OF NORTH AMERICA – LEGENDS
And It Still Is That Way. Collected by Byrd Baylor. (A)
588
Baker, Olaf. Where the Buffalo Begin. (2-4)
587
de Paola, Tomie. Legend of the Bluebonnet. (2-4)
156, 419, 837, 1041
de Paola, Tomie. Legend of the Indian Paintbrush. (2-4)
588

Goble, Paul. Gift of the Sacred Dog. (1-4)
588, 1047

Goble, Paul. The Girl Who Loved Wild Horses. (1-4)
1, 137, 255, 267, 269, 271

Longfellow, Henry Wadsworth. Hiawatha. (K-6)
591

McDermott, Gerald. Arrow to the Sun. (1-4)
1, 269, 587, 1041

Steptoe, John. The Story of Jumping Mouse. (1-3)
419

Van Laan, Nancy. Rainbow Crow. (2-4)
1041

**INDIANS OF NORTH AMERICA—LENAPE—
LEGENDS**

Van Laan, Nancy. Rainbow Crow. (2-4)
1041

**INDIANS OF NORTH AMERICA—NAVAJO—
FICTION**

Armer, Laura Adams. Waterless Mountain. (6)
269

Miles, Miska. Annie and the Old One. (3-5)
15, 21, 232, 271, 278, 587, 620, 714, 978, 1016, 1047,
1055

O'Dell, Scott. Sing Down the Moon. (5-6)
245, 358, 411, 542, 767, 937, 1023

**INDIANS OF NORTH AMERICA—OGLALA—
BIOGRAPHY**

Meadowcroft, Enid LaMonte. Crazy Horse: Sioux
Warrior. (2-4)
11

INDIANS OF NORTH AMERICA—PAPAGO

Baylor, Byrd. The Desert Is Theirs. (1-4)
588, 1041

**INDIANS OF NORTH AMERICA—PAWNEE—
FICTION**

Cohen, Carol Lee. The Mud Pony. (1-3)
587

INDIANS OF NORTH AMERICA—POETRY

Dancing Teepees: Poems of American Indian Youth.
Ed. by Virginia H. Sneve. (3-6)
588

**INDIANS OF NORTH AMERICA—POWHATAN—
BIOGRAPHY**

Fritz, Jean. The Double Life of Pocahontas. (3-6)
588, 755

**INDIANS OF NORTH AMERICA—PUEBLO—
LEGENDS**

McDermott, Gerald. Arrow to the Sun. (1-4)
1, 269, 587, 1041

**INDIANS OF NORTH AMERICA—SOCIAL
CONDITIONS**

Ashabrenner, Brent. To Live in Two Worlds. (6)
588

Kroeber, Theodore. Ishi, Last of His Tribe. (6)
679, 1024

**INDIANS OF NORTH AMERICA—SOCIAL
CONDITIONS—FICTION**

O'Dell, Scott. Sing Down the Moon. (5-6)
245, 358, 542, 767, 937, 1023

**INDIANS OF NORTH AMERICA—WAMPANOAG—
BIOGRAPHY**

Bulla, Clyde Robert. Squanto, Friend of the Pilgrims.
(3-5)
417

Kessel, Joyce. Squanto and the First Thanksgiving.
(2-4)
588

**INDIANS OF NORTH AMERICA—YAHI—
BIOGRAPHY**

Kroeber, Theodore. Ishi, Last of His Tribe. (6)
679, 1024

INDIANS OF NORTH AMERICA—YOUTH

Ashabrenner, Brent. To Live in Two Worlds (6)
588

INDIANS OF SOUTH AMERICA—FICTION

Clark, Ann Nolan. Secret of the Andes. (6)
269

INDIANS OF SOUTH AMERICA—LEGENDS

Finger, Charles. Tales of Silver Lands. (5-6)
269

INFANTS—FICTION

Aruego, Jose. Rockabye Crocodile. (P-2)
587

Day, Alexander. Carl Goes Shopping. (P-1)
1005

Cleary, Beverly. Socks. (3-4)
261, 330, 592

Fisher, Iris. Katie Bo. (P-2)
588

Hoban, Russell. A Baby Sister for Frances. (P-1)
590

Hutchins, Pat. Where's the Baby? (P-2)
587

Mayer, Mercer. The New Baby. (P-1)
1030

McCully, Emily Arnold. The New Baby. (P-1)
588

Parish, Peggy. Amelia Bedelia and the Baby. (1-3)
3, 591, 997

Petersham, Maud. The Box with Red Wheels. (P-2)
587

Shreve, Susan. Lilly and the Runaway Baby. (2-4)
838

Smith, Janice Lee. The Monster in the Third Dresser
Drawer and Other Stories about Adam Joshua. (2-4)
283

Titherington, Jeanne. A Place for Ben. (P-2)
587

Zolotow, Charlotte. But Not Billy. (P-2)
587

INUIT—FICTION

Andrews, Jan. Very Last First Time. (K-3)
415, 588

George, Jean Craighead. Julie of the Wolves. (6)
2, 88, 221, 269, 277, 393, 405, 406, 565, 606, 775,
923

Paulsen, Gary. Dogsong. (6)
413, 908

Rogers, Jean. Runaway Mittens. (P-2)
588

Scott, Ann Herbert. On My Mother's Lap. (P-K)
254

INUIT—LEGENDS

Munsch, Robert. A Promise Is a Promise. (1-3)
845

San Souci, Robert. Song of Sedna. (2-4)
1048

INSECTS—FICTION

Bodecker, N. M. The Mushroom Center Disaster. (2-4)
587

Carter, David. How Many Bugs in a Box. (P-1)
1056

Dahl, Roald. James and the Giant Peach. (4-6)
14, 64, 99, 183, 256, 268, 320, 473, 680, 717, 922,
1012

INSECTS—MISCELLANY

Cutting, Brian. A Small World. (1-3)
1057

INSECTS—POETRY

Fleischman, Paul. Joyful Noise: Poems for Two Voices.
(4-6)
269, 587, 1018

INTERPLANETARY VOYAGES—FICTION

Bradbury, Ray. The Martian Chronicles. (6)
1027

INVENTORS AND INVENTIONS

Caney, Steven. Steven Caney's Invention Book. (4-6)
1026

Fritz, Jean. What's the Big Idea, Ben Franklin? (3-6)
11, 15, 500, 848

Provenson, Alice. The Glorious Flight. (K-3)
1, 269, 271, 415

INVENTORS AND INVENTIONS—FICTION

Sadler, Marilyn. Alistair's Time Machine. (K-3)
1057

IRELAND—FOLKLORE

Balian, Lorna. Leprechauns Never Lie. (K-3)
271, 1001

Boden, Alice. The Field of Buttercups. (P-2)
408

Kennedy, Richard. The Leprechaun's Story. (K-2)
266, 271

IRELAND—HISTORY—1800-1899—FICTION

McKenna, Marita Conlon. Under the Hawthorn Tree.
(4-6)
6

IRISH AMERICANS—FICTION

Stolz, Mary. Noonday Friends. (4-6)
405

ISLANDS—FICTION

Avi. Shadrach's Crossing. (6)
417, 588

Brown, Margaret Wise. The Little Island. (1-3)
1, 269, 711, 739

Brunhoff, Jean de. The Story of Babar. (P-2)
12, 407, 587

Buck, Pearl. The Big Wave. (4-6)
310, 405, 413, 553, 771, 851

Cooney, Barbara. Island Boy. (1-3)
588

Farley, Walter. The Black Stallion. (4-6)
504, 867, 1019, 1055

Hedderwick, Mairi. Katie Morag Delivers the Mail.
(P-2)
587

Henry, Marguerite. Misty of Chincoteague. (3-5)
14, 235

Kellogg, Steven. The Island of the Skog. (1-3)
267, 271, 407, 587

Martel, Cruz. Yagua Days. (2-4)
667

McCloskey, Robert. Time of Wonder. (A)
1, 269

Montgomery, Lucy M. Anne of Green Gables. (4-6)
201, 368, 413

O'Dell, Scott. Island of the Blue Dolphins. (5-6)
2, 17, 63, 99, 212, 268, 269, 349, 405, 523, 594, 604,
718, 921, 958, 1019

Sperry, Armstrong. Call It Courage. (5-6)
2, 5, 17, 56, 226, 269, 339, 405, 554, 594, 601,
721, 901, 1014

Steig, William. Abel's Island. (3-5)
47, 587, 668

Taylor, Theodore. The Cay. (5-6)
16, 82, 197, 277, 340, 413, 582, 904, 1015, 1046

Wiggin, Kate Douglas Smith. Rebecca of Sunnybrook
Farm. (5-6)
414

ITALIAN-AMERICANS—FICTION

de Paola, Tomie. Watch Out for the Chicken Feet in
Your Soup. (K-2)
588

ITALY

Anno, Mitsumasa. Anno's Italy. (A)
587

ITALY—FICTION

Brighton, Catherine. Five Secrets in a Box. (3-6)
412

Collodi, Carlo. The Adventures of Pinnochio. (3-6)
999, 1017

Collodi, Carlo. The Adventures of Pinnochio. Illus. by
Robert Innocenti. (3-6)
587

ITALY—FOLKLORE

de Paola, Tomie. Strega Nona. (1-4)
11, 13, 18, 97, 255, 265, 271, 408, 442, 657, 714

JACK AND THE BEANSTALK ADAPTATIONS

Briggs, Raymond. Jim and the Beanstalk. (P-2)
11

JACK FROST (LEGENDARY CHARACTER)

Van Allsburg, Chris. The Stranger. (A)
587

JACKSON, ANDREW

Quackenbush, Andrew. Who Let Muddy Boots into the
White House? (5-6)
588

MATHEMATICAL CONCEPTS — BILLION (THE NUMBER)
Schwartz, David M. How Much Is a Million? (A)
1056
MATHEMATICAL CONCEPTS — COUNTING
Anno. Anno's Counting Book. (P-2)
11, 407, 589, 707, 989, 1056
Aylesworth, Jim. One Crow: A Counting Rhyme. (P-2)
587
Berenstain, Stan. Bears on Wheels. (P-2)
1056
Butler, M. Christina. Too Many Eggs. (P-1)
412
Carter, David. How Many Bugs in a Box? (P-1)
1056
Cleveland, David. The April Rabbits. (P-1)
258
Crowther, Robert. The Most Amazing Hide and Seek Counting Book. (P-1)
1056
Feelings, Muriel L. Moja Means One: A Swahili Counting Book. (1-3)
11
Giganti, Paul. How Many Snails? A Counting Book. (P-1)
1057
Kitamura, Satoshi. When Sheep Cannot Sleep. (P-1)
1056
Lindbergh, Reeve. The Midnight Farm. (P-K)
1056
Langstaff, John. Over in the Meadow. (P-1)
1006
Mack, Stan. Ten Bears in My Bed. (P-2)
1056
Mathews, Louise. Bunches and Bunches of Bunnies. (K-2)
272, 1056
Owens, Annie. Annie's One to Ten. (P-1)
1056
Rees, Mary. Ten in a Bed. (P-2)
587
Schwartz, David M. How Much Is a Million? (A)
1056
Testa, Fulvio. If You Take a Pencil. (1-3)
117
Trinca, Rod. One Woolly Wombat. (P-1)
1056
MATHEMATICAL CONCEPTS — DIVISION
Hutchins, Pat. The Doorbell Rang. (P-2)
410, 1056
MATHEMATICAL CONCEPTS — GEOMETRY
Carle, Eric. The Secret Birthday Message. (P-1)
415, 1044, 1056
MATHEMATICAL CONCEPTS — MEASUREMENT
Lionni, Leo. Inch by Inch. (P-1)
258, 407, 1056
Myller, Rolf. How Big Is a Foot? (K-3)
415
MATHEMATICAL CONCEPTS — MILLION (THE NUMBER)
Schwartz, David M. How Much Is a Million? (A)
1056

Schwartz, David. If You Made a Million. (3-6)
412
MATHEMATICAL CONCEPTS — MONEY
Berenstain, Stan. The Berenstain Bears Trouble with Money. (P-3)
272
Marshall, James. Willis. (1-3)
272
Mathis, Sharon Bell. The Hundred Penny Box. (4-6)
471, 641, 719
Schwartz, David A. If You Made a Million. (3-6)
412
Viorst, Judith. Alexander Who Use to be Rich Last Sunday. (P-3)
257, 267, 588, 1056
MATHEMATICAL CONCEPTS — MULTIPLICATION
Mathews, Louise. Bunches and Bunches of Bunnies. (K-2)
272, 1056
Travas, Irene. Emma's Christmas. (P-2)
1056
MATHEMATICAL CONCEPTS — NUMBER CONCEPT
Kasza, Keiko. The Wolf's Chicken Stew. (P-1)
1056
Schwartz, David M. How Much Is a Million? (A)
1056
MATHEMATICAL CONCEPT — NUMBERS
Haskins, Jim. Count Your Way through Japan. (2-4)
588
MATHEMATICAL CONCEPT — RULERS (INSTRUMENTS) — FICTION
Giff, Patricia Reilly. In the Dinosaur's Paw. (2-4)
274, 281
MATHEMATICAL CONCEPT — TIME
Pluckrose, Henry. Time. (P-1)
272
MATHEMATICAL CONCEPTS — TIME — FICTION
Carle, Eric. The Grouchy Ladybug. (P-2)
272, 415, 791, 1004, 1056
Hernandez, Xavier. Barmi: A Mediterranean City through the Ages. (3-6)
412
Lyon, George Ella. Father Time and the Day Boxes. (P-2)
410
Bowers, Kathleen Rice. At This Very Minute. (P-2)
410
Sadler, Marilyn. Alistair's Time Machine. (K-3)
1057
MATHEMATICAL CONCEPT — TRILLION (THE NUMBER)
Schwartz, David M. How Much Is a Million? (A)
1056
MATURATION — FICTION
Avi. The Fighting Ground. (6)
343, 588, 1052
Aseltine, Lorraine. First Grade Can Wait. (P-1)
587
Byars, Betsy. After the Goat Man. (5-6)
414

Ets, Marie Hall. *Gilberto and the Wind.* (P-1)
255, 731

Ets, Marie Hall. *Nine Days to Christmas.* (1-3)
1, 269, 588

Lewis, Thomas P. *Hill of Fire.* (1-3)
415, 640

O'Dell, Scott. *The Black Pearl.* (5-6)
5, 238, 387, 505, 899

O'Dell, Scott. *The King's Fifth.* (5-6)
413

Steinbeck, John. *The Pearl.* (6)
89, 397, 406, 585, 1022

MICE—FICTION

Bunting, Eve. *The Mother's Day Mice.* (P-2)
587, 1001

Carle, Eric. *Do You Want to Be My Friend?* (P-K)
587, 1005

Cleary, Beverly. *Mouse and the Motorcycle.* (2-5)
37, 169, 259, 418, 479, 587, 875

Cleary, Beverly. *Ralph S. Mouse.* (3-5)
261, 483

Cleary, Beverly. *Runaway Ralph.* (3-5)
173, 487

Goodall, John S. *Shrewbettina's Birthday.* (P-1)
587

Holabird, Katherine. *Angelina's Birthday Surprise.* (K-2)
1044

Kellogg, Steven. *The Island of the Skog.* (1-3)
267, 271, 407, 587

Kraus, Robert. *Another Mouse to Feed.* (P-2)
588

Kraus, Robert. *Whose Mouse Are You?* (P-1)
13

Kroll, Steven. *The Biggest Pumpkin Ever.* (K-2)
724, 783, 1001

Lawson, Robert. *Ben and Me.* (4-6)
52, 179, 289, 417, 453, 588, 883, 1055

Lionni, Leo. *Alexander and the Wind-up Mouse.* (P-1)
12, 255, 271, 587, 715, 1003

Lionni, Leo. *Frederick.* (P-2)
95, 139, 266, 443, 587

Lionni, Leo. *Tillie and the Wall.* (P-2)
587

Lobel, Arnold. *Mouse Soup.* (K-2)
840

Lobel, Arnold. *The Rose in My Garden.* (K-3)
1056

McCully, Emily Arnold. *The New Baby.* (P-1)
588

Mendoza, Joyce. *Need a House? Call Ms. Mouse.* (P-2)
410, 588

Miller, Edna. *Mousekin Takes a Trip.* (P-2)
1057

Miller, Edna. *Mousekin's Birth.* (K-3)
415

Miller, Edna. *Mousekin's Woodland Sleepers.* (P-2)
1057

Numeroff, Laura Joffe. *If You Give a Mouse a Cookie.* (P-2)
18, 94, 255, 258, 271, 410, 795, 1004, 1056

O'Brien, Robert C. *Mrs. Frisby and the Rats of NIMH.* (4-6)
2, 16, 66, 99, 213, 268, 269, 374, 414, 568, 681, 776, 925, 1021

Selden, George. *Cricket in Times Square.* (3-6)
57, 239, 314, 414, 461, 587, 869

Steig, William. *Abel's Island.* (3-5)
47, 587, 668

Steig, William. *Amos and Boris.* (1-3)
11, 407, 409

Steig, William. *Doctor DeSoto.* (P-3)
271, 634, 729, 817

Titus, Eve. *Anatole and the Cat.* (1-3)
11

Walsh, Ellen Stoll. *Mouse Paint.* (P-2)
1005

White, E. B. *Stuart Little.* (3-6)
8, 43, 161, 256, 494, 712, 1013

MICE—FOLKLORE

Aesop. *The City Mouse and the Country Mouse.* (2-4)
250, 1002

Aesop. *The Lion and the Mouse.* (2-4)
250, 1002

Brown, Marcia. *Once a Mouse.* (1-3)
1, 267, 269, 271, 648

Cauley, Lorinda Bryan. *The Town Mouse and the Country Mouse.* (1-3)
591, 1033

Steptoe, John. *The Story of Jumping Mouse.* (1-3)
419

MIDDLE AGES—FICTION

De Angeli, Marguerite. *Door in the Wall.* (4-6)
2, 217, 269, 369, 514, 595, 754, 909, 1053

Grahame, Kenneth. *The Reluctant Dragon.* (3-5)
1015

Gray, Elizabeth Janet. *Adam of the Road.* (6)
269, 1053

Phillips, Louis. *The Brothers Wrong and Wrong Again.* (1-3)
271

MIND READING—FICTION

Key, Alexander. *The Forgotten Door.* (6)
466

MISBEHAVIOR—FICTION

Allard, Harry. *Miss Nelson Is Back.* (1-3)
432

Allard, Harry. *Miss Nelson Is Missing.* (1-3)
26, 96, 132, 265, 266, 271, 410, 432, 647, 715, 822, 1008

Bemelmans, Ludwig. *Madeline and the Bad Hat.* (P-2)
590

Blume, Judy. *Tales of a Fourth Grade Nothing.* (2-5)
44, 98, 176, 256, 260, 275, 333, 418, 496, 592, 862

Cassedy, Sylvia. *Behind the Attic Wall.* (5-6)
162

Caudill, Rebecca. *Did You Carry the Flag Today, Charley?* (P-2)
587

Cleary, Beverly. *Otis Spofford.* (3-5)
532

Clymer, Eleanor. *My Brother Stevie.* (3-5)
325

MONSTERS—FICTION

Bang, Molly. Wiley and the Hairy Man. (1-3)
419

Christian, Mary Blount. Swamp Monsters. (1-3)
409

Crowe, Robert L. Clyde Monster. (P-1)
408

Gackenbach, Dick. Harry and the Terrible Whatzit. (K-1)
254, 271, 819

Galdone, Joanne. The Tailypo: A Ghost Story. (P-2)
413

Hutchins, Pat. The Very Worst Monster. (P-2)
11

Hutchins, Pat. Where's the Baby? (P-2)
587

Kellogg, Steven. The Island of the Skog. (1-3)
267, 271, 407, 587

Kellogg, Steven. Mysterious Tadpole. (K-3)
255, 273

Kellogg, Steven. Ralph's Secret Weapon. (K-2)
271

Mayer, Mercer. Liza Lou and the Yeller Belly Swamp. (1-3)
255

Mayer, Mercer. There's a Nightmare in My Closet. (P-1)
11, 94, 108, 254, 267, 408, 445, 659, 703, 1003

Mosel, Arlene. The Funny Little Woman. (K-3)
1, 269, 272, 409

Most, Bernard. Boo. (P-1)
408

Pinkwater, Daniel Manus. The Hoboken Chicken Emergency. (3-5)
168

Pinkwater, Daniel. I Was a Second Grade Werewolf. (1-3)
271

Prelutsky, Jack. The Baby Uggs Are Hatching. (1-3)
271, 590

Sendak, Maurice. Where the Wild Things Are. (P-3)
1, 12, 18, 27, 95, 118, 255, 265, 269, 271, 407, 449, 664, 704, 708, 1009

Smith, Janice Lee. Monster in the Third Dresser Drawer: And Other Stories about Adam Joshua. (2-4)
283

Turkle, Brinton. Do Not Open. (K-2)
255

Ungerer, Tomi. Zarelda's Ogre. (P-2)
11

Yolen, Jane. Commander Toad in Space. (1-2)
255, 259

MONTHS OF THE YEAR—POETRY

See also Days of the Week, Mathematical Concepts—Time

Coleridge, Sara. January Brings the Snow: A Book of Months. (P-1)
272, 1057

Provenson, Alice. The Year at Maple Hill Farm. (K-2)
1056, 1057

Sendak, Maurice. Chicken Soup with Rice. (P-1)
18, 109, 271, 995

MONTICELLO (VA.)

Fisher, Leonard Everett. Monticello. (A)
588

MOON

Branley, Franklin. The Moon Seems to Change. (K-3)
597

Branley, Franklin. What the Moon Is Like. (K-3)
597

MOON—FICTION

Asch, Frank. Moon Bear
258

Asch, Frank. Mooncake. (K-1)
597

Berger, Barbara. Grandfather Twilight. (P-2)
587

Brown, Margaret Wise. Good Night Moon. (P-2)
254, 705, 997

Brown, Margaret Wise. Wait til the Moon Is Full. (P-2)
587

Carle, Eric. Papa, Please Get the Moon for Me. (K-2)
1006

McDermott, Gerald. Anansi the Spider. (1-3)
422

MOON PHASES

Branley, Franklin. The Moon Seems to Change. (K-3)
597

MOOSE—FICTION

Rogers, Jean. The Secret Moose. (3-5)
259

Wiseman, Bernard. Morris Goes to School. (P-2)
273

MOSQUITOES—FOLKLORE

Aardema, Verna. Why Mosquitoes Buzz in People's Ears. (1-3)
1, 14, 145, 255, 269, 407, 666, 712, 1010, 1045

MOTHER'S DAY—FICTION

Bunting, Eve. The Mother's Day Mice. (P-2)
587, 1001

Hautzig, Esther. A Gift for Mama. (3-6)
294

Kroll, Steven. Happy Mother's Day. (P-2)
588

MOTION PICTURES—FICTION

Deary, Terry. Calamity Jane. (4-6)
9

MOTORCYCLING—FICTION

Cleary, Beverly. Mouse and the Motorcycle. (2-5)
37, 169, 259, 418, 479, 587, 875

MOUNTAINEERING—FICTION

Ullman, James Ramsey. Banner in the Sky. (4-6)
898

MOUNTAIN LIFE—FICTION

Lobel, Arnold. Ming Lo Moves the Mountain. (K-2)
265, 1056

Rabin, Ruth Yaffe. High in the Mountains. (K-3)
587

Rylant, Cynthia. When I Was Young in the Mountains. (K-3)
416

Spyri, Johanna. Heidi. (4-6)
414, 587

Ullman, James Ramsey. Banner in the Sky. (4-6)
898

MOVING—FICTION
Aliki. We Are Best Friends. (K-2)
588, 663, 970
Asch, Frank. Goodbye House. (P-2)
588
Blume, Judy. Iggie's House. (4-6)
260, 275
Blume, Judy. Then Again, Maybe I Won't. (5-6)
260
Calhoun, Mary. Julie's Tree. (K-2)
587
Coerr, Eleanor. The Josefina Story Quilt. (1-3)
259, 588
Fritz, Jean. The Cabin Faced West. (2-4)
337, 417, 509, 588
Fritz, Jean. Homesick: My Own Story. (4-6)
373, 411, 587, 758
Garrigue, Sheila. Between Friends. (5-6)
405, 587
Greenfield, Eloise. Grandmama's Joy. (1-3)
588
Hughes, Shirley. Moving Molly. (P-2)
265
Hurwitz, Johanna. Aldo Applesauce. (4-6)
147
Johnston, Tony. The Quilt Story. (P-2)
410
Lawrence, James. Binky Brothers. (1-3)
409
Lord, Bette Bao. In the Year of the Boar and Jackie Robinson. (3-6)
14, 98, 268, 348, 411, 677, 719, 774, 917, 1020
Provenson, Alice. Shaker Lane. (P-2)
416, 588
Sandin, Joan. The Long Way to a New Land. (P-2)
588, 981
Sharmat, Marjorie Weinman. Gila Monsters Meet You at the Airport. (K-2)
140, 419
Shura, Mary Francis. The Search for Grissi. (3-6)
880
Slote, Alfred. Moving In. (5-6)
414, 587
Smith, Miriam. Annie and Moon. (P-2)
588
Surat, Michele Marie. Angel Child, Dragon Child. (1-3)
977
Wilder, Laura Ingalls. By the Shores of Silver Lake. (3-6)
262, 417
Wilder, Laura Ingalls. Little House on the Prairie. (3-6)
256, 266, 350, 414, 476, 857, 1020
Zolotow, Charlotte. A Tiger Called Thomas. (P-2)
587

MURDER—FICTION
Babbitt, Natalie. Tuck Everlasting. (4-6)
78, 188, 270, 276, 361, 414, 545, 690, 945, 1020
Henry, Marguerite. Brighty of the Grand Canyon. (3-6)
414, 508

MUSEUMS
Aliki. Digging Up Dinosaurs. (1-4)
596
Aliki. My Visit to the Dinosaurs. (K-3)
596

MUSEUMS—FICTION
Adler, David. Cam Jansen and the Mystery of the Dinosaur Bones. (2-4)
290, 831
Hoff, Syd. Danny and the Dinosaur. (K-2)
13, 127, 427, 1005
Konigsburg, Elaine. From the Mixed-Up Files of Mrs. Basil E. Frankweiler. (4-6)
2, 16, 60, 211, 269, 345, 405, 414, 515, 595, 674, 721, 912, 1017

MUSIC
Field, E. Wynken, Blynken and Nod. (K-2)
591
Langstaff, John. Over in the Meadow. (P-1)
744, 1006
Langstaff, John. Oh! A Hunting We Will Go! (P-2)
254
Mack, Stan. Ten Bears in My Bed. (P-2)
1056
Westcott, Nadine Bernard. I Know an Old Lady Who Swallowed a Fly. (P-3)
271

MUSIC—FICTION
Keats, Ezra Jack. Whistle for Willie. (P-2)
94, 267, 665, 1003
Selden, George. Cricket in Times Square. (3-6)
57, 239, 314, 414, 461, 587, 869
Trivas, Irene. Emma's Christmas. (P-2)
1056

MUSICAL INSTRUMENTS—ACCORDIANS
Williams, Vera. Something Special for Me. (K-3)
969

MUSICAL INSTRUMENTS—BASSOON
Kellogg, Steven. Ralph's Secret Weapon. (K-2)
271

MUSICAL INSTRUMENTS—CELLO
MacLachlan, Patricia. The Facts and Fictions of Minna Pratt. (5-6)
911

MUSICAL INSTRUMENTS—HARMONICA
McCloskey, Robert. Lentil. (1-3)
271, 587

MUSICAL INSTRUMENTS—TRUMPET
White, E. B. Trumpet of the Swan. (3-6)
77, 187, 498

MUSICAL INSTRUMENTS—VIOLINS
Greenwald, Sheila. Give Us a Great Big Smile, Rosy Cole. (2-4)
587

MUSICIANS—FICTION
Greenwald, Sheila. Give Us a Great Big Smile, Rosy Cole. (2-4)
587
MacLachlan, Patricia. The Facts and Fictions of Minna Pratt. (5-6)
911

McKinley, Robin. The Hero and the Crown. (6)
2, 269, 411, 1027

Munsch, Robert. The Paper Bag Princess. (1-3)
843

Phillips, Louis. The Brothers Wrong and Wrong Again.
(1-3)
271

Sargent, Sarah. Weird Henry Berg. (3-5)
1027

Small, David. Paper John. (P-2)
410

Williams, Jay. Everyone Knows What a Dragon Looks
Like. (1-3)
257

Wilson, Sarah. Beware the Dragons. (K-2)
1036

Yolen, Jane. The Greyling. (4-6)
5

NAMES — FICTION

Bayer, Jane. A, My Name Is Alice. (P-2)
410, 588

Davis, Gibbs. The Other Emily. (K-2)
271

Hurwitz, Johanna. The Adventures of Ali Baba
Bernstein. (3-4)
146, 274

Lester, Helen. A Porcupine Named Fluffy. (P-2)
131

NAMES — FOLKLORE

Grimm, Jacob. Rumplestiltskin. (1-4)
252

Mosel, Arlene. Tikki Tikki Tembo. (P-2)
255, 271, 447, 660, 1010

Zelinsky, Paul. Rumplestiltskin. (P-3)
587

Zemach, Harve. Duffy and the Devil. (1-4)
1, 269, 587

NATIONAL MONUMENTS

Maestro, Betsy. The Story of the Statue of Liberty.
(P-3)
588

Munro, Roxie. Inside Outside Book of Washington
D.C. (2-6)
588

NATURE — DRAWING

Arnosky, Jim. Sketching Outdoors in Autumn. (A)
587

NAVIGATION — BIOGRAPHY

Latham, Jean Lee. Carry On, Mr. Bowditch. (6)
269, 751, 902

NEIGHBORHOODS — FICTION

Pinkwater, Daniel. The Big Orange Splot. (K-2)
271, 588

NETHERLANDS — BIOGRAPHY

Frank, Anne. Anne Frank: Diary of a Young Girl. (6)
83, 206, 386, 406, 555, 1024

NETHERLANDS — FICTION

De Jong, Meindert. The Wheel on the School. (4-6)
269

Green, Norma. The Hole in the Dike. (P-2)
587

Hort, Lenny. Boy Who Held Back the Sea. (K-3)
588

NEW YEAR'S DAY

See also Chinese New Year

Kelley, Emily. Happy New Year. (3-5)
588

NEW YEAR'S DAY — FICTION

Anno, Mitsumasa. All in a Day. (3-5)
588

NEW YEAR'S DAY — FOLKLORE

Andersen, Hans Christian. The Little Match Girl. (1-4)
263

Andersen, Hans Christian. The Little Match Girl. Illus.
by Rachel Isadora. (1-4)
587

NEWBERY AWARD

Alexander, Lloyd. The High King. (6)
2, 269, 372

Armer, Laura Adams. Waterless Mountain. (6)
269

Armstrong, William H. Sounder. (5-6)
90, 99, 225, 269, 399, 405, 406, 419, 574, 612, 688,
722, 892, 941

Bailey, Carolyn. Miss Hickory. (4-6)
269

Blos, Joan W. A Gathering of Days. (6)
2, 269

Brink, Carol Ryrie. Caddie Woodlawn. (4-6)
209, 269, 338, 417, 511, 594, 600, 1021

Byars, Betsy. The Summer of the Swans. (5-6)
2, 9, 17, 99, 228, 269, 360, 414, 544, 587, 721,
944, 1017

Chrisman, Arthur Bowie. Shen of the Sea. (5-6)
269

Clark, Ann Nolan. Secret of the Andes. (6)
269

Cleary, Beverly. Dear Mr. Henshaw. (4-6)
2, 17, 58, 210, 261, 269, 315, 405, 415, 513, 587,
594, 673, 720, 773, 906, 1013

Coatsworth, Elizabeth. The Cat Who Went to Heaven.
(3-5)
269

Cooper, Susan. The Grey King. (6)
2, 269, 413

Daugherty, James. Daniel Boone. (2-4)
2, 269

De Angeli, Marguerite. Door in the Wall. (4-6)
2, 217, 269, 369, 514, 595, 754, 909, 1053

De Jong, Meindert. The Wheel on the School. (4-6)
269

Du Bose, William Pene. The Twenty-One Balloons.
(4-6)
269, 362, 895, 1021

Edmonds, Walter D. The Matchlock Gun. (2-4)
269

Enright, Elizabeth. Thimble Summer. (4-6)
269

Estes, Eleanor. Ginger Pye. (5-6)
269

Field, Rachel. Hitty: Her First Hundred Years. (4-6)
269

Finger, Charles. Tales of Silver Lands. (5-6)
269

Fleischman, Paul. Joyful Noise: Poems for Two Voices.
(4-6)
269, 587, 1018

Fleischman, Sid. The Whipping Boy. (4-6)
2, 215, 256, 269, 365, 414, 502, 780, 865, 1014

Forbes, Esther. Johnny Tremain. (4-6)
220, 256, 269, 392, 417, 564, 605, 760, 959, 1023, 1052

Fox, Paula. The Slave Dancer. (6)
2, 227, 269, 573, 939, 1023

Freedman, Russell. Lincoln: A Photobiography. (4-6)
2, 269, 588, 1024

George, Jean Craighead. Julie of the Wolves. (6)
2, 88, 221, 269, 277, 393, 405, 406, 565, 606, 775,
923

Gray, Elizabeth Janet. Adam of the Road. (6)
269, 1053

Hamilton, Virginia. M. C. Higgins the Great. (6)
269

Hawes, Charles Boardman. The Dark Frigate. (6)
269

Henry, Marguerite. King of the Wind. (4-6)
2, 222, 269, 566, 889, 1013

Hunt, Irene. Up a Road Slowly. (6)
269

James, Will. Smoky, the Cowhorse. (6)
269

Keith, Harold. Rifles for Watie. (6)
269, 413, 417

Kelly, Eric P. The Trumpeter of Krakow. (6)
269

Konigsburg, Elaine. From the Mixed-Up Files of Mrs.
Basil E. Frankweiler. (4-6)
2, 16, 60, 211, 269, 345, 405, 414, 515, 595, 674,
721, 912, 1017

Krumgold, Joseph. And Now Miguel. (5-6)
269

Krumgold, Joseph. Onion John. (5-6)
269

Latham, Jean Lee. Carry On, Mr. Bowditch. (6)
269, 751, 902

Lawson, Robert. Rabbit Hill. (4-6)
70, 223, 269, 414, 536

L'Engle, Madeline. A Wrinkle in Time. (4-6)
2, 9, 17, 80, 231, 256, 268, 269, 270, 404, 414, 580,
595, 693, 722, 897, 1021, 1061

Lenski, Lois. Strawberry Girl. (4-6)
269

Lewis, Elizabeth. Young Fu of the Upper Yangtze. (6)
269

Lofting, Hugh. The Voyages of Doctor Doolittle. (5-6)
269

MacLachlan, Patricia. Sarah, Plain and Tall. (3-5)
2, 17, 75, 99, 214, 256, 268, 269, 270, 328, 405,
414, 490, 588, 592, 686, 717, 779, 847, 1013

McKinley, Robin. The Hero and the Crown. (6)
2, 269, 411, 1027

Meigs, Cornelia. Invincible Louisa. (6)
269

Mukerji, Dhan. Gay-Neck: The Story of a Pigeon. (6)
269

Neville, Emily Cheney. It's Like This, Cat. (5-6)
218, 269, 524

O'Brien, Robert C. Mrs. Frisby and the Rats of NIMH.
(4-6)
2, 16, 66, 99, 213, 268, 269, 374, 414, 568, 681,
776, 925, 1021

O'Dell, Scott. Island of the Blue Dolphins. (5-6)
2, 17, 63, 99, 212, 268, 269, 349, 405, 523, 594, 604,
718, 921, 958, 1019

Paterson, Katherine. Bridge to Terabithia. (5-6)
2, 17, 55, 208, 256, 268, 269, 336, 405, 507, 587,
594, 671, 719, 884, 1019, 1050, 1058

Paterson, Katherine. Jacob Have I Loved. (6)
2, 87, 219, 269, 418, 563

Raskin, Ellen. The Westing Game. (5-6)
2, 229, 269, 377, 381, 586, 947, 1025

Sawyer, Ruth. Roller Skates. (5-6)
269

Seredy, Kate. The White Stag. (6)
269

Shannon, Monica. Dobry. (6)
269

Sorenson, Virginia. Miracles on Maple Hill. (4-6)
269

Spear, Elizabeth George. The Bronze Bow. (6)
269

Spear, Elizabeth George. The Witch of Blackbird Pond.
(5-6)
2, 79, 230, 269, 384, 406, 417, 579, 594, 617, 896,
950, 1021

Sperry, Armstrong. Call It Courage. (5-6)
2, 5, 17, 56, 226, 269, 339, 405, 554, 594, 601,
721, 901, 1014

Taylor, Mildred. Roll of Thunder, Hear My Cry. (5-6)
2, 17, 74, 224, 269, 398, 411, 413, 539, 611, 685,
962, 1020

Trevino, Elizabeth Borton de. I, Juan de Pareja. (6)
269

Van Loon, Hendrik. The Story of Mankind. (A)
269

Voigt, Cynthia. Dicey's Song. (5-6)
2, 84, 216, 269, 390, 584, 907, 956

Willard, Nancy. A Visit to William Blake's Inn. (5-6)
2, 269

Yates, Elizabeth. Amos Fortune, Free Man. (4-6)
2, 269, 417, 588, 750

NEWSPAPERS—FICTION

Leedy, Loreen. The Furry News: How to Make a
Newspaper. (P-2)
412

NIGHT

Branley, Franklin. What Makes Day and Night. (K-3)
597

Horwitz, Joshua. Night Markets. (3-5)
588

NIGHT—FICTION

Berger, Barbara. Grandfather Twilight. (P-2)
587

Brinckloe, Julie. Fireflies. (P-2)
730

Brown, Margaret Wise. Wait til the Moon Is Full. (P-2)
587

Barrett, Judi. Animals Should Definitely Not Wear Clothing. (P-1)
271

Bayer, Jane. A, My Name Is Alice. (P-1)
410, 588

Brown, Margaret Wise. The Important Book. (P-K)
412, 1005, 1054

Burningham, John. Would You Rather... (P-2)
408

Carle, Eric. Do You Want to Be My Friend? (P-K)
587, 1005

Carle, Eric. The Grouchy Ladybug. (P-2)
272, 415, 791, 1004, 1056

Cherry, Lynne. The Great Kapok Tree. (K-3)
416, 1011, 1037

De Regniers, Beatrice. May I Bring a Friend? (P-2)
1, 12, 269, 407, 710, 800, 1004

Elting, Mary. Q Is for Duck: An Alphabet Guessing Game. (K-3)
1056

Emberley, Barbara. Drummer Hoff. (P-1)
1, 254, 269, 587

Flack, Marjorie. Ask Mr. Bear. (P-1)
12, 254, 587, 1005

Gwynne, Fred. A Chocolate Moose for Dinner. (A)
271

Hutchins, Pat. The Doorbell Rang. (P-2)
410, 1056

Hogrogian, Nonny. One Fine Day. (K-3)
1, 267, 269, 408, 435, 589, 649

Hoguet, Susan Ramsey. I Unpacked Grandmother's Trunk. (K-3)
410, 590

Krauss, Ruth. A Hole Is to Dig. (P-2)
587

Langstaff, John. Over in the Meadow. (P-1)
744, 1006

Lobel, Arnold. On Market Street. (P-1)
11, 410

Martin, Bill. Brown Bear, Brown Bear, What Do You See? (P-2)
12, 94, 258, 412, 708, 997, 1056

Serfozo, Mary. Who Said Red? (P-1)
412

Shaw, Charles G. It Looked Like Spilt Milk. (P-2)
18, 254, 587

Silverstein, Shel. Who Wants a Cheap Rhinoceros? (P-2)
410

Tolstoy, Alexi. The Great Big Enormous Turnip. (P-2)
254

Tresselt, Alvin. The Mitten. (P-2)
254, 410, 801

PAUL BUNYAN (LEGENDARY CHARACTER)
Blassingame, Wyatt. John Henry and Paul Bunyan Play Baseball. (1-4)
271

Emberley, Barbara. The Story of Paul Bunyan. (P-2)
11

Kellogg, Steven. Paul Bunyan. (K-3)
588, 650

PEACE
Grahame, Kenneth. The Reluctant Dragon. (3-5)
1015

Hickman, Janet. Zoar Blue. (5-6)
417

Leaf, Munro. The Story of Ferdinand the Bull. (P-2)
271, 441, 587, 656, 827

PEARL DIVING
O'Dell, Scott. The Black Pearl. (5-6)
5, 238, 387, 505, 899

Steinbeck, John. The Pearl. (6)
89, 397, 406, 585, 1022

PECOS BILL (LEGENDARY CHARACTER)
Blassingame, Wyatt. Pecos Bill Catches a Hidebehind. (1-4)
271

Kellogg, Steven. Pecos Bill. (2-6)
587

PEER PRESSURE
Bauer, Marion Dane. On My Honor. (6)
270, 353, 405, 411, 413, 927, 1015

Brown, Marc. Arthur's Eyes. (K-2)
97, 410

De Clements, Barthe. Nothing's Fair in the Fifth Grade. (4-6)
170, 270, 418

Levoy, Myron. Alan and Naomi. (6)
367

Neufeld, John. Edgar Allen. (5-6)
342

Smith, Robert Kimmel. The War with Grandpa. (4-6)
363, 418, 546, 691, 722, 946

PEET, BILL
Peet, Bill. Bill Peet: An Autobiography. (4-6)
587

PELICANS—FICTION
Lobel, Arnold. Fables. "The Pelican and the Crane." (3-6)
1002

Wildsmith, Bryan. Pelican. (P-2)
11, 271

PENGUINS
Bonners, Susan. A Penguin Year. (1-4)
1042

PENGUINS—FICTION
Atwater, Richard Tupper. Mr. Popper's Penguins. (3-5)
242, 324, 414, 527, 876, 1042

PERU—FICTION
Clark, Ann Nolan. Secret of the Andes. (6)
269

PETS
Arnold, Caroline. Pets without Homes. (1-4)
588

PETS—FICTION
Alexander, Martha. No Ducks in Our Bathtub. (K-2)
255

Baker, Leslie. The Third Story Cat. (P-2)
267

Balian, Lorna. The Aminal. (P-2)
271, 408

Balian, Lorna. Sometimes It's Turkey, Sometimes It's Feathers. (P-2)
271, 1001

Baylor, Byrd. Amigo. (K-2)
409, 723

Blades, Ann. Mary of Mile 18. (1-3)
587

Brett, Jan. Annie and the Wild Animals. (K-3)
255, 587

Bridwell, Norman. Clifford at the Circus. (P-2)
273

Bridwell, Norman. Clifford, the Big Red Dog. (P-2)
107

Bridwell, Norman. Clifford's Birthday Party. (P-2)
998

Campbell, Rod. The Pop-Up Pet Shop. (P-2)
1028

Cleary, Beverly. Ribsy. (3-5)
261

Cuyler, Marjorie. Freckles and Willie. (P-2)
271

Day, Alexander. Carl Goes Shopping. (P-1)
1005

Gag, Wanda. Millions of Cats. (P-2)
254, 265, 587, 997

Gardiner, John Reynolds. Stone Fox. (3-6)
7, 15, 42, 270, 331, 411, 414, 417, 493, 587, 860, 1012, 1055

Hazen, Barbara Shook. Tight Times. (K-2)
265, 588

Keats, Ezra Jack. Whistle for Willie. (P-2)
95, 267, 665, 1003

Kellogg, Steven. Can I Keep Him? (K-3)
271

Kellogg, Steven. Mysterious Tadpole. (K-3)
255, 273

Morey, Walt. Gentle Ben. (5-6)
198, 516, 887

Most, Bernard. My Very Own Octopus. (P-2)
408

Ness, Evaline. Sam, Bangs and Moonshine. (K-3)
1, 41, 160, 269, 271, 489, 587, 715, 825

Neville, Emily Cheney. It's Like This, Cat. (5-6)
218, 269, 524

Noble, Trina Hakes. The Day Jimmy's Boa Ate the Wash. (K-2)
13, 120, 271, 588, 1054

North, Sterling. Rascal. (4-6)
72, 537, 932

Orbach, Ruth. Please Send a Panda. (P-2)
408

Sharmat, Marjorie Weinman. Nate the Great and the Fishy Prize. (1-3)
411

Shura, Mary Francis. The Search for Grissi. (3-6)
880

Smyth, Glenda. A Pet for Mrs. Arbuckle. (P-2)
419

Taylor, Theodore. Trouble with Tuck. (4-6)
1014

Ungerer, Tomi. Crictor. (K-2)
408, 590

Van Allsburg, Chris. The Garden of Abdul Gasazi. (1-3)
11, 257, 271

Wagner, Jane. J. T. (3-6)
34, 298, 472, 856

Wallace, Bill. Ferrets in the Bedroom, Lizards in the Fridge. (4-6)
270

Ward, Lynd. The Biggest Bear. (1-3)
1, 13, 142, 255, 269, 271, 623, 812, 1003

Yorinks, Arthur. Hey, Al. (1-3)
1, 269, 271, 587

Zion, Gene. Harry, the Dirty Dog. (P-2)
12, 254, 998

PHOTOGRAPHERS – FICTION

Greenwald, Sheila. Give Us a Great Big Smile, Rosy Cole. (2-4)
587

PHYSICALLY IMPAIRED – BLIND – BIOGRAPHY

Graff, Stewart. Helen Keller. (4-6)
295

Hunter, Edith. Child of the Silent Night: The Story of Laura Bridgman. (4-6)
1024

Little, Jean. Little by Little: A Writer's Childhood. (5-6)
587

PHYSICALLY IMPAIRED – BLIND – EDUCATION

Brown, Marion Marsh. Silent Storm. (4-6)
405

Davidson, Margaret. Helen Keller's Teacher. (4-6)
873

PHYSICALLY IMPAIRED – BLIND – FICTION

Garfield, James B. Follow My Leader. (4-6)
411

MacLachlan, Patricia. Through Grandpa's Eyes. (1-3)
271, 588, 747

Martin, Bill. Knots on a Counting Rope. (1-3)
257

Taylor, Theodore. Trouble with Tuck. (4-6)
1014

Wilder, Laura Ingalls. By the Shores of Silver Lake. (3-6)
262, 417

PHYSICALLY IMPAIRED – DEAF

Greenberg, Judith E. What Is the Sign for Friend? (1-3)
588

Peterson, Jeanne Whitehouse. I Have a Sister, My Sister Is Deaf. (1-4)
415

PHYSICALLY IMPAIRED – DEAF – BIOGRAPHY

Graff, Stewart. Helen Keller. (4-6)
295

Hunter, Edith. Child of the Silent Night: The Story of Laura Bridgman. (4-6)
1024

PHYSICALLY IMPAIRED – DEAF – EDUCATION

Davidson, Margaret. Helen Keller's Teacher. (4-6)
873

McDermott, Gerald. The Stonecutter. (1-4)
587

Pomerantz, Charlotte. The Chalk Doll. (1-3)
588

Provenson, Alice. Shaker Lane. (P-2)
416, 588

Steinbeck, John. The Pearl. (6)
89, 397, 406, 585, 1022

Stolz, Mary. Noonday Friends. (4-6)
405

Twain, Mark. The Prince and the Pauper. (6)
1022

POVERTY — FOLKLORE

Grass, Ruth. Hansel and Gretel. (P-2)
587

Grimm, Jacob. Hansel and Gretel. (P-2)
252, 264, 999

Lesser, Rika. Hansel and Gretel. (P-2)
18, 587

McDermott, Gerald. The Stonecutter. (1-4)
587

PRAIRIE DOGS — FICTION

Baylor, Byrd. Amigo. (K-2)
409, 723

PRAIRIE ECOLOGY

George, Jean Craighead. One Day in the Prairie. (4-6)
587

PREDICTABLE STORIES

Asbjornsen, P. C. Three Billy Goats Gruff. (1-4)
252, 707, 807

Asbjornsen, P. C. Three Billy Goats Gruff. Illus. by Janet Stevens. (P-2)
587

Brett, Jan. Annie and the Wild Animals. (K-3)
255, 587

Brown, Margaret Wise. Good Night Moon. (P-2)
254, 705, 997

Campbell, Rod. My Presents. (P-1)
1057

Carle, Eric. The Very Hungry Caterpillar. (P-2)
11, 12, 18, 94, 123, 254, 265, 407, 589, 705, 998, 1035, 1056, 1057

Gag, Wanda. Millions of Cats. (P-2)
254, 265, 587, 997

Galdone, Paul. Henny Penny. (P-2)
587

Galdone, Paul. The Little Red Hen. (P-2)
1033

Galdone, Paul. The Three Bears. (P-2)
265, 587

The Gingerbread Boy. (P-2)
10, 251, 705, 999

Grimm, Jacob. The Breman Town Musicians. (2-4)
252

Henny Penny. (P-2)
10, 251

Hutchins, Pat. Don't Forget the Bacon. (P-2)
271, 788

Krauss, Ruth. The Carrot Seed. (P-2)
12, 407, 998, 1054

The Little Red Hen. (P-2)
10, 251, 708, 999

Mosel, Arlene. Tikki Tikki Tembo. (P-2)
255, 271, 447, 660, 1010

Petersham, Maud. The Box with Red Wheels. (P-2)
587

Schmidt, Karen Lee. The Gingerbread Man. (P-2)
18

Sendak, Maurice. Chicken Soup with Rice. (P-1)
18, 109, 271, 995

Seuss, Dr. Green Eggs and Ham. (P-1)
267, 998

Slobodkina, Esphyr. Caps for Sale. (P-2)
12, 18, 254, 587, 627, 696, 710, 785, 997, 1011

Steig, William. Doctor DeSoto. (P-3)
271, 634, 729, 817

The Three Bears. (P-2)
251, 706, 999

Tresselt, Alvin. The Mitten. (P-2)
257, 410, 801

Westcott, Nadine Bernard. I Know an Old Woman Who Swallowed a Fly. (P-3)
271

Zemach, Margot. The Little Red Hen. (P-2)
587

Zolotow, Charlotte. But Not Billy. (P-2)
587

PREJUDICE — FICTION

Armstrong, William H. Sounder. (5-6)
90, 99, 225, 269, 399, 405, 406, 419, 574, 612, 722, 892, 941

Blume, Judy. Iggie's House. (4-6)
260, 270

Estes, Eleanor. The Hundred Dresses. (3-5)
61, 297, 411, 520, 855, 1015

Naidoo, Beverly. Journey to Jo'Burg. (5-6)
761

Neufeld, John. Edgar Allen. (5-6)
342

Sebestyen, Ouida. Words by Heart. (5-6)
414. 953

Speare, Elizabeth George. Sign of the Beaver. (4-6)
6, 16, 98, 244, 356, 413, 414, 417, 419, 572, 588, 687, 936, 1013, 1059

Taylor, Mildred. The Gold Cadillac. (4-6)
417, 588

Taylor, Mildred. Let the Circle Be Unbroken. (4-6)
413

Taylor, Mildred. Roll of Thunder, Hear My Cry. (5-6)
2, 17, 74, 224, 269, 398, 411, 413, 539, 611, 685, 962, 1020

Taylor, Theodore. The Cay. (5-6)
16, 82, 197, 277, 340, 413, 582, 904, 1015, 1046

Uchida, Yoshiko. A Jar of Dreams. (5-6)
417, 759

Uchida, Yoshiko. Journey Home. (5-6)
417

Uchida, Yoshiko. Journey to Topaz. (5-6)
414, 417, 588, 762

Wilson, Sarah. Beware the Dragons. (K-2)
1036

PRESIDENTS

Parker, Nancy Winslow. The President's Car. (4-6)
588

PRESIDENTS – U.S. – BIOGRAPHY

Adler, David A. A Picture Book of Abraham Lincoln.
(1-3)
426, 588

Adler, David A. A Picture Book of George Washington.
(1-3)
588

Adler, David A. Thomas Jefferson, Father of Our
Democracy. (6)
588

D'Aulaire, Ingri. Abraham Lincoln. (2-4)
1, 11, 269, 591

Devaney, John. Franklin Delano Roosevelt. (5-6)
588

Freedman, Russell. Lincoln: A Photobiography. (4-6)
2, 269, 588, 1024

Gross, Ruth Belov. If You Grew Up with George
Washington. (2-4)
588

Quackenbush, Robert. Don't You Dare Shoot That
Bear. (6)
588

Quackenbush, Robert. Who Let Muddy Boots into the
White House. (5-6)
588

PRINCES AND PRINCESSES

See also Kings, Queens, Rulers, etc.

Andersen, Hans Christian. The Princess and the Pea.
(1-4)
253, 263, 408

Fleischman, Sid. The Whipping Boy. (4-6)
2, 215, 256, 269, 365, 414, 502, 780, 865, 1014

Grimm, Jacob. Snow White and the Seven Dwarfs.
(P-2)
252, 264, 999

Karlin, Barbara. Cinderella. (P-2)
18

Mayer, Mercer. The Twelve Dancing Princesses. (1-4)
587

Munsch, Robert. The Paper Bag Princess. (1-3)
267, 843

Perrault, Charles. Cinderella. (P-2)
716, 999

Perrault, Charles. Cinderella or the Little Glass Slipper.
Pictures by Marcia Brown. (P-2)
1, 269

Perrault, Charles. The Sleeping Beauty. (P-2)
999

Thurber, James. Many Moons. (2-4)
1, 269, 587, 987

Twain, Mark. The Prince and the Pauper. (6)
1022

PRISONS – FICTION

Babbitt, Natalie. Tuck Everlasting. (4-6)
78, 188, 270, 276, 361, 414, 545, 690, 945, 1020

Richler, Mordecai. Jacob Two Two Meets the Hooded
Fang. (4-6)
414

PROBLEM SOLVING – FICTION

Avi. Wolf Rider. (7)
1025

Campbell, Rod. Dear Zoo. (P-1)
1028, 1057

Carlson, Nancy. Loudmouth George and the Sixth
Grade Bully. (K-2)
271

Chapman, Carol. Herbie's Troubles. (K-2)
271

Cleary, Beverly. Henry and the Clubhouse. (3-5)
261, 470

Cooney, Nancy Evans. The Blanket Had to Go. (P-2)
254

Dahl, Roald. Danny, the Champion of the World. (4-6)
1016

Dahl, Roald. The BFG. (4-6)
8

de Paola, Tomie. Marianna May and Nursey. (P-2)
410

Hardendorff, Jeanne B. The Bed Just So. (P-2)
408

Lord, John Vernon. The Giant Jam Sandwich. (K-3)
271, 1056

McCloskey, Robert. Lentil. (1-3)
271, 587

Nixon, Joan Lowery. The Stalker. (6)
1025

Payne, Emmy. Katy No-Pocket. (K-2)
18, 587, 736

Peterson, John. The Littles. (4-6)
267, 300, 477

Smith, Robert Kimmel. The War with Grandpa. (4-6)
363, 418, 546, 691, 722, 946

Sobol, Donald. Encyclopedia Brown, Boy Detective.
(3-5)
271, 275, 462

Thiele, Colin. Farmer Schulz's Duck. (K-3)
587

Thurber, James. Many Moons. (2-4)
1, 269, 587, 987

Titus, Eve. Anatole and the Cat. (1-3)
11

Tolstoy, Alexi. The Great Big Enormous Turnip.
(P-2)
254

Wood, Audrey. King Bidgood's in the Bath. (P-2)
587, 591

PROMISES

Bauer, Marion Dane. On My Honor. (6)
270, 353, 405, 411, 415, 927, 1015

Grimm, Jacob. The Frog Prince. (1-4)
264

Munsch, Robert. A Promise Is a Promise. (1-3)
845

PUERTO RICANS – UNITED STATES – FICTION

Martel, Cruz. Yagua Days. (2-4)
667

Mohr, Nicholasa. Felita. (2-4)
293

PUERTO RICO—FICTION
Martel, Cruz. Yagua Days. (2-4)
667
PUMPKINS—FICTION
Johnston, Tony. The Vanishing Pumpkin. (P-2)
271, 1054
Kroll, Steven. The Biggest Pumpkin Ever. (K-2)
724, 783, 1001
Titherington, Jeanne. Pumpkin, Pumpkin. (P-2)
18, 272, 1057
Williams, Linda. The Little Old Lady Who Was Not
Afraid of Anything. (P-2)
410, 1054
PUPPETS AND PUPPET PLAYS—FICTION
Babbitt, Natalie. Nellie: A Cat on Her Own. (K-2)
1006
Collodi, Carlo. The Adventures of Pinnochio. (3-6)
999, 1017
Collodi, Carlo. The Adventures of Pinnochio. Illus. by
Roberto Innocenti. (3-6)
587
Jeschke, Susan. Perfect the Pig. (1-3)
436
Paterson, Katherine. The Master Puppeteer. (6)
413
PURITANS—FICTION
Spear, Elizabeth George. The Witch of Blackbird Pond.
(5-6)
2, 79, 230, 269, 384, 406, 417, 579, 594, 617, 896,
950, 1021
PUZZLES
Campbell, Rod. Dear Zoo. (P-1)
1028, 1057
Carter, David A. Surprise Party. (P-2)
412
Elting, Mary. Q Is for Duck: An Alphabet Guessing
Game. (K-3)
1056
Geisert, Arthur. Pigs from A to Z. (1-3)
587
Hoban, Tana. Look Again. (P-2)
410
Raskin, Ellen. The Westing Game. (5-6)
2, 229, 269, 377, 381, 586, 947, 1025
Sharmat, Marjorie Weinman. Nate the Great and the
Phony Clue. (1-3)
273, 841
QUESTS IN FICTION
Alexander, Lloyd. The High King. (6)
2, 269, 372
Babbitt, Natalie. The Search for Delicious. (4-6)
1027
Cooper, Susan. The Dark Is Rising. (5-6)
389
Cooper, Susan. Over Sea, Under Stone. (5-6)
595
Saint Exupery, Antoine De. The Little Prince. (4-6)
395, 645, 1016
Steptoe, John. Story of Jumping Mouse. (1-3)
419

Tolkien, J. R. R. The Hobbit. (4-6)
391, 559, 1022
Winthrop, Elizabeth. Castle in the Attic. (4-6)
419, 587, 1027
QUILTS—FICTION
Coerr, Eleanor. The Josefina Story Quilt. (1-3)
259, 588
Ernst, Lisa Campbell. Sam Johnson and the Blue
Ribbon Quilt. (P-2)
416
Flournoy, Valerie. Patchwork Quilt. (K-3)
265, 271
Johnston, Tony. The Quilt Story. (P-2)
410
Jonas, Ann. The Quilt. (P-2)
587
RABBITS—FICTION
Adams, Adrienne. The Great Valentine's Day Balloon
Race. (K-3)
271
Aesop. The Rabbit and the Tortoise. (2-4)
250, 1002
Bates, Lucy. Little Rabbit's Loose Tooth. (K-2)
13, 18, 254, 272, 407, 706, 1004
Brown, Marc. The Bionic Bunny Show. (K-3)
415
Brown, Margaret Wise. Goodnight Moon. (P-1)
254, 705, 997
Brown, Margaret Wise. Home for a Bunny. (P-2)
1001
Brown, Margaret Wise. Runaway Bunny. (P-K)
439, 587, 701
Carlson, Nancy. Loudmouth George and the Sixth
Grade Bully. (K-2)
271
Cazet, Denys. December 24th. (P-2)
588
Cleveland, David. The April Rabbits. (P-1)
258
Friedrich, Priscilla. The Easter Bunny That Overslept.
(P-2)
587
Gag, Wanda. ABC Bunny. (P-1)
587
Heyward, Dubose. The Country Bunny and the Little
Gold Shoe. (P-2)
271, 1001
Howe, James. Bunnicula. (3-6)
149, 256, 311, 407, 418, 509, 587, 672, 718, 868
Jarrell, Randall. Gingerbread Rabbit. (P-2)
411
Keller, Holly. Cromwell's Glasses. (P-2)
588
Lawson, Robert. Rabbit Hill. (4-6)
70, 223, 269, 414, 536
Leedy, Loreen. The Bunny Play. (P-2)
587
Lionni, Leo. Let's Make Rabbits. (P-2)
410

Mathews, Louise. Bunches and Bunches of Bunnies. (K-2)
272, 1056

Potter, Beatrix. The Tale of Benjamin Bunny. (P-1)
587

Potter, Beatrix. The Tale of Peter Rabbit. (P-2)
12, 18, 95, 258, 407, 589, 590, 1003, 1010

Tafuri, Nancy. Rabbit's Morning. (P-2)
254

Tompert, Ann. Nothing Sticks Like a Shadow. (K-2)
742

Zolotow, Charlotte. Mr. Rabbit and the Lovely Present. (P-2)
12, 407, 1004

RABBITS—POETRY

Fisher, Aileen. Rabbits, Rabbits. (2-4)
11

RACCOONS—FICTION

Brown, Margaret Wise. Wait til the Moon Is Full. (P-2)
587

North, Sterling. Rascal. (4-6)
72, 537, 932

St. George, Judith. The Halloween Pumpkin Smasher. (2-4)
271

Sharmat, Marjorie. The 329th Friend. (K-2)
271, 408

Wells, Rosemary. Timothy Goes to School. (P-1)
254, 1006

RACE AWARENESS—POETRY

Adoff, Arnold. All the Colors of the Race. (4-6)
587

RACING—FICTION

Adams, Adrienne. The Great Valentine's Day Balloon Race. (K-3)
271

Aesop. The Rabbit and the Tortoise. (2-4)
250, 1002

Coerr, Eleanor. The Big Balloon Race. (K-3)
415

Crews, Donald. Bicycle Race. (K-2)
11

Turkle, Brinton. Rachel and Obadiah. (K-3)
417

RAIN AND RAINFALL

Simon, Seymour. Storms. (2-6)
587

RAIN AND RAINFALL—FICTION

Blegvad, Lenore. Rainy Day Kate. (K-2)
588

Burningham, John. Mr. Gumpy's Motorcar. (K-3)
415

Lloyd, David. Hello, Goodbye. (P-2)
587

Kalan, Robert. Rain. (P-1)
1057

Martin, Bill. Listen to the Rain. (P-3)
587

Spier, Peter. Peter Spier's Rain. (P-1)
407

Thaler, Mike. In the Middle of a Puddle. (P-2)
587

Zolotow, Charlotte. The Quarreling Book. (K-2)
1010

RAIN FORESTS

George, Jean Craighead. One Day in the Tropical Rain Forest. (4-6)
1048

RAIN FORESTS—FICTION

Cherry, Lynne. The Great Kapok Tree. (K-3)
416, 1011, 1037

RAINBOWS

Brooks, Ron. Annie's Rainbows. (P-2)
408

Freeman, Don. A Rainbow of My Own. (P-1)
587, 1057

Udry, Janice May. Let's Be Enemies. (P-1)
588

RANCH LIFE—FICTION

Erickson, John. Hank, the Cowdog. (4-6)
166

Krumgold, Joseph. And Now Miguel. (5-6)
269

RATS—FICTION

Allen, Jeffrey. Nosey Mrs. Rat. (K-2)
271

Grahame, Kenneth. The Wind in the Willows. (4-6)
196, 383, 548, 587, 616

O'Brien, Robert C. Mrs. Frisby and the Rats of NIMH. (4-6)
2, 16, 66, 99, 213, 268, 269, 374, 414, 568, 681, 776, 925, 1021

RAYS (FISHES)—FICTION

O'Dell, Scott. The Black Pearl. (5-6)
5, 238, 387, 505, 899

READING

Gibbons, Gail. Check It Out! The Book about Libraries. (1-3)
410

READING—FICTION

Bauer, Carolyn Feller. Too Many Books. (P-2)
267

Bunting, Eve. The Wednesday Surprise. (P-2)
416

Duvoisin, Roger. Petunia. (K-2)
11, 12, 407, 587, 1006

Giff, Patricia Reilly. The Beast in Mrs. Rooney's Room. (2-4)
409, 411, 811

Giff, Patricia Reilly. Today Was a Terrible Day. (1-2)
271

Gilson, Jamie. Do Bananas Chew Gum? (4-6)
256

Levinson, Nancy Smiler. Clara and the Bookwagon. (1-3)
417, 588

Maestro, Betsy. Harriet Reads Signs. (P-1)
588

O'Neill, Catherine. Mrs. Dunphy's Dog. (P-2)
410

Seuss, Dr. I Can Read with My Eyes Shut. (P-2)
11

Kline, Suzy. Horrible Harry in Room 2B. (1-3)
97

Konigsburg, Elaine. Altogether One at a Time. (4-6)
411

Konigsburg, Elaine. From the Mixed-Up Files of Mrs. Basil E. Frankweiler. (4-6)
2, 16, 60, 211, 269, 345, 405, 414, 515, 595, 674, 721, 912, 1017

Konigsburg, Elaine. Jennifer, Hecate, Macbeth, William McKinley and Me, Elizabeth. (4-6)
234, 411, 526

Konigsburg, Elaine. Throwing Shadows. (5-6)
587

MacLachlan, Patricia. Arthur for the Very First Time. (4-6)
882

MacLachlan, Patricia. The Facts and Fictions of Minna Pratt. (5-6)
911

MacLachlan, Patricia. Mama One, Mama Two. (P-2)
588

MacLachlan, Patricia. Seven Kisses in a Row. (2-4)
287, 587

MacLachlan, Patricia. Through Grandpa's Eyes. (1-3)
271, 588, 747

Martel, Cruz. Yagua Days. (2-4)
667

Mathis, Sharon Bell. Hundred Penny Box. (4-6)
471, 641, 719

Mathis, Sharon Bell. Sidewalk Story. (3-5)
411

McKenna, Colleen O'Shaughnessy. Fourth Grade Is a Jinx. (3-5)
587

Naidoo, Beverly. Journey to Jo'Burg. (5-6)
321, 761

Ness, Evaline. Sam, Bangs and Moonshine. (K-3)
1, 41, 160, 269, 271, 489, 587, 715, 825

Neufeld, John. Edgar Allen. (5-6)
342

Neville, Emily Cheney. It's Like This, Cat. (5-6)
218, 269, 524

Park, Barbara. Skinnybones. (4-6)
859, 1055

Paterson, Katherine. Bridge to Terabithia. (5-6)
2, 17, 55, 208, 256, 268, 269, 336, 405, 507, 587, 594, 671, 719, 884, 1019, 1050, 1058

Paterson, Katherine. Come Sing, Jimmy Jo. (5-6)
388

Paterson, Katherine. Great Gilly Hopkins. (5-6)
241, 346, 557, 587, 913

Paterson, Katherine. Park's Quest. (6)
377

Robinson, Barbara. The Best Christmas Pageant Ever. (4-6)
163, 454, 669, 850

Robinson, Barbara. My Brother Louis Measures Worms. (4-6)
277

Sachar, Louis. There's a Boy in the Girls' Bathroom. (5-6)
893

Sachs, Marilyn. The Bear's House. (4-5)
270, 405

Shura, Mary Francis. Chester. (4-6)
587

Shura, Mary Francis. The Search for Grissi. (3-6)
880

Shyer, Marlene Fanta. Welcome Home, Jellybean. (5-6)
364

Slote, Alfred. Hang Tough, Paul Mather. (4-6)
276

Slote, Alfred. Moving In. (5-6)
414, 587

Smith, Doris Buchanan. A Taste of Blackberries. (4-6)
177, 306, 405, 411, 863, 1017, 1055

Smith, Robert Kimmel. The War with Grandpa. (4-6)
363, 418, 546, 722, 691, 946

Snyder, Zilpha Keatley. The Egypt Game. (5-6)
240, 411, 1025

Stolz, Mary. Bully on Barkham Street. (4-6)
587

Stolz, Mary. A Dog on Barkham Street. (4-6)
414, 587

Viorst, Judith. Alexander and the Terrible, Horrible, No Good, Very Bad Day. (P-3)
11, 18, 19, 94, 133, 255, 265, 271, 407, 618, 716, 1008, 1054

Viorst, Judith. Alexander Who Used to Be Rich Last Sunday. (P-3)
257, 267, 588, 1056

Viorst, Judith. Rosie and Michael. (K-2)
271

Voigt, Cynthia. Dicey's Song. (5-6)
2, 84, 216, 269, 390, 584, 907, 956

Voigt, Cynthia. The Homecoming. (5-6)
411, 560, 915

Wagner, Jane. J. T. (3-6)
34, 298, 472, 856

Wallace, Bill. A Dog Called Kitty. (4-6)
414

Wallace, Bill. Ferrets in the Bedroom, Lizards in the Fridge. (4-6)
270

REBELLION—FICTION

Cassedy, Sylvia. Behind the Attic Wall. (5-6)
162

Paterson, Katherine. The Great Gilly Hopkins. (5-6)
241, 346, 557, 587, 913

REBUSES

Marzollo, Jean. The Rebus Treasury. (P-K)
410

Mother Goose. The Real Mother Goose Picture Word Rhymes. (P-2)
587

Partch, Virgil F. The Christmas Cookie Sprinkle Snitcher. (P-2)
408

RECYCLING—FICTION

Bocecker, N. M. The Mushroom Center Disaster. (2-4)
587

Fitzhugh, Louise. Harriet the Spy. (4-6)
167, 405, 888

Gardiner, John Reynolds. Top Secret. (3-5)
881

Giff, Patricia Reilly. The Beast in Ms. Rooney's Room. (2-4)
409, 411, 811

Giff, Patricia Reilly. Fourth Grade Celebrity. (4-6)
467

Giff, Patricia Reilly. In the Dinosaur's Paw. (2-4)
274, 281

Giff, Patricia Reilly. Lazy Lions, Lucky Lambs. (2-4)
821

Giff, Patricia Reilly. Today Was a Terrible Day. (1-2)
271

Gilson, Jamie. Do Bananas Chew Gum? (4-6)
256

Gilson, Jamie. Thirteen Ways to Sink a Sub. (4-6)
178, 418

Hahn, Mary Downing. Daphne's Book. (4-6)
341

Hoban, Russell. Bread and Jam for Frances. (P-1)
13, 18, 95, 124, 255, 625, 711, 1003

Honeycutt, Natalie. The All New Jonah Twist. (3-5)
270

Hurwitz, Johanna. Also Applesauce. (4-6)
147

Hurwitz, Johanna. Class Clown. (2-4)
587

Hurwitz, Johanna. To Catch a Crook. (2-4)
414, 587

Kline, Suzy. Horrible Harry in Room 2B. (1-3)
97

Lord, Bette Bao. In the Year of the Boar and Jackie Robinson. (3-6)
14, 98, 268, 348, 411, 677, 719, 774, 917, 1020

Lovelace, Maud Hart. Heavens to Betsy. (5-6)
413

McKenna, Colleen O'Shaughnessy. Fourth Grade Is a Jinx. (3-5)
587

Noble, Trina Hakes. The Day Jimmy's Boa Ate the Wash. (K-2)
13, 18, 120, 271, 588, 1054

Nordstrom, Ursula. Secret Language. (4-6)
414

Oppenheim, Joanne. Mrs. Peloki's Snake. (K-2)
271

Parish, Peggy. Teach Us, Amelia Bedelia. (1-3)
3, 591

Park, Barbara, Skinnybones. (4-6)
859, 1055

Pinkwater, Daniel. I Was a Second Grade Werewolf. (1-3)
271

Rabe, Bernice. The Balancing Girl. (K-2)
966

Sachar, Louis. Sideways Stories from Wayside School. (3-6)
98

Sachar, Louis. There's a Boy in the Girls' Bathroom. (5-6)
893

Sachs, Marilyn. The Bear's House. (4-5)
270, 405

Say, Allen. The Bicycle Man. (K-3)
588

Schwartz, Amy. Bea and Mr. Jones. (K-2)
265, 271, 419, 967

Sharmat, Marjorie. Maggie Marmelstein for President. (5-6)
323, 858

Sharmat, Marjorie. Rosy Cole's Great American Guilt Club. (2-4)
587

Shura, Mary Francis. The Search for Grissi. (3-6)
880

Snyder, Carol. Ike and Mama and the Trouble at School. (4-6)
419

Snyder, Zilpha Keatley. The Egypt Game. (5-6)
240, 411, 1025

Sorenson, Virginia. Plain Girl. (4-6)
765

Stevenson, James. That Dreadful Day. (K-2)
271

Surat, Michele Marie. Angel Child, Dragon Child. (1-3)
977

Udry, Janice. What Mary Jo Shared. (K-2)
12, 407

Weiss, Nicki. Barney Is Big. (P-2)
588

Weiss, Leatie. My Teacher Sleeps at School. (1-3)
126

Wells, Rosemary. Timothy Goes to School. (P-1)
254, 1006

Wiseman, Bernard. Morris the Moose Goes to School. (1-3)
273

Wittman, Sally. The Boy Who Hated Valentine's Day. (P-2)
272

Yashima, Taro. Crow Boy. (1-3)
13, 31, 96, 255, 407, 587, 632, 979

SCHOOL—MAINSTREAMING IN EDUCATION
Lasker, Joe. Nick Joins In. (K-2)
588

SCHOOL—SLOW LEARNERS
Cohen, Miriam. It's George. (K-2)
588

SCHOOL COUNSELORS
Sachar, Louis. There's a Boy in the Girls' Bathroom. (5-6)
893

SCIENCE
Berenstain, Stan. The Berenstain Bears' Science Fair. (1-3)
1057

SCIENCE EXPERIMENTS

Berenstain, Stan. The Berenstain Bears' Science Fair. (1-3)
1057

Branley, Franklyn. Mickey's Magnet. (1-3)
1057

Faverty, Richard. Professor Bubble's Official Bubble Handbook. (3-5)
1040

Simon, Seymour. Soap Bubble Magic. (K-2)
587

SCIENCE EXPERIMENTS – FICTION

Gardiner, John Reynolds. Top Secret. (3-5)
881

SCIENCE FICTION

Bradbury, Ray. The Martian Chronicles. (6)
1027

Christopher, John. The White Mountains. (5-6)
189, 382, 595

Gardiner, John Reynolds. Top Secret. (3-5)
881

Harding, Lee. Fallen Spaceman. (1-3)
409

Karl, Jean. Beloved Benjamin Is Waiting. (5-6)
587

Key, Alexander. The Forgotten Door. (6)
466

L'Engle, Madeline. A Wrinkle in Time. (4-6)
2, 9, 17, 80, 213, 256, 268, 269, 270, 404, 414, 580, 595, 693, 722, 897, 1021, 1061

Paton Walsh, Jill. The Green Book. (4-6)
419

Sadler, Marilyn. Alistair's Time Machine. (K-3)
1057

Service, Pamela F. Stinker from Space. (3-5)
414, 1027

Yolen, Jane. Commander Toad in Space. (1-2)
255, 259

SCIENTISTS – BIOGRAPHY

Aliki. A Weed Is a Flower: The Life of George Washington Carver. (3-5)
588

SCOTLAND – FICTION

Hunter, Mollie. The Kelpie's Pearls. (5-6)
414

Hunter, Mollie. A Stranger Came Ashore. (6)
942

Stevenson, Robert Louis. Kidnapped. (6)
1022

Yolen, Jane. The Greyling. (4-6)
5)

SCOTLAND – FOLKLORE

Nic Leodhas, Sorche. Always Room for One More. (K-2)
1, 269

SEA STORIES

Andrews, Jan. Very Last First Time. (K-3)
415, 588

Babbitt, Natalie. Eyes of the Amaryllis. (4-6)
5

Byars, Betsy. Animal, Vegetable and John D. Jones. (5-6)
414

Gramatky, Hardie. Little Toot. (P-1)
997

Haas, Irene. The Maggie B. (P-2)

Kipling, Rudyard. The Crab That Played With the Sea: A Just So Story. (1-4)
408, 1046

Lionni, Leo. Swimmy. (P-2)
11, 415, 443, 588, 598, 702, 1057

McCloskey, Robert. Burt Dow, Deep Water Man. (1-3)
410

McCloskey, Robert. Time of Wonder. (A)
1, 269

O'Dell, Scott. Island of the Blue Dolphins. (5-6)
2, 17, 63, 99, 212, 268, 269, 349, 405, 523, 594, 604, 718, 921, 958, 1019

Peet, Bill. Kermit, the Hermit. (K-2)
96, 1055

Roop, Peter. Keep the Lights Burning, Abbie. (1-3)
97, 415, 980

Sperry, Armstrong. Call It Courage. (5-6)
2, 5, 17, 56, 226, 269, 339, 405, 554, 594, 601, 721, 901, 1014

Steig, William. Amos and Boris. (1-3)
11, 407, 409

Taylor, Theodore. The Cay. (5-6)
16, 82, 197, 277, 340, 413, 582, 904, 1015, 1046

Tresselt, Alvin. Hide and Seek Fog. (P-2)
587

Turkle, Brinton. Do Not Open. (K-2)
255

Yolen, Jane. The Greyling. (4-6)
5

Zion, Gene. Harry by the Sea. (P-2)
792

SEAMAN – BIOGRAPHY

Latham, Jean Lee. Carry On, Mr. Bowditch. (6)
269, 751, 902

SEASHORE BIOLOGY

Malnig, Anita. Where the Waves Break: Life at the Edge of the Sea. (3-6)
598

SEASONS

Branley, Franklin. Sunshine Makes the Seasons. (K-3)
597

Gibbons, Gail. The Seasons of Arnold's Apple Tree. (P-2)
1029, 1057

SEASONS – FICTION

Anno, Mitsumasa. Anno's Counting Book. (P-2)
11, 407, 589, 707, 989, 1056

Brown, Margaret Wise. The Little Island. (1-3)
1, 269, 711, 739

Carle, Eric. The Tiny Seed. (P-2)
415, 1057

Fowler, Susi Gregg. When Summer Ends. (P-2)
1029

Griffin, Sandra Ure. Earth Circles. (A)
412

Hall, Donald. Ox-cart Man. (K-3)
1, 269, 271, 416, 588, 714

Johnston, Tony. Yonder. (K-3)
588

Lobel, Arnold. Frog and Toad All Year. (K-2)
4, 466, 591

Maestro, Betsy. Through the Year with Harriet. (P-1)
11

McCurdy, Michael. Hannah's Farm. (1-3)
588

Pearson, Susan. My Favorite Time of the Year. (P-2)
588

Provenson, Alice. The Year at Maple Hill Farm. (K-2)
1056, 1057

Ryder, Joanne. Simon Underground. (K-3)
415

Udry, Janice May. A Tree Is Nice. (K-2)
1, 12, 269, 415, 1057

Van Allsburg, Chris. The Stranger. (A)
587

SEASONS – POETRY

Bennett, Lee Hopkins. The Sky Is Full of Song. (1-3)
407, 995

Livingston, Myra Cohn. A Circle of Seasons. (2-6)
587, 1056

Sendak, Maurice. Chicken Soup with Rice. (P-1)
109, 271

SEEDS – FICTION

Carle, Eric. The Tiny Seed. (P-2)
415, 1057

Krauss, Ruth. The Carrot Seed. (P-2)
12, 407, 998, 1054

SELF ACCEPTANCE – FICTION

Blume, Judy. Freckle Juice. (2-4)
33, 96, 260, 274, 280, 410, 469, 818

Blume, Judy. The One in the Middle Is the Green Kangaroo. (K-3)
97, 260, 265, 267, 285, 480, 823

Brown, Marc. Arthur's Nose. (K-2)
271, 1006

Carle, Eric. The Mixed-Up Chameleon. (P-2)
1005

Carlson, Nancy. I Like Me. (P-2)
588

Carrick, Carol. Left Behind. (1-3)
588

Danziger, Paula. The Cat Ate My Gymsuit. (5-6)
512, 903

Davis, Gibbs. The Other Emily. (K-2)
271

Giff, Patricia Reilly. Fourth Grade Celebrity. (4-6)
467

Gilson, Jamie. Do Bananas Chew Gum? (4-6)
256

Hamilton, Virginia. Zeely. (4-6)
694

Howe, James. I Wish I Were a Butterfly. (K-3)
588, 1011, 1054

Hurwitz, Johanna. The Adventures of Ali Baba Bernstein. (3-4)
146, 274

Kent, Jack. The Caterpillar and the Polliwog. (P-2)
726, 786

Konigsburg, E. S. Throwing Shadows. (5-6)
587

Kraus, Robert. Leo, the Late Bloomer. (P-1)
12, 111, 407, 587, 1004, 1054

Lionni, Leo. Alexander and the Wind-up Mouse. (P-1)
12, 255, 271, 587, 715, 1003

Lionni, Leo. Pezzetino. (P-2)
408, 419

Mayer, Mercer. All By Myself. (P-1)
1030

Peet, Bill. Chester, the Worldly Pig. (1-3)
13, 271, 409, 1006

Sharmat, Marjorie. The 329th Friend. (1-3)
271, 408

Sharmat, Marjorie. Helga High Up. (P-2)
271

Sorenson, Virginia. Plain Girl. (4-6)
765

Viorst, Judith. Alexander and the Terrible, Horrible, No Good, Very Bad Day. (P-3)
11, 18, 19, 94, 133, 255, 265, 271, 407, 618, 716, 1008, 1054

Waber, Bernard. You Look Ridiculous Said the Rhinocerous to the Hippopotamus. (P-2)
419

SELF DEFENSE – FICTION

Byars, Betsy. The 18th Emergency. (4-6)
151, 870

SELF RELIANCE – FICTION

Mayer, Mercer. All By Myself. (P-1)
1030

SEQUOYAH

Hunt, Bernice Kohn. Talking Leaves: The Story of Sequoyah. (3-5)
407

SHADOWS – FICTION

Anno, Mitsumasa. In Shadowland. (1-4)
587

Asch, Bernard. Bear Shadow. (P-2)
271, 781, 1057

Jukes, Mavis. No One Is Going to Nashville. (2-5)
842

Seely, Laura L. The Book of Shadowboxes: A Story of the ABC's. (P-1)
412

SHADOWS – FOLKLORE

Cendrars, Blaise. Shadow. (1-3)
1, 269, 415

SHARING – FICTION

Hutchins, Pat. The Doorbell Rang. (P-2)
410, 1056

Lionni, Leo. It's Mine. (K-3)
415

Silverstein, Shel. The Giving Tree. (A)
271, 419, 1013, 1034

SHARING – FOLKLORE

Brown, Marcia. Stone Soup. (K-3)
13, 96, 255, 271, 440, 655, 712, 1009

SHARKS

Cole, Joanna. Hungry, Hungry Sharks. (K-3)
598

McGovern, Ann. Sharks. (K-3)
598

SHEEP—FICTION

Kitamura, Satoshi. When Sheep Cannot Sleep. (P-1)
1056

Maestro, Betsy. Lambs for Dinner. (P-2)
254

SHOEMAKERS—FOLKLORE

Grimm, Jacob. The Elves and the Cobbler. (1-4)
264

SHOES—FICTION

Daly, Nicki. Not So Fast, Songolo. (K-3)
588

Matsuno, Masako. A Pair of Red Clogs. (P-K)
255

Winthrop, Elizabeth. Shoes. (P-2)
587

SHOPPING—FICTION

Allard, Harry. I Will Not go to Market Today. (P-2)
271

Daly, Nicki. Not So Fast, Songolo. (K-3)
588

Day, Alexander. Carl Goes Shopping. (P-1)
1005

Hutchins, Pat. Don't Forget the Bacon. (P-2)
271, 788

Lobel, Arnold. On Market Street. (P-1)
11, 410

SHORT STORIES

Cameron, Ann. More Stories Julian Tells. (2-4)
592

Cameron, Ann. The Stories Julian Tells. (2-4)
267, 409, 588

Konigsburg, E. S. Throwing Shadows. (5-6)
587

Levoy, Myron. Witch of Fourth Street. (4-6)
307

Smith, Janice Lee. The Monster in the Third Dresser
Drawer: And Other Stories about Adam Joshua. (2-4)
283

SHREWS—FICTION

Goodall, John S. Shrewbettina's Birthday. (P-1)
587

SIGN LANGUAGE

Patterson, Dr. Francine. Koko's Kitten. (3-5)
15, 737

SIGNS

Hoban, Tana. I Read Signs. (P-1)
588

SINGING GAMES

Seeger, Ruth Crawford. American Folk Songs for
Children in Home, School and Nursery School. (A)
413

SKUNKS—FICTION

Service, Pamela F. Stinker from Space. (3-5)
414, 1027

SLAVERY

Lester, Julius. To Be a Slave. (6)
588

SLAVERY—BIOGRAPHY

Ferris, Jeri. Go Free or Die. (5-6)
588

McGovern, Ann. Runaway Slave: The Story of Harriet
Tubman. (2-4)
11

Petry, Ann. Harriet Tubman: Conductor on the
Underground Railroad. (4-6)
411, 914

Yates, Elizabeth. Amos Fortune, Free Man. (4-6)
2, 269, 417, 588, 750

SLAVERY—FICTION

Borton, Elizabeth Borton de. I, Juan de Paraja.
(6)
269

Collier, James. Jump Ship to Freedom. (5-6)
588

Collier, James. War Comes to Willy Freeman. (4-6)
768

Fox, Paula. The Slave Dancer. (6)
2, 227, 269, 573, 939, 1023

Hamilton, Virginia. House of Dies Drear. (5-6)
675, 1025

Monjo, F. N. The Drinking Gourd. (1-3)
32, 417

Turner, Ann. Nettie's Trip South. (5-6)
417

SLED DOG RACING

Cooper, Michael. Racing Sled Dogs. (4-6)
587

SLED DOG RACING—FICTION

Gardiner, John Reynolds. Stone Fox. (3-6)
7, 15, 42, 270, 331, 411, 414, 417, 493, 587, 860, 1012,
1055

Paulsen, Gary. Dogsong. (6)
413, 908

SLEEP—FICTION

Field, E. Wynken, Blynken and Nod. (K-2)
591

Hardendorff, Jeanne B. The Bed Just So. (P-2)
408

Kraus, Robert. Milton the Early Riser. (P-1)
267

Shepperson, Rob. The Sandman. (P-2)
272

Irving, Washington. Rip Van Winkle. (5-6)
587

Wood, Audrey. The Napping House. (P-2)
95, 254, 258, 587, 710, 1054, 1056

Zolotow, Charlotte. The Sleepy Book. (P-2)
587

SLEEP—FOLKLORE

Perrault, Charles. The Sleeping Beauty. (P-2)
999

SMOKING—FICTION

Cleary, Beverly. Ramona and Her Father.
(3-6)
71, 256, 261, 267, 414

SMUGGLING—FICTION

Avi. Shadrach's Crossing. (6)
417, 588

SNAKES

Noble, Trinka Hakes. The Day Jimmy's Boa Ate the Wash. (K-2)
13, 18, 120, 271, 588, 1054

Oppenheim, Joanne. Mrs. Peloki's Snake. (K-2)
271

Ungerer, Tomi. Crictor. (K-2)
408, 590

Wildsmith, Brian. Python's Party. (P-2)
11

SNOW/BLIZZARDS – FICTION

Briggs, Raymond. The Snowman. (P-1)
102

Burton, Virginia. Katy and the Big Snow. (P-2)
255, 699, 1003

Clifford, Eth. Help! I'm a Prisoner in the Library. (3-5)
1014

Goffstein, M. B. Our Snowman. (P-2)
410

Hader, Berta. The Big Snow. (K-2)
1, 269

Keats, Ezra. Snowy Day. (P-2)
1, 12, 18, 128, 265, 269, 407, 654, 804, 998, 1057

Krauss, Ruth. The Happy Day. (P-2)
254

Morgan, Allen. Sadie and the Snowman. (K-3)
415

Steig, Irene. Brave Irene. (K-3)
271

Stevens, Carla. Anna, Grandpa and the Big Storm. (P-2)
588

Tresselt, Alvin. White Snow, Bright Snow. (P-2)
1, 269

Wilder, Laura Ingalls. The Long Winter. (3-6)
262, 417, 478, 608

Zolotow, Charlotte. Something Is Going to Happen. (P-2)
1029

SNOW – FOLKLORE

Van Laan, Nancy. Rainbow Crow. (2-4)
1041

SNOWMEN – FICTION

Briggs, Raymond. The Snowmen. (P-1)
102, 587, 994

Goffstein, M. B. Our Snowman. (P-2)
410

Kellogg, Steven. The Mystery of the Missing Red Mitten. (P-1)
254, 258

Mendez, Phil. The Black Snowman. (1-3)
588

Morgan, Allen. Sadie and the Snowman. (K-3)
415

SOLAR SYSTEM

Branley, Franklin. The Planets Seem to Change. (1-4)
597

SONGS

Diane Goode Book of Folk Tales and Songs. (2-5)
588

Field, E. Wynken, Blynken and Nod. (K-2)
591

Langstaff, John. Oh! A Hunting We Will Go. (P-2)
254

Langstaff, John. Over in the Meadow. (P-1)
744, 1006

Mack, Stan. Ten Bears in My Bed. (P-2)
1056

Nic Leodhas, Sorche. Always Room for One More. (K-2)
1, 269

Rounds, Glen. I Know an Old Lady Who Swallowed a Fly. (P-2)
587

Seeger, Ruth Crawford. American Folk Songs for Children in Home, School and Nursery School. (A)
413

Sewall, Marcia. Animal Song. (P-2)
587

Westcott, Nadine Bernard. I Know an Old Woman Who Swallowed a Fly. (P-3)
271

Wolff, Ashley. The Bells of London. (P-2)
587

SONGS – NATIONAL

Key, Francis Scott. Star Spangled Banner. Illus. by Peter Spier. (A)
416, 588

SOUTH AFRICA

Daly, Nicki. Not So Fast, Songolo. (K-3)
588

SOUTH AFRICA – RACE RELATIONS

Naidoo, Beverly. Journey to Jo'Burg. (5-6)
321, 761

SOUTH AMERICA – AMAZON RIVER

Cherry, Lynne. The Great Kapok Tree. (K-3)
416, 1011, 1037

SPACE COLONIES – FICTION

Bradbury, Ray. The Martian Chronicles. (6)
1027

SPACE FLIGHT

Barton, Byron. I Want to Be an Astronaut. (P-2)
588, 1057

Ride, Sally. To Space and Back with Sally Ride. (3-5)
597

SPACE FLIGHT – FICTION

Sadler, Marilyn. Alistair's Time Machine. (K-3)
1057

Young, Ruth. A Trip to Mars. (P-2)
412

SPACE FLIGHT TO THE MOON

Murphy, Jill. What's Next Baby Bear? (K-2)
808

SPACE SHUTTLES

Ride, Sally. To Space and Back with Sally Ride. (3-5)
597

SPACE VEHICLES – MODELS

West, Robin. Far Out: How to Create Your Own Star World. (4-6)
588

SPAIN – FICTION

Hancock, Sibyl. Esteban and the Ghost. (K-3)
419

Clifton, Lucille. Everett Anderson's Goodbye. (P-2)
588
Cole, Joanna. Gooly Gump Swallowed a Fly. (P-2)
410
Degen, Bruce. Jamberry. (P-2)
698
Field, Rachel. General Store. (P-3)
588
Flora, James. The Great Green Turkey Creek Monster. (1-3)
271
Hague, Michael. Alphabears. (P-1)
587
Hughes, Shirley. Out and About. (P-2)
587
Hutchins, Pat. Don't Forget the Bacon. (P-2)
271, 788
Kraus, Robert. Whose Mouse Are You? (P-1)
13
Lear, Edward. The Quangle Wangle's Hat. Illus. by Helen Oxenbury. (P-2)
587
Lear, Edward. The Quangle Wangle's Hat. Illus. by Janet Stevens. (P-2)
587
Lindbergh, Reeve. The Midnight Farm. (P-K)
1056
Lobel, Arnold. On Market Street. (P-1)
11, 410
Lobel, Arnold. The Rose in My Garden. (K-3)
1056
Lord, John Vernon. The Giant Jam Sandwich. (K-3)
271, 1056
Martin, Bill. Brown Bear, Brown Bear, What Do You See? (P-2)
12, 94, 258, 412, 708, 997, 1056
Martin, Bill. Chicka Chicka Boom Boom. (P-2)
412, 1054
Partch, Virgil F. The Christmas Cookie Sprinkle Snitcher. (P-2)
408
Peet, Bill. Hubert's Hair Raising Adventure. (K-3)
271
Peet, Bill. Kermit, the Hermit. (K-2)
96, 1055
Peet, Bill. The Luckiest One of All. (2-4)
271, 587
Peet, Bill. No Such Things. (1-3)
271
Peet, Bill. The Pinkish Purplish Bluish Egg. (K-3)
271
Ryder, Joanne. Chipmunk Song. (K-3)
415
Seuss, Dr. And to Think That I Saw It on Mulberry Street. (P-3)
587
Seuss, Dr. Butter Battle Book. (K-3)
419
Seuss, Dr. Cat in the Hat. (P-2)
590
Seuss, Dr. Green Eggs and Ham. (P-1)
267, 998

Seuss, Dr. Horton Hatches the Egg. (P-3)
18, 407, 419
Seuss, Dr. Horton Hears a Who. (P-3)
13
Seuss, Dr. How the Grinch Stole Christmas. (1-3)
266
Seuss, Dr. I Can Read with My Eyes Shut. (P-2)
11
Seuss, Dr. If I Ran the Zoo. (P-3)
996
Seuss, Dr. In a People House. (P-1)
998
Seuss, Dr. The Lorax. (P-3)
419, 590, 1006
Silverstein, Shel. Who Wants a Cheap Rhinoceros? (P-2)
410
Trinca, Rod. One Wooly Wombat. (P-1)
1056
Winthrop, Elizabeth. Shoes. (P-2)
587

STORKS—FICTION
De Jong, Meindert. The Wheel on the School. (4-6)
269

STORKS—FOLKLORE
Aesop. The Fox and the Stork. (2-4)
250

STORYTELLING—FICTION
Tompert, Ann. Grandfather Tang's Story. (1-4)
1056

SUBURBAN LIFE
Blume, Judy. Iggie's House. (4-6)
260, 275
Blume, Judy. Otherwise Known as Sheila the Great. (4-6)
171, 260
Blume, Judy. Then Again, Maybe I Won't. (6)
260
Cleary, Beverly. Ellen Tebbits. (3-5)
261, 414
Cleary, Beverly. Henry and the Clubhouse. (3-5)
261, 470
Cleary, Beverly. Henry Huggins. (3-5)
154
De Clements, Barthe. Nothing's Fair in the Fifth Grade. (4-6)
170, 270, 418
Park, Barbara. Skinnybones. (4-6)
859, 1055
Rockwell, Anne. Our Garage Sale. (P-1)
272
Stolz, Mary. Bully on Barkham Street. (4-6)
587
Stolz, Mary. A Dog on Barkham Street. (4-6)
414, 587

SULLIVAN, ANNIE
Brown, Marion Walsh. Silent Storm. (4-6)
405
Davidson, Margaret. Helen Keller's Teacher. (4-6)
873

SUMMER — FICTION

Cameron, Ann. Julian's Glorious Summer. (2-4)
282, 411

Factor, June. Summer. (P-2)
588

McCloskey, Robert. Time of Wonder. (A)
1, 269

Moore, Elaine. Grandma's House. (P-2)
588

Zion, Gene. Harry by the Sea. (P-2)
792

SUN

Branley, Franklin. The Sun, Our Nearest Star. (K-3)
597

Branley, Franklin. Sunshine Makes the Seasons. (K-3)
597

Gibbons, Gail. Sun Up, Sun Down. (P-2)
1057

Simon, Seymour. Sun. (K-3)
597

SUN — FICTION

Anno, Mitsumasa. In Shadowland. (1-4)
587

Baylor, Byrd. The Way to Start a Day. (3-6)
588

Euvremeyer, Teryl. Sun's Up. (P-1)
587

Novak, Matt. Claude and Sun. (P-1)
410

SUPERSTITIONS

Schwartz, Alvin. Cross Your Fingers, Spit in Your Hat. (4-6)
588

SURVIVAL — FICTION

Bunting, Eve. How Many Days to America? A Thanksgiving Story. (1-3)
266, 588

Burnford, Sheila. The Incredible Journey. (5-6)
7, 86, 181, 347, 418, 562, 603, 919, 957

Collier, James. War Comes to Willy Freeman. (4-6)
768

Eckert, Allan W. Incident at Hawk's Hill. (6)
561, 918

Farley, Walter. The Black Stallion. (4-6)
504, 867, 1019, 1055

Fox, Paula. The Slave Dancer. (6)
2, 227, 269, 573, 939, 1023

Garfield, Leon. Young Nick and Jubilee. (4-6)
6

George, Jean Craighead. Julie of the Wolves. (6)
2, 88, 221, 269, 277, 393, 405, 406, 565, 606, 775, 923

George, Jean Craighead. My Side of the Mountain. (5-6)
236, 268, 352, 570, 609, 777, 877, 1020

Knight, Eric. Lassie Come Home. (4-6)
1021

London, Jack. Call of the Wild. (5-6)
81, 207, 406, 581, 1022

McKenna, Marita. Under the Hawthorn Tree. (4-6)
6

Mowat, Farley. Lost in the Barrens. (5-6)
184

Naidoo, Beverly. Journey to Jo'Burg. (5-6)
761

O'Dell, Scott. Island of the Blue Dolphins. (5-6)
2, 17, 63, 99, 212, 268, 269, 349, 405, 523, 594, 604, 718, 921, 958, 1019

O'Dell, Scott. Sarah Bishop. (5-6)
6, 417, 933

Paton Walsh, Jill. The Green Book. (4-6)
419

Paulsen, Gary. Hatchet. (5-6)
85, 249, 371, 413, 558, 1055

Shub, Elizabeth. White Stallion. (1-3)
46

Speare, Elizabeth George. Sign of the Beaver. (4-6)
6, 16, 98, 244, 356, 413, 414, 417, 419, 572, 588, 687, 936, 1013, 1059

Steig, William. Abel's Island. (3-5)
47, 587, 668

Taylor, Theodore. The Cay. (5-6)
16, 82, 197, 277, 340, 413, 582, 904, 1015, 1046

Voigt, Cynthia. The Homecoming. (5-6)
411, 560, 915

Warner, Gertrude. Boxcar Children. (2-4)
29

SWALLOWS — FICTION

Politi, Leo. Song of the Swallows. (K-3)
1, 269, 407

SWANS — FICTION

Andersen, Hans Christian. The Ugly Duckling. (1-4)
253, 263, 448, 661

Andersen, Hans Christian. The Wild Swans. (1-4)
263

White, E. B. Trumpet of the Swan. (3-6)
77, 187, 498

SWEDEN — FICTION

Lindgren, Astrid. Pippi Longstocking. (3-5)
8, 39, 157, 326, 482, 593, 651, 844

SWEDISH — AMERICANS

Sandin, Joan. The Long Way to a New Land. (P-2)
588, 981

SWITZERLAND — ALPS — FICTION

Spyri, Johanna. Heidi. (4-6)
414, 587

SWITZERLAND — MATTERHORN — FICTION

Ullman, James Ramsey. Banner in the Sky. (4-6)
898

TALL TALES

Blassingame, Wyatt. John Henry and Paul Bunyan Play Baseball. (1-4)
271

Blassingame, Wyatt. Pecos Bill Catches a Hidebehind. (1-4)
271

Emberley, Barbara. The Story of Paul Bunyan. (P-2)
11

Felton, Harold W. Big Mose: Hero Fireman. (1-4)
271

Fleischman, Sid. Chancy and the Grand Rascal. (4-6)
753

Fleischman, Sid. McBroom and the Big Wind. (3-6)
271

Flora, James. Grandpa's Farm. (K-3)
271

Gage, Wilson. Mrs. Gaddy and the Fast Growing Vine. (1-3)
271

Gelman, Rita Goldin. The Biggest Sandwich Ever. (P-2)
408

Kellogg, Steven. Paul Bunyan. (K-3)
588, 650

Kellogg, Steven. Pecos Bill. (2-6)
587, 588

Rounds, Glen. Mr. Yowder and the Windwagon. (4-6)
588

Schwartz, Alvin. Whoppers, Tall Tales and Other Lies. (2-6)
271

Stevenson, James. The Great Big Especially Beautiful Easter Egg. (K-3)
271

TANGRAMS

Tompert, Ann. Grandfather Tang's Story. (1-4)
1056

TANTRUMS

Burnett, Frances Hodgson. The Secret Garden. (4-6)
9, 200, 379, 413, 414, 540, 587, 718, 934, 1019

Cleary, Beverly. Beezus and Ramona. (2-4)
96, 148, 452

TEACHERS—BIOGRAPHY

Davidson, Margaret. Helen Keller's Teacher. (4-6)
873

Ferris, Jeri. What Do You Mean? A Story about Noah Webster. (5-6)
588

Meltzer, Milton. Mary McLeod Bethune. (5-6)
588

TEACHERS—FICTION

Allard, Harry. Miss Nelson Has a Field Day. (1-3)
273

Allard, Harry. Miss Nelson Is Back. (1-3)
432

Allard, Harry. Miss Nelson Is Missing. (1-3)
26, 96, 132, 265, 266, 271, 410, 432, 647, 715, 822, 1008

Christian, Mary Blount. Swamp Monsters. (1-3)
409

Cleary, Beverly. Ramona the Brave. (3-5)
304, 484

Danziger, Paula. The Cat Ate My Gymsuit. (5-6)
512, 903

Gilson, Jamie. Thirteen Ways to Sink a Sub. (4-6)
178, 418

McKenna, Colleen O'Shaughnessy. Fourth Grade Is a Jinx. (3-5)
587

Parish, Peggy. Teach Us, Amelia Bedelia. (1-3)
3, 591

Sachs, Marilyn. The Bear's House. (4-5)
270, 405

Thaler, Mike. A Hippopotamus Ate the Teacher. (K-2)
835

Weiss, Leatie. My Teacher Sleeps in School. (1-3)
126

TEASING

Burch, Robert. Queenie Peavy. (5-6)
684

Caple, Kathy. The Biggest Nose. (P-2)
272

Cleary, Beverly. Otis Spofford. (3-5)
532

Estes, Eleanor. The Hundred Dresses. (3-5)
61, 297, 411, 520, 855, 1015

Hurwitz, Johanna. Aldo Applesauce. (4-6)
147

Sperry, Armstrong. Call It Courage. (5-6)
2), 5, 17, 56, 226, 269, 339, 405, 554, 594, 601, 721, 901, 1014

TEDDY BEARS

Dillon, Barbara. The Teddy Bear Tree. (3-5)
256

Douglass, Barbara. Good as New. (P-K)
1031

Freeman, Don. Corduroy. (P-2)
12, 23, 94, 254, 258, 273, 407, 408, 425, 587, 590, 630, 1008

Freeman, Don. A Pocket for Corduroy. (P-2)
11, 265, 408, 425, 706, 803, 1003

Gretz, Susanna. Teddy Bears Cure a Cold. (P-1)
272

Hague, Kathleen. Alphabears. (P-1)
587

Hoban, Lillian. Arthur's Honey Bear. (1-3)
125, 423

Ingpen, Robert. The Idle Bear. (P-2)
587

Milne, A. A. Winnie the Pooh. (1-4)
13, 192, 407, 414, 998

Milne, A. A. The World of Pooh: The Complete Winnie-the-Pooh and House at Pooh Corner. (1-4)
587

Stevenson, James. The Night After Christmas. (P-2)
587

Waber, Bernard. Ira Sleeps Over. (K-2)
11, 12, 18, 25, 94, 119, 254, 265, 271, 407, 428, 642, 710, 820, 1007

Zalben, Jane Breskin. A Perfect Nose for Ralph. (P-2)
408

TEETH

Bate, Lucy. Little Rabbit's Loose Tooth. (K-2)
13, 18, 254, 272, 407, 706, 1004

Birdseye, Tom. Airmail to the Moon. (P-2)
587

Brown, Marc. Arthur's Tooth. (P-2)
255, 273

McPhail, David. The Bear's Toothache. (K-2)
782

Williams, Barbara. William's Toothache. (P-2)
982

TELEVISION — FICTION

Brown, Marc. The Bionic Bunny Show. (K-3)
415

Miles, Betty. The Secret Life of the Underwear Champ. (4-6)
491

THANKSGIVING DAY

Gibbons, Gail. Thanksgiving Day. (P-2)
271, 588

THANKSGIVING DAY — FICTION

Balian, Lorna. Sometimes It's Turkey, Sometimes It's Feathers. (P-2)
271, 1001

Brown, Marc. Arthur's Thanksgiving. (P-2)
271

Bunting, Eve. How Many Days to America? A Thanksgiving Story. (1-3)
266, 588

Cohen, Barbara. Molly's Pilgrim. (2-4)
267, 417, 588, 592

Devlin, Harry. Cranberry Thanksgiving. (1-3)
271

Kroll, Steven. Oh! What a Thanksgiving. (P-2)
588

Kroll, Steven. One Tough Turkey. (P-2)
271

Sharmat, Marjorie. One Terrific Thanksgiving. (P-3)
271

Spinelli, Eileen. Thanksgiving at the Tapleton's. (K-3)
271

THANKSGIVING DAY — CRAFTS

Cauley, Lorinda Bryan. Things to Make and Do for Thanksgiving. (2-5)
271

THANKSGIVING DAY — POETRY

Prelutsky, Jack. It's Thanksgiving. (1-3)
271, 588, 1001

THEATER

Brown, Marc. Arthur's Thanksgiving. (P-2)
271

Cohen, Miriam. Starring First Grade. (P-2)
1054

Leedy, Loreen. The Bunny Play. (P-2)
587

Ormerod, Jan. The Story of Chicken Licken. (P-1)
587

Robinson, Barbara. The Best Christmas Pageant Ever. (4-6)
163, 454, 669, 850

Slate, Joseph. How Little Porcupine Played Christmas. (P-2)
272

Waber, Bernard. Lyle Finds His Mother. (K-2)
274, 590

THREE BEARS ADAPTATIONS

Turkle, Brinton. Deep in the Forest. (P-2)
104, 267, 1006

THUNDERSTORMS

Simon, Seymour. Storms. (2-6)
587

THUNDERSTORMS — FICTION

Stolz, Mary. Storm in the Night. (K-3)
587

TIGERS — FICTION

Kraus, Robert. Leo, the Late Bloomer. (P-1)
12, 111, 407, 587, 1004, 1054

TIME TRAVEL — FICTION

Banks, Lynne Reid. Return of the Indian. (4-6)
73, 276, 538

Banks, Lynne Reid. Secret of the Indians. (4-6)
541

L'Engle, Madeline. A Wrinkle in Time. (4-6)
2, 9, 17, 80, 231, 256, 268, 269, 270, 404, 414, 580, 595, 693, 722, 897, 1021, 1061

Lunn, Janet. The Root Cellar. (5-6)
417

TOADS

Lobel, Arnold. Days with Frog and Toad. (K-2)
4, 591

Lobel, Arnold. Frog and Toad All Year. (K-2)
4, 446, 591

Lobel, Arnold. Frog and Toad Are Friends. (K-2)
4, 13, 24, 96, 446, 591, 638, 707, 1007, 1056

Lobel, Arnold. Frog and Toad Together. (K-2)
4, 255, 259, 274, 446, 591, 985, 1003

Yolen, Jane. Commander Toad in Space. (1-2)
255, 259

TONGUE TWISTERS

Obligado, Lillian. Faint Frogs Feeling Feverish. (1-3)
257, 266

TOOLS

Gibbons, Gail. Tool Book. (P-K)
588

TOOTH FAIRY — FICTION

Bate, Lucy. Little Rabbit's Loose Tooth. (K-2)
13, 18, 254, 272, 407, 706, 1004

Birdseye, Tom. Airmail to the Moon. (P-2)
587

TORNADOES

Branley, Franklyn. Tornado Alert. (P-4)
587

George, Jean Craighead. Tornadoes. (4-6)
587

TOYS AND MOVABLE BOOKS

Ahlberg, Janet. The Jolly Postman. (A)
271, 410, 412, 1005, 1011

Asch, Frank. I Can Blink. (P-1)
412

Brown, Ruth. If at First You Do Not See. (K-3)
1057

Butler, M. Christina. Too Many Eggs: A Counting Book. (P-1)
412

Campbell, Rod. The Pop-Up Pet Shop. (P-2)
1028

Carle, Eric. Papa, Please Get the Moon for Me. (K-2)
1006

Carle, Eric. The Secret Birthday Message. (P-1)
415, 1044, 1056

Carle, Eric. The Very Busy Spider. (P-2)
18, 258, 410, 412, 415, 507, 1003

Carle, Eric. The Very Hungry Caterpillar. (P-2)
11, 12, 18, 94, 123, 254, 265, 407, 589, 705, 998, 1035, 1056, 1057

Carter, David. How Many Bugs in a Box? (P-1)
1056

Carter, David A. Surprise Party. (P-2)
412

Crowther, Robert. The Most Amazing Hide and Seek Alphabet Book. (P-1)
589

Crowther, Robert. The Most Amazing Hide and Seek Counting Book. (P-1)
1056

Hill, Eric. Spot Goes to the Circus. (P-1)
1028

Hoban, Tana. Look! Look! Look! (P-1)
587

Hooper, Meredith. Seven Eggs. (P-2)
410

Provenson, Alice. Leonardo Da Vinci. (3-6)
412

Roth, Harold. Let's Look All Around the House. (P-1)
588

TOYS

Blocksma, Mary. Action Contraption. (2-5)
587

TOYS—FICTION

Andersen, H. C. The Steadfast Tin Soldier. (1-4)
14

Banks, Lynne Reid. Indian in the Cupboard. (4-6)
62, 98, 182, 256, 270, 319, 411, 413, 522, 678, 718, 920, 1019

Banks, Lynne Reid. Return of the Indian. (4-6)
73, 276, 538

Banks, Lynne Reid. Secret of the Indian. (4-6)
541

Cleary, Beverly. Mouse and the Motorcycle. (2-5)
37, 169, 259, 418, 479, 587, 875

Dillon, Barbara. The Teddy Bear Tree. (3-5)
256

Douglass, Barbara. Good as New. (P-K)
1031

Eager, Edward. Knight's Castle. (4-6)
411

Field, Rachel. Hitty: Her First Hundred Years. (4-6)
269

Freeman, Don. Corduroy. (P-2)
12, 23, 94, 254, 258, 273, 407, 408, 425, 587, 590, 630, 1008

Freeman, Don. A Pocket for Corduroy. (P-2)
265, 408, 425, 803, 1003

Hoban, Lillian. Arthur's Honey Bear. (1-3)
125, 423

Hutchins, Pat, Changes, Changes. (P-1)
106, 587, 588, 589, 991

Ingpen, Robert. The Idle Bear. (P-2)
587

Lionni, Leo. Alexander and the Wind-up Mouse. (P-1)
12, 255, 271, 587, 715, 1003

Milne, A. A. Winnie the Pooh. (1-4)
13, 192, 407, 414, 998

Milne, A. A. The World of Pooh: The Complete Winnie-the-Pooh and House at Pooh Corner. (1-4)
587

Piper, Kitty. The Little Engine That Could. (P-1)
95, 587, 997

Rey, Margaret. Curious George Flies a Kite. (P-2)
815

Sachs, Marilyn. The Bear's House. (4-5)
270, 405

Serfozo, Mary. Who Said Red. (P-1)
412

Seymour, Peter. The Magic Toyshop. (P-2)
1006

Stevenson, James. The Night After Christmas. (P-2)
587

Waber, Bernard. Ira Sleeps Over. (K-2)
12, 18, 25, 94, 119, 254, 265, 407, 428, 642, 710, 820, 1007

Williams, Margery. Velveteen Rabbit. (2-4)
14, 191, 268, 271, 335, 499, 662, 713, 1007

Zalben, Jane Breskin. A Perfect Nose for Ralph. (P-2)
408

Zolotow, Charlotte. William's Doll. (P-2)
12, 706, 976, 1009

TRACTORS—FICTION

Burton, Virginia. Katy and the Big Snow. (P-2)
255, 699, 1003

TRAFFIC SIGNS

Hoban, Tana. I Read Signs. (P-1)
588

TRAINS

Gibbons, Gail. Trains. (1-3)
588

TRAINS—FICTION

Burton, Virginia. Choo Choo. (K-3)
415

Crews, Donald. Freight Train. (P-K)
12, 254, 588, 697, 705

Goble, Paul. Death of the Iron Horse. (K-3)
588

Piper, Watty. The Little Engine That Could. (P-1)
94, 587, 997

Van Allsburg, Chris. The Polar Express. (A)
1, 269, 271, 438, 591, 1016

TRAMPS

Carlson, Natalie Savage. The Family under the Bridge.
270

TRANSPORTATION

Ames, Lee. Draw 50 Vehicles. (4-6)
588

Barton, Byron. Airport. (P-2)
588

Brown, Laurene Krasny. Dinosaurs Travel. (1-5)
588

100 Words about Transportation. (P-1)
588

Parker, Nancy Winslow. The President's Car. (4-6)
588

TRANSPORTATION—FICTION

Levinson, Riki. I Go with My Family to Grandma's. (P-2)
588

Scarry, Richard. Richard Scarry's Cars, and Trucks and Things That Go. (P-2)
588, 1030

TREASURE TROVE—FICTION
Hamilton, Virginia. House of Dies Drear. (5-6)
675, 1025

TREES
Aliki. The Story of Johnny Appleseed. (2-4)
407, 805

Burns, Diane. Arbor Day. (3-5)
588

de Paola, Tomie. The Family Christmas Tree Book. (3-5)
588

Kellogg, Steven. Johnny Appleseed. (1-3)
18, 272, 588, 1034

Lasky, Kathryn. Sugaring Time. (4-6)
746

LeSueur, Meridel. Little Brother of the Wilderness: The Story of Johnny Appleseed. (4-6)
417, 588

Romanova, Natalia. Once There Was a Tree. (K-3)
743

TREES—FICTION
Andersen, Hans Christian. The Fir Tree. (1-4)
263

Calhoun, Mary. Julie's Tree. (K-2)
587

Cherry, Lynne. The Great Kapok Tree. (K-3)
1011, 1037

Ernst, Kathryn. Mr. Tamarin's Trees. (P-2)
408

Gibbons, Gail. The Seasons of Arnold's Apple Tree. (P-2)
1029, 1057

Holling, Holling Clancy. Tree in the Trail. (5-6)
588

Lloyd, David. Hello, Goodbye. (P-2)
587

Maynard, Joyce. New House. (P-2)
588

Silverstein, Shel. The Giving Tree. (A)
271, 419, 1013, 1034

Seuss, Dr. The Lorax. (P-3)
419, 590, 1006

Taylor, Mildred. Song of the Trees. (4-6)
411, 891

Udry, Janice May. A Tree Is Nice. (K-2)
1, 12, 269, 415, 1057

York, Carol Beach. Johnny Appleseed. (2-4)
11

TRICKSTERS
Jacobs, Leland B. April Fool! (P-2)
271

TRICKSTERS—FICTION
Turkle, Brinton. Do Not Open. (K-2)
255

TRICKSTERS—FOLKLORE
Galdone, Paul. Three Aesop Fox Fables. (1-4)
271

Haley, Gail. A Story, A Story. (K-3)
1, 269, 409, 592, 1045

Kellogg, Steven. Chicken Little. (K-3)
409, 587, 589

Ormerod, Jan. The Story of Chicken Licken. (P-1)
587

TROLLS—FICTION
de Paola, Tomie. Helga's Dowery. (1-3)
587

Marshall, Edward. Troll Country. (K-2)
828

TROLLS—FOLKLORE
Asbjornsen, P. C. The Three Billy Goats Gruff. (1-4)
252

Grimm, Jacob. Snow White and Rose Red. (1-4)
264

TRUCKS
Gibbons, Gail. Trucks. (P-1)
588

TRUCKS—FICTION
Lyon, David. The Biggest Truck. (P-2)
588

Merrill, Jean. The Pushcart War. (5-6)
378, 930

Scarry, Richard. Richard Scarry's Cars and Trucks and Things That Go. (P-2)
588, 1030

TRUTH, SOJOURNER
Ferris, Jeri. Walking the Road to Freedom. (5-6)
588

TSUNAMIS—FICTION
Buck, Pearl. The Big Wave. (4-6)
310, 405, 413, 553, 771, 851

Hodges, Margaret. The Wave. (4-6)
5, 402

TUBMAN, HARRIET (ROSS)
Ferris, Jeri. Go Free or Die. (5-6)
588

McGovern, Ann. Runaway Slave: The Story of Harriet Tubman. (2-4)
11

Petry, Ann. Harriet Tubman: Conductor on the Underground Railroad. (4-6)
411, 914

TURKEYS—FICTION
Balian, Lorna. Sometimes It's Turkey, Sometimes It's Feathers. (P-2)
271, 1001

Kroll, Steven. One Tough Turkey. (P-2)
271

TURTLES—FICTION
Blume, Judy. Tales of a Fourth Grade Nothing. (2-5)
44, 98, 176, 256, 260, 275, 333, 418, 496, 592, 862

Burch, Robert. Ida Early Comes Over the Mountain. (5-6)
414
Burch, Robert. Queenie Peavy. (5-6)
684

UNITED STATES – GREAT SMOKY MOUNTAINS – FICTION
Cleaver, Vera. Where the Lilies Bloom. (5-6)
769, 948

UNITED STATES – ILLINOIS – FICTION
Bauer, Marion Dane. On My Honor. (6)
270, 353, 405, 411, 413, 927, 1015
Hunt, Irene. Across Five Aprils. (5-6)
48, 246, 413, 417, 549, 599, 749, 954

UNITED STATES – INDIANA – FICTION
Henry, Jo Anne Landers. Log Cabin in the Woods. (4-6)
588

UNITED STATES – KANSAS – FICTION
Fleischman, Sid. Chancy and the Grand Rascal. (4-6)
753
Nixon, Joan Lowery. A Family Apart. (5-6)
405, 417, 588, 756
Wilder, Laura Ingalls. Little House on the Prairie. (3-6)
256, 262, 350, 414, 417, 476, 857, 1020

UNITED STATES – KENTUCKY – BIOGRAPHY
Daugherty, James. Daniel Boone. (2-4)
2, 269

UNITED STATES – LOUISIANA – POETRY
Jacobs, Howard, ed. The Cajun Night Before Christmas. (1-3)
587

UNITED STATES – MAINE – FICTION
Field, Rachel. Hitty: Her First Hundred Years. (4-6)
269
McCloskey, Robert. Time of Wonder. (A)
1, 269
Speare, Elizabeth George. Sign of the Beaver. (4-6)
6, 16, 98, 244, 356, 413, 414, 417, 419, 572, 588, 687, 936, 1013, 1059
Wiggin, Kate Douglas Smith. Rebecca of Sunnybrook Farm. (5-6)
414

UNITED STATES – MAINE – MATINICUS ROCK LIGHTHOUSE – BIOGRAPHY
Roop, Peter. Keep the Lights Burning, Abbie. (1-3)
97, 415, 980

UNITED STATES – MARYLAND – FICTION
Voigt, Cynthia. Dicey's Song. (5-6)
2, 84, 216, 269, 390, 584, 907, 956

UNITED STATES – MASSACHUSETTS
Waters, Kate. Sarah Morton's Day. (1-3)
416

UNITED STATES – MASSACHUSETTS – BIOGRAPHY
Bulla, Clyde Robert. Squanto, Friend of the Pilgrims. (3-5)
417
Fritz, Jean. And Then What Happened, Paul Revere? (3-6)
51, 419

Kessel, Joyce. Squanto and the First Thanksgiving. (2-4)
588

UNITED STATES – MASSACHUSETTS – FICTION
Fast, Howard. April Morning. (6)
551, 955
Forbes, Esther. Johnny Tremain. (4-6)
220, 256, 269, 392, 417, 564, 605, 760, 959, 1023, 1052
Fritz, Jean. Early Thunder. (6)
417
Turkle, Brinton. Rachel and Obadiah. (K-3)
417

UNITED STATES – MICHIGAN – FICTION
Whelan, Gloria. Next Spring an Oriole. (2-4)
284

UNITED STATES – MINNESOTA – FICTION
Paulsen, Gary. The Winter Room. (6)
93
Wilder, Laura Ingalls. On the Banks of Plum Creek. (3-6)
262, 411, 417

UNITED STATES – MISSISSIPPI – FICTION
Taylor, Mildred. The Friendship. (4-6)
417, 1023
Taylor, Mildred. Let the Circle Be Unbroken. (4-6)
413
Taylor, Mildred. Roll of Thunder, Hear My Cry. (5-6)
2, 17, 74, 224, 269, 398, 411, 539, 611, 685, 962, 1020
Taylor, Mildred. Song of the Trees. (4-6)
411, 891

UNITED STATES – MISSISSIPPI RIVER – FICTION
Twain, Mark. Adventures of Tom Sawyer. (5-6)
76, 205, 385, 550, 587

UNITED STATES – MISSOURI – FICTION
Nixon, Joan Lowery. Caught in the Act. (4-6)
417
Twain, Mark. Adventures of Tom Sawyer. (5-6)
76, 205, 385, 550, 587

UNITED STATES – NEBRASKA – FICTION
Talbot, Charlene Joy. An Orphan for Nebraska. (4-6)
417

UNITED STATES – NEW ENGLAND
Siegel, Beatrice. Fur Trappers and Traders. (4-6)
588
Tudor, Tasha. A Time to Keep: The Tasha Tudor Book of Holidays. (A)
266

UNITED STATES – NEW ENGLAND – FICTION
Alcott, Louisa May. Little Women. (5-6)
414, 1022
Hall, Donald. Ox-cart Man. (K-3)
1, 269, 271, 416, 588, 714
Monjo, F. N. Drinking Gourd. (1-3)
32, 417

UNITED STATES – NEW HAMPSHIRE – FICTION
Bailey, Carolyn. Miss Hickory. (4-6)
269
Blos, Joan W. A Gathering of Days. (6)
2, 269

UNITED STATES – NEW JERSEY – FICTION
Blume, Judy. Superfudge. (2-5)
175, 260, 332, 418, 495, 861
Gauche, Patricia Lee. This Time, Tempe Wick? (3-5)
417
UNITED STATES – NEW MEXICO – FICTION
Krumgold, Joseph. And Now Miguel. (5-6)
269
O'Dell, Scott. Sing Down the Moon. (5-6)
245, 358, 411, 542, 767, 937, 1023
UNITED STATES – NEW YORK – BIOGRAPHY
Stevenson, James. Higher on the Door. (3-4)
587
Stevenson, James. When I Was Nine. (3-4)
587
Yates, Elizabeth. My Diary, My Life. (6)
413
UNITED STATES – NEW YORK – FICTION
Edmonds, Walter D. Matchlock Gun. (2-4)
269
Irving, Washington. Rip Van Winkle. (5-6)
587
Mazer, Harry. Cave Under the City. (5-6)
417
O'Dell, Scott. Sarah Bishop. (5-6)
6, 417, 933
Wilder, Laura Ingalls. Farmer Boy. (3-6)
757
UNITED STATES – NEW YORK – CATSKILL MOUNTAINS – FICTION
George, Jean Craighead. My Side of the Mountain. (5-6)
236, 268, 352, 570, 609, 777, 877, 1020
UNITED STATES – NEW YORK – NEW YORK CITY
Horwitz, Joshua. Night Markets. (3-5)
588
Munro, Roxie. Inside Outside Book of New York. (2-6)
588
UNITED STATES – NEW YORK – NEW YORK CITY – FICTION
Clymer, E. Luke Was There. (4-6)
351
Konigsburg, Elaine. From the Mixed-Up Files of Mrs. Basil E. Frankweiler. (4-6)
2, 16, 60, 211, 269, 345, 405, 411, 515, 595, 674, 721, 912, 1017
Konigsburg, Elaine. Jennifer, Hecate, Macbeth, William McKinley and Me, Elizabeth. (4-6)
234, 411, 526
Holman, Felice. Slake's Limbo. (6)
186, 359, 938
Hurwitz, Johanna. The Adventures of Ali Baba Bernstein. (3-4)
146, 274
Levoy, Myron. Alan and Naomi. (6)
397
Levoy, Myron. Witch of Fourth Street. (4-6)
307
Martel, Cruz. Yagua Days. (2-4)
667
Merrill, Jean. The Pushcart War. (5-6)
378, 930

Neville, Emily Cheney. It's Like This, Cat. (5-6)
218, 269, 524
Sawyer, Ruth. Roller Skates. (5-6)
269
Selden, George. Cricket in Times Square. (3-6)
57, 239, 314, 414, 461, 587, 869
Snyder, Carol. Ike and Mama and the Trouble at School. (4-6)
419
Stevens, Carla. Anna, Grandpa and the Big Storm. (P-2)
588
Stolz, Mary. Noonday Friends. (4-6)
405
Taylor, Sydney. All-of-a-Kind Family. (4-6)
308
Waber, Bernard. The House on East Eighty-Eighth Street. (K-2)
590
Wagner, Jane. J. T. (3-6)
34, 298, 472, 856
White, E. B. Stuart Little. (3-6)
8, 43, 161, 256, 494, 712, 1013
UNITED STATES – NEW YORK – NEW YORK CITY – BROOKLYN – FICTION
Shura, Mary Francis. The Search for Grissi. (3-6)
880
UNITED STATES – NEW YORK – NEW YORK CITY – HARLEM – FICTION
Childress, Alice. A Hero Ain't Nothin' but a Sandwich. (6)
413
UNITED STATES – NEW YORK – NEW YORK CITY – MANHATTAN – FICTION
Rosenbloom, Joseph. Maxillian: You Are the Greatest. (4-6)
413
UNITED STATES – OHIO – FICTION
Hamilton, Virginia. House of Dies Drear. (5-6)
675, 1025
Hamilton, Virginia. M. C. Higgins the Great. (6)
269
Sanders, Scott Russell. Aurora Means Dawn. (1-3)
416, 588
UNITED STATES – OKLAHOMA – FICTION
Rawls, Wilson. Summer of the Monkeys. (4-6)
418, 543, 943
UNITED STATES – OZARK MOUNTAINS – FICTION
Rawls, Wilson. Where the Red Fern Grows. (5-6)
7, 92, 98, 204, 403, 405, 578, 615, 692, 949, 965, 1019, 1060
UNITED STATES – PENNSYLVANIA – FICTION
Avi. Encounters at Easton. (5-6)
417, 588
Avi. Night Journeys. (5-6)
417, 588
Bell, Frederic. Jenny's Corner. (4-6)
417
Fritz, Jean. The Cabin Faced West. (2-4)
337, 417, 510, 588
Sorenson, Virginia. Miracles on Maple Hill. (4-6)
269

Briggs, Raymond. The Snowman. (P-1)
102, 587, 994

Burton, Virginia. Katy and the Big Snow. (P-2)
255, 699, 1003

Clifford, Eth. Help! I'm a Prisoner in the Library. (3-5)
1014

Delton, Judy. My Mom Hates Me in January. (K-2)
271

Goffstein, M. B. Our Snowman. (P-2)
410

Hader, Berta. The Big Snow. (K-2)
1, 269

Keats, Ezra. Snowy Day. (P-2)
1, 12, 18, 128, 265, 269, 407, 654, 804, 998, 1057

Kellogg, Steven. The Mystery of the Missing Red Mitten. (P-1)
254, 258

Krauss, Ruth. The Happy Day. (P-2)
254

Morgan, Allen. Sadie and the Snowman. (K-3)
415

Steig, William. Brave Irene. (K-3)
271

Stevens, Carla. Anna, Grandpa and the Big Storm. (P-2)
588

Tresselt, Alvin. The Mitten. (P-2)
254, 410, 801

Tresselt, Alvin. White Snow, Bright Snow. (P-2)
1, 269

Wilder, Laura Ingalls. The Long Winter. (3-6)
262, 417, 478, 608

Zolotow, Charlotte. Something Is Going to Happen. (P-2)
1029

WINTER – POETRY

Frost, Robert. Stopping by the Woods on a Snowy Evening. Illus. by Susan Jeffers. (A)
587

WISHES

Brittain, Bill. The Wish Giver. (4-6)
366, 414, 419

Giff, Patricia Reilly. In the Dinosaur's Paw. (2-4)
274, 281

Haas, Irene. The Maggie B. (P-2)
408

Orbach, Ruth. Please Send a Panda. (P-2)
408

Steig, William. Sylvester and the Magic Pebble. (K-2)
1, 13, 97, 144, 255, 265, 269, 271, 272, 444, 587, 590, 658, 708, 806, 1009

WITCHES

Balian, Lorna. Humbug Potion. (1-3)
410

Balian, Lorna. Humbug Witch. (P-1)
271

Calhoun, Mary. Wobble the Witch Cat. (K-2)
11

Coombs, Patricia. Dorrie and the Goblin. (1-3)
271

Gutherie, Donna. The Witch Who Lives Down the Hall. (1-3)
272, 419

Hautzig, Deborah. Little Witch's Big Night. (P-2)
1001

Himmelman, John. Amanda and the Witch Switch. (P-2)
271

Johnston, Tony. The Vanishing Pumpkin. (P-2)
271, 1054

Lewis, C. S. The Lion, the Witch and the Wardrobe. (4-6)
16, 65, 199, 277, 322, 414, 474, 587, 595, 607, 717, 874, 1020

Paul, Korky. Winnie the Witch. (P-2)
410

Peet, Bill. Big Bad Bruce. (1-3)
97, 255, 271, 714, 998

Peet, Bill. The Whingdingdilly. (1-3)
271, 408, 1007

Speare, Elizabeth George. The Witch of Blackbird Pond. (5-6)
2, 79, 230, 269, 384, 406, 417, 579, 594, 617, 896, 950, 1021

Wood, Audrey. Heckedy Peg. (K-3)
265, 266

WITCHES – FOLKLORE

de Paola, Tomie. Strega Nona. (1-4)
11, 13, 18, 97, 255, 265, 271, 408, 442, 657, 714

de Paola, Tomie. Strega Nona's Magic Lessons. (K-3)
415

Grimm, Jacob. Hansel and Gretel. (P-2)
252, 264, 999

Grimm, Jacob. Rapunzel. (1-4)
264, 408

Lester, Rika. Hansel and Gretel. (P-2)
18

WIZARDS

Baum, L. Frank. Wonderful Wizard of Oz. (3-6)
275, 414, 587, 593, 951

Cazet, Denys. Doctor Change. (1-3)
410

Hunter, Mollie. A Stranger Came Ashore. (6)
942

Madden, Don. The Wartville Wizard. (K-3)
1037

Stockton, Frank R. The Beeman of Orn. (5-6)
984

WOLVES – FICTION

Aiken, Joan. Wolves of Willoughby Chase. (4-6)
6. 952

Allard, Harry. It's Nice to Have a Wolf around the House. (P-2)
587

Blades, Ann. Mary of Mile 18. (P-3)
587

George, Jean Craighead. Julie of the Wolves. (6)
2, 88, 221, 269, 277, 393, 405, 406, 565, 606, 775, 923

Kasza, Keiko. The Wolf's Chicken Stew. (P-1)
1056

Campbell, Rod. Dear Zoo. (P-1)
1028, 1057
Carrick, Carol. Patrick's Dinosaurs. (K-2)
265, 596, 802, 1057
Hoban, Tana. A Children's Zoo. (P-2)
587

Seuss, Dr. If I Ran the Zoo. (P-3)
95, 996
Thaler, Mike. A Hippopotamus Ate the Teacher. (K-2)
835
ZOOS—POETRY
Prelutsky, Jack. Zoo Doings. (K-3)
271

Author Listing

If you are looking for ideas to use with specific children's books, check this section under the author, the joint author, or the illustrator. Folktales and fairy tales, illustrated by a particular artist, are included in addition to a generic title, such as "Cinderella." Following the author and book title, provided are the grade level and resource book codes that lead to idea books listed in the Literature Materials Guide beginning on page 171.

Aardema, Verna. Bringing the Rain to Kapiti Plain. (1-3) 588, 626, 715, 725, 1056
———. Why Mosquitoes Buzz in People's Ears. (1-3) 1, 14, 145, 255, 269, 407, 666, 712, 1010, 1045
Aaseng, Nate. Basketball: You Are the Coach. (4-6) 413
Ackerman, Karen. Song and Dance Man, The. (K-2) 269, 587, 1011
Adams, Adrienne. Great Valentine's Day Balloon Race, The. (K-3) 271
Adler, C.S. Silver Coach. (5-6) 357
Adler, David A. Cam Jansen and the Mystery at the Monkey House. (2-4) 813, 830
———. Cam Jansen and the Mystery of the Circus Clown. (2-4) 97
———. Cam Jansen and the Mystery of the Dinosaur Bones. (2-4) 290, 831
———. Picture Book of Abraham Lincoln, A. (1-3) 416, 588
———. Picture Book of George Washington, A. (1-3) 588
———. Picture Book of Martin Luther King, A. (1-3) 416, 588
———. Thomas Jefferson, Father of Our Democracy. (6) 588
Adoff, Arnold. All the Colors of the Race. (4-6) 587
———. My Black Me. (5-6) 588
Aesop. Aesop's Fables. (2-4) 591
———. Aesop's Fables. Illus. by Michael Hague. (2-4) 591
———. Ants and the Grasshopper, The. (K-3) 1002
———. Bee and the Dove, The. (2-4) 1002
———. City Mouse and the Country Mouse, The. (2-4) 250, 1002
———. Crow and the Pitcher, The. (2-4) 1002
———. Fox and the Grapes, The. (2-4) 250, 1002
———. Fox and the Stork, The. (2-4) 250
———. Goose That Laid the Golden Egg, The. (K-3) 250, 1002
———. Lion and the Mouse, The. (2-4) 250, 1002
———. Proud Turtle, The. (2-4) 1002
———. Rabbit and the Tortoise, The. (2-4) 250, 1002
———. Town Mouse and the Country Mouse, The. (1-3) 591, 1033
———. Town Mouse and the Country Mouse, The. Illus. by Lorinda Bryan Cauley. (1-3) 591, 1033
Ahlberg, Allan, and Janet Ahlberg. Each Peach, Pear, Plum. (K-2) 587, 789
———. Jolly Postman, The. (A) 271, 410, 412, 1005, 1011
Ahlberg, Janet and Allan Ahlberg. Each Peach, Pear, Plum. (K-2) 587, 789

———. Jolly Postman, The. (A) 271, 410, 412, 1005, 1011
Aitken, Joan. Wolves of Willoughby Chase, The. (4-6) 6, 952
Alcott, Louisa May. Little Women. (5-6) 414, 1022
Alexander, Lloyd. High King, The. (6) 2, 269, 372
Alexander, Martha. Blackboard Bear. (K-2) 113
———. How My Library Grew. (P-2) 588
———. No Ducks in Our Bathtub. (K-2) 255
Alexander, Sue. Nadia the Willful. (K-3) 419
Aliki. Corn Is Maize: The Gift of the Indians. (1-4) 728
———. Digging Up Dinosaurs. (1-4) 596
———. Dinosaur Bones. (K-3) 587
———. Dinosaurs Are Different. (K-3) 596
———. Fossils Tell of Long Ago. (1-3) 596
———. Many Lives of Benjamin Franklin, The. (P-5) 588
———. My Visit to the Dinosaurs. (K-3) 596
———. Story of Johnny Appleseed, The. (2-4) 407, 805
———. Two of Them, The. (P-2) 588
———. We Are Best Friends. (K-2) 588, 663, 970
———. Weed Is a Flower: The Life of George Washington Carver, A. (3-5) 588
Aliki (illus.). Aunt Nina and Her Nieces and Nephews, by Franz Brandenburg. (P-2) 588
Allard, Harry. I Will Not Go to Market Today. (P-2) 271
———. It's So Nice to Have a Wolf Around the House. (P-2) 587
———. Miss Nelson Has a Field Day. (1-3) 273
Allard, Harry, and James Marshall. Miss Nelson Is Back. (1-3) 432
———. Miss Nelson Is Missing. (1-3) 26, 96, 132, 265, 266, 271, 410, 432, 647, 715, 822, 1008
Allen, Jeffrey, and James Marshall. Nosey Mrs. Rat. (K-2) 271
Allen, Pamela. Who Sank the Boat? (P-2) 415, 1056
Allen, Thomas B. Where Children Live. (P-2) 588
Altman, Susan. Extraordinary Black Americans From Colonial to Contemporary Times. (5-6) 588
Ames, Lee. Draw 50 Vehicles. (4-6) 588
Ancona, George. American Family Farm, The. (4-6) 588
———. Bananas from Manolo to Margie. (3-5) 407, 588
———. Dancing Is. (3-5) 588
Ancona, George (illus.). Pioneer Children of Appalachia, by Joan Anderson. (4-6) 588
Andersen, Hans Christian. Emperor's New Clothes, The. (K-3) 253, 263, 635, 1007

MacLachlan, Patricia. Arthur for the Very First Time. (4-6) 882

———. Facts and Fictions of Minna Pratt, The. (5-6) 911

———. Mama One, Mama Two. (P-2) 588

———. Sarah, Plain and Tall. (3-5) 2, 17, 75, 99, 214, 256, 268, 269, 270, 328, 405, 414, 490, 588, 592, 686, 717, 779, 847, 1013

———. Seven Kisses in a Row. (2-4) 287, 587

———. Through Grandpa's Eyes. (1-3) 271, 747, 588

Madden, Don. Wartville Wizard, The. (K-3) 1037

Maestro, Betsy, and Guilio Maestsro. Harriet Reads Signs and More Signs. (P-1) 588

———. Lambs for Dinner. (P-2) 254

———. Story of the Statue of Liberty, The. (P-3) 588

———. Taxi: A Book of City Words. (1-3) 588

———. Through the Year with Harriet. (P-1) 11

Maestro, Guilio (illus.). Rockets and Satellites, by Franklin Branley. (1-4) 597

———. Sunshine Makes the Seasons, by Franklin Branley. (K-3) 597

———. Tornado Alert, by Franklin Branley. (P-4) 597

Maestro, Guilio, and Betsy Maestro. Harriet Reads Signs and More Signs. (P-1) 588

———. Lambs for Dinner. (P-2) 254

———. Story of the Statue of Liberty, The. (P-3) 588

———. Taxi: A Book of City Words. (1-3) 588

———. Through the Year with Harriet. (P-1) 11

Mahy, Margaret. Jam. (P-3) 271

Malnig, Anita. Where the Waves Break: Life at the Edge of the Sea. (3-6) 598

Manes, Stephen. Be a Perfect Person in Just Three Days. (3-5) 288, 418, 450, 720, 770, 849, 1014, 1055

Mango, Karen. Codes, Ciphers and Other Secrets. (4-6) 587

Mari, Isla. Little Red Balloon, The. (P-1) 408

Marshall, Edward. Troll Country. (K-2) 828

Marshall, James. George and Martha. (P-2) 255, 259, 587, 1032

———. Goldilocks and the Three Bears. (P-2) 588

———. What's the Matter with Carruthers? (P-2) 587

———. Willis. (1-3) 272

Marshall, James (illus.). Cinderella, by Barbara Karlin. (P-2) 18

———. Dinner at Alberta's, by Russell Hoban. (K-2) 587, 816

———. I Will Not Go to Market Today, by Harry Allard. (P-2) 271

———. It's So Nice to Have a Wolf Around the House, by Harry Allard. (P-2) 587

———. James Marshall's Mother Goose, by Mother Goose. (P-2) 587

———. Troll Country, by Edward Marshall. (K-2) 828

Marshall, James, and Harry Allard. Miss Nelson Is Back. (1-3) 432

———. Miss Nelson Is Missing. (1-3) 26, 96, 132, 265, 266, 271, 410, 432, 647, 715, 822, 1008

———. Nosey Mrs. Rat. (K-2) 271

Martel, Cruz. Yagua Days. (2-4) 667

Martin, Bill. Brown Bear, Brown Bear, What Do You See? (P-2) 12, 94, 258, 412, 708, 997, 1056

———. Knots on a Counting Rope. (1-3) 257

Martin, Bill, and John Archambault. Chicka Chicka Boom Boom. (P-2) 412, 1054

———. Listen to the Rain. (P-3) 587

———. Up and Down on the Merry-Go-Round. (P-2) 587

———. White Dynamite and the Curly Kid. (K-3) 271

Marzollo, Jean. Rebus Treasury, The. (P-K) 410

Mathews, Louise. Bunches and Bunches of Bunnies. (K-2) 272, 1056

Mathis, Sharon Bell. Hundred Penny Box. (4-6) 471, 641, 719

———. Sidewalk Story. (3-5) 411

Matsuno, Masako. Pair of Red Clogs, A. (P-K) 255

Mayer, Marianna. Twelve Dancing Princesses, The. (1-4) 587

Mayer, Mercer. All By Myself. (P-1) 1030

———. Boy, a Dog and a Frog, A. (P-1) 990

———. East O' the Sun and West O' the Moon. (4-6) 267

———. Frog Goes to Dinner. (P-1) 100

———. Hiccup. (P-1) 103

———. I Was So Mad. (P-2) 110

———. Liza Lou and the Yeller Belly Swamp. (1-3) 255

———. New Baby, The. (P-1) 1030

———. There's a Nightmare in My Closet. (P-1) 11, 95, 108, 254, 267, 408, 445, 659, 703, 1003

———. There's an Alligator Under My Bed. (P-1) 587, 1004

———. When I Get Bigger. (P-1) 588

Mayer, Mercer (illus.). Everyone Knows What a Dragon Looks Like, by Jay Williams. (1-3) 257

Mayers, Florence Cassin. National Air Space Museum ABC, The. (2-6) 588

Maynard, Joyce. New House. (P-2) 588

Mazer, Harry. Cave Under the City. (5-6) 417

McClenathan, Louise. Easter Pig, The. (1-3) 271

McCloskey, Robert. Blueberries for Sal. (P-2) 11, 12, 255, 265, 271, 587, 624, 784, 998

———. Burt Dow, Deep Water Man. (1-3) 410

———. Homer Price. (3-6) 411, 518, 854, 1012

———. Lentil. (1-3) 271, 587

———. Make Way for Ducklings. (P-1) 1, 12, 95, 269, 271, 272, 407, 415, 430, 646, 799, 1008

———. Time of Wonder. (1-3) 1, 269

McCord, David. Speak Up. (A) 11

McCully, Emily Arnold. New Baby, The. (P-1) 588

McCurdy, Michael. Hannah's Farm. (1-3) 588

McDermott, Gerald. Anansi the Spider. (1-3) 422

———. Arrow to the Sun. (1-4) 1, 269, 587, 1041

———. Stonecutter, The. (1-4) 587

McDermott Gerald (illus.). Twelve Dancing Princesses, The, by Marianna Mayer. (1-4) 587

———. Three Little Kittens. (P-2) 1000

———. Tomie dePaola's Mother Goose. (P-2) 587, 589

Mowat, Farley. Lost in the Barrens. (5-6) 184

———. Owls in the Family. (4-6) 172, 413, 481, 592, 878

Mueller, Virginia. Playhouse for Monster, A. (P-1) 588

Mukerji, Dhan. Gay-Neck, the Story of a Pigeon. (6+) 269

Munro, Roxie. Inside Outside Book of New York. (2-6) 588

———. Inside Outside Book of Washington, D.C. (2-6) 588

Munsch, Robert. Love You Forever. (K-2) 1009

———. Paperbag Princess, The. (1-3) 267, 843

———. Promise is a Promise, A. (1-3) 845

Murphy, Jill. What Next Baby Bear? (K-2) 808

Musgrove, Margaret. Ashanti to Zulu. (3-6) 1, 269, 621, 1026

Myers, Bernice. Sidney Rella and the Glass Sneakers. (1-4) 271

Myller, Rolf. How Big Is a Foot? (K-3) 415

Naidoo, Beverly. Journey to Jo'burg. (5-6) 321, 761

Nelson, Theresa. And One for All. (5-6) 417

———. Devil Storm. (5-6) 417

Nelson, Vaunda M. Always Gramma. (P-2) 416

Nerlove, Miriam. Hannukkah. (1-3) 588

Ness, Evaline. Sam, Bangs and Moonshine. (K-3) 1, 41, 160, 269, 271, 489, 587, 715, 825

Neufeld, John. Edgar Allen. (5-6) 342

Neville, Emily Cheneq. It's Like This, Cat. (5-6) 218, 269, 524

Newman, Robert. Case of the Baker St. Irregular. (6) 413, 1025

Nic Leodhas, Sorche. Always Room for One More. (K-2) 1, 269

Nixon, Joan Lowery. Beats Me, Claude. (1-3) 587

———. Caught in the Act. (4-6) 417

———. Family Apart, A. (5-6) 405, 417, 588, 756

———. In the Face of Danger. (4-6) 417

———. Stalker, The. (6) 1025

Noble, Trinka Hakes. Day Jimmy's Boa Ate the Wash, The. (K-2) 13, 18, 120, 271, 588, 1054

Nordstrom, Ursula. Secret Language. (4-6) 414

North, Sterling. Rascal. (4-6) 72, 537, 932

Norton, Mary. Borrowers, The. (3-6) 54, 193, 414, 506, 587, 593, 900

Novak, Matt. Claude and Sun. (P-1) 410

Numeroff, Laura Joffe. If You Give a Mouse a Cookie. (P-2) 18, 255, 258, 271, 410, 795, 1004, 1056

O'Brien, Robert C. Mrs. Frisby and the Rats of NIMH. (4-6) 2, 16, 66, 99, 213, 268, 269, 374, 414, 568, 681, 776, 925, 1021,

O'Dell, Scott. Black Pearl, The. (5-6) 5, 238, 505, 899, 387

———. Island of the Blue Dolphins. (5-6) 2, 17, 63, 99, 212, 268, 269, 349, 405, 523, 594, 604, 718, 921, 958, 1019

———. King's Fifth, The. (5-6) 413

———. Sarah Bishop. (5-6) 6, 417, 933

———. Sing Down the Moon. (5-6) 245, 358, 411, 542, 767, 937, 1023

———. Zia. (6) 417

O'Neill, Catherine. Mrs. Dunphy's Dog. (P-2) 410

O'Neill, Mary. Hailstones and Halibut Bones. (P-6) 11, 587, 1018

Obligado, Lillian. Faint Frogs Feeling Feverish. (1-3) 257, 266

Okie, Susan, and Sally Ride. To Space and Back with Sally Ride. (3-5) 597

Oppenheim, Joanne. Mrs. Peloki's Snake. (K-2) 271

Orbach, Ruth. Please Send a Panda. (P-2) 408

Ormerod, Jan. Moonlight. (P-1) 992

———. Story of Chicken Licken, The. (P-1) 587

Owen, Anne. Annie's One to Ten. (P-1) 1056

Oxenbury, Helen (illus.). Quangle Wangle's Hat, The, by Edward Lear. (1-4) 587

Parish, Peggy. Amelia Bedelia. (1-3) 11, 20, 97, 255, 421, 587, 591, 619, 712, 809, 1008, 1054, 1057

———. Amelia Bedelia and the Baby. (1-3) 3, 591, 997

———. Amelia Bedelia Goes Camping. (1-3) 135

———. Amelia Bedelia Helps Out. (1-3) 3, 591

———. Come Back, Amelia Bedelia. (1-3) 591

———. Good Work, Amelia Bedelia. (1-3) 3, 274

———. Teach Us, Amelia Bedelia. (1-3) 3, 591

Park, Barbara. Skinnybones. (4-6) 859, 1055

Parker, Nancy Winslow. Paul Revere's Ride. (A) 587

———. President's Car, The. (4-6) 588

Parker, Nancy Winslow (illus.). My Mom Travels a Lot, by Caroline Feller Bauer. (K-2) 115

Parkes, Brenda, and Judith Smith. Enormous Watermelon, The. (K-3) 412, 1057

Parnall, Peter. Feet. (P-2) 587

Parnall, Peter (illus.). Desert Is Theirs, The, by Byrd Baylor. (1-4) 588, 1041

———. Everybody Needs a Rock, by Byrd Baylor. (1-4) 415

———. Hawk, I'm Your Brother, by Byrd Baylor. (1-4) 733

———. I'm in Charge of Celebrations, by Byrd Baylor. (3-6) 257, 266, 588

———. Way to Start a Day, The, by Byrd Baylor. (3-6) 588

Parsons, Alexandra. Amazing Spiders. (1-4) 1054

Partch, Virgil F. Christmas Cookie Sprinkle Snitcher, The. (P-2) 408

Patent, Dorothy. Horse of a Different Color, A. (4-6) 587

Quackenbush, Robert. Don't You Dare Shoot That Bear. (6) 588
———. Mark Twain: What Kind of Name Is That? A Story of Samuel Langhorn Clemens. (6) 587
———. Quit Pulling My Leg! A Story of Davy Crockett. (5-6) 588
———. Who Let Muddy Boots into the White House?: A Story of Andrew Jackson (5-6) 588

Rabe, Bernice. Balancing Girl, The. (K-2) 966
Raboff, Ernest Lloyd. Pierre Auguste Renoir. (4-6) 595
Radin, Ruth Yaffe. High in the Mountains. (K-3) 587
Ransome, Arthur. Fool of the World and the Flying Ship, The. (2-5) 1, 269, 407
———. Fool of the World and the Flying Ship, The. Illus. by Uri Shulevitz. (2-5) 1, 269, 407
Raskin, Ellen. Nothing Ever Happens on My Block. (K-2) 591
———. Spectacles. (K-2) 415, 1057
———. Westing Game, The. (5-6) 2, 229, 269, 377, 381, 586, 947, 1025
Rawls, Wilson. Summer of the Monkeys. (4-6) 418, 543, 943
———. Where the Red Fern Grows. (5-6) 7, 92, 98, 204, 403, 405, 578, 615, 692, 949, 965, 1019, 1060
Rayner, Mary. Mr. and Mrs. Pig's Evening Out. (K-2) 11, 255
Rees, Mary. Ten in a Bed. (P-2) 587
Reit, Seymour. Behind Rebel Lines: The Incredible Story of Emma Edmonds. (5-6) 588, 1051
Rey, H.A. Curious George. (P-2) 12, 95, 122, 272, 426, 590
———. Curious George Takes a Job. (P-2) 255
Rey, Margaret. Curious George Flies a Kite. (P-2) 815
———. Curious George Goes to the Hospital. (P-2) 11
Rice, Eve. Benny Bakes a Cake. (P-2) 254
Rice, James. Cajun Night Before Christmas. (1-3) 587
———. Cajun Night Before Christmas. Illus. by Howard Jacobs. (1-3) 587
Richler, Mordecai. Jacob Two Two Meets the Hooded Fang. (4-6) 414
Richter, Conrad. Light in the Forest. (6) 194, 394, 406, 567, 763
Riddell, Chris. Bird's New Shoes. (P-2) 410
Ride, Sally, and Susan Okie. To Space and Back with Sally Ride. (3-5) 597
Riley, James Whitcomb. Gobble-uns'll Git You Ef You Don't Watch Out, The. (2-4) 591
Robbins, Ken. At the Ballpark. (2-5) 587
Robbins, Ruth. Baboushka and the Three Kings. (2-4) 1, 269, 588
Robinson, Barbara. Best Christmas Pageant Ever, The. (4-6) 163, 454, 669, 850
———. My Brother Louis Measures Worms. (4-6) 277
Rockwell, Anne. Bump in the Night, The. (P-2) 408

———. Hugo at the Window. (P-2) 587
———. My Spring Robin. (P-K) 1029
———. Our Garage Sale. (P-1) 272
———. Three Bears and 15 Other Stories, The. (K-3) 589, 590
Rockwell, Thomas. How to Eat Fried Worms. (4-6) 99, 259, 296, 414, 418, 519, 676, 836, 1014, 1055
Rogasky, Barbara (reteller). Rapunzel. (1-4) 487, 587
———. Water of Life, The. (4-6) 414, 587
Rodgers, Mary. Freaky Friday. (5-6) 16, 153, 344, 468, 871
Rogers, Fred. Going to the Doctor. (P-1) 272
Rogers, Jean. Runaway Mittens. (P-2) 588
———. Secret Moose, The. (1-3) 259
Rogow, Zack. Oranges. (2-4) 588
Romonova, Natalia. Once There Was a Tree. (K-2) 743
Roop, Connie, and Peter Roop. Buttons for General Washington. (4-6) 588
———. Keep the Lights Burning, Abbie. (1-3) 97, 415, 980
Roop, Peter, and Connie Roop. Buttons for General Washington. (4-6) 588
———. Keep the Lights Burning, Abbie. (1-3) 97, 415, 980
Rosenbloom, Joseph. Maxillian: You Are the Greatest. (4-6) 413
Ross, Dave. Book of Hugs, A. (P-1) 408
Roth, Harold. Let's Look All Around the House. (P-1) 588
Rounds, Glen. I Know an Old Lady Who Swallowed a Fly. (P-2) 587
———. Mr. Yowder and the Windwagon. (4-6) 588
Rounds, Glen (illus.). Cross Your Fingers, Spit in Your Hat, by Alvin Schwartz. (4-6) 588
———. Whoppers, Tall Tales and Other Lies, by Alvin Schwartz. (2-6) 271
Roy, Ron. Breakfast with My Father. (P-2) 588
Ruben, Patricia. True or False. (P-2) 408
Rupprecht, Siegfried P. Tale of the Vanishing Rainbow, The. (K-2) 588
Ryder, Joanne. Chipmunk Song. (K-3) 415
———. Simon Underground. (K-3) 415
Rylant, Cynthia. Birthday Presents. (P-1) 588, 1057
———. Mr. Griggs Work. (P-2) 416
———. Night in the Country. (P-2) 416
———. Relatives Came, The. (K-3) 255, 265, 266, 271, 588
———. This Year's Garden. (P-2) 588
———. When I Was Young in the Mountains. (K-3) 416
———. When I Was Young in the Mountains. Illus. by Diane Goode. (K-3) 416

Sabin, Louis. Wonders of the Sea. (2-4) 598
Sachar, Louis. Sideways Stories From Wayside School. (3-6) 98

———. On the Banks of Plum Creek. (3-6) 262, 411, 417

———. These Happy Golden Years. (3-6) 262, 417

Wildsmith, Brian. Hunter and His Dog. (P-2) 419

———. Lazy Bear, The. (P-2) 254

———. Pelican. (P-2) 11, 271

———. Python's Party. (P-2) 11

———. Wild Animals. (P-2) 587

Will. Finders Keepers. (K-2) 1, 269

Willard, Nancy (illus.). Visit to William Blake's Inn, A, by Alice Provenson and Martin Provenson. (5-6) 2, 269

Williams, Barbara. Albert's Toothache. (P-2) 255, 982

———. Valentine for Cousin Archie, A. (K-3) 271

Williams, Garth (illus.). Amigo, by Byrd Baylor. (K-2) 409, 723

———. Bedtime for Frances, by Russell Hoban. (P-1) 11, 96, 590, 622, 695, 1007

———. By the Shores of Silver Lake, by Laura Ingalls Wilder. (3-6) 262, 417

———. Charlotte's Web, by E. B. White. (3-6) 8, 11, 15, 30, 97, 233, 268, 274, 313, 414, 457, 593, 602, 720, 853, 1012, 1050

———. Cricket in Times Square, by George Selden. (3-6) 57, 239, 314, 414, 461, 587, 869

———. Farmer Boy, by Laura Ingalls Wilder. (3-6) 757

———. First Four Years, The, by Laura Ingalls Wilder. (3-6) 417

———. Little House in the Big Woods, by Laura Ingalls Wilder. (3-6) 35, 195, 259, 262, 407, 417, 475, 592, 644, 711

———. Little House on the Prairie, by Laura Ingalls Wilder. (3-6) 256, 262, 350, 414, 417, 476, 857, 1020

———. Little Town on the Prairie, by Laura Ingalls Wilder. (3-6) 262, 417

———. Long Winter, The, by Laura Ingalls Wilder. (3-6) 262, 417, 478, 608

———. On the Banks of Plum Creek, by Laura Ingalls Wilder. (3-6) 262, 411, 417

———. Over and Over, by Charlotte Zolotow. (P-2) 588

———. Stuart Little, by E. B. White. (3-6) 8, 43, 161, 256, 494, 712, 1013

———. These Happy Golden Years, by Laura Ingalls Wilder. (3-6) 262, 417

———. Wait 'til the Moon Is Full, by Margaret Wise Brown. (P-2) 587

Williams, Jay. Everyone Knows What a Dragon Looks Like. (1-3) 257

Williams, Jennifer, and Vera Williams. Stringbean's Trip to the Shining Sea. (3-6) 412, 588

Williams, Linda. Little Old Lady Who Was Not Afraid of Anything, The. (P-2) 410, 1054

Williams, Margery. Velveteen Rabbit. (2-4) 14, 191, 268, 271, 335, 499, 662, 713, 1007

Williams, Vera. Chair for My Mother. (P-3) 22, 255, 265, 271, 588, 628, 713, 787, 814

———. Cherries and Cherry Pits. (1-3) 409

———. Something Special for Me. (K-3) 969

Williams, Vera, and Jennifer Williams. Stringbean's Trip to the Shining Sea. (3-6) 412, 588

Wilner, Isabel. Poetry Troupe, The. (A) 11

Wilson, Sarah. Beware the Dragons! (K-2) 1036

Winer, Yvonne, and Carol Aitken McLean-Carr. Never Snap at a Bubble. (K-2) 1040

Winter, Paula. Bear and the Fly, The. (P-1) 105

Winthrop, Elizabeth. Best Friend Club, The. (P-2) 588

———. Castle in the Attic. (4-6) 419, 587, 1027

———. Katherine's Doll. (P-2) 587

———. Lizzie and Harold. (P-2) 588

———. Shoes. (P-2) 587

Wiseman, Bernard. Morris the Moose Goes to School. (1-3) 273

Wittman, Sally. Boy Who Hated Valentine's Day. (P-2) 272

Wojciechowska, Maia. Shadow of a Bull. (6) 2, 269, 571, 935

Wolff, Ashley. Bells of London, The. (P-2) 587

Wolfson, Evelyn. From Abenaki to Zuni. (4-6) 588

Wood, Audrey. Heckedy Peg. (K-3) 265, 266

———. King Bidgood's in the Bath. (P-2) 587, 591

———. Napping House. (P-2) 95, 254, 258, 587, 710, 1054

———. Quick as a Cricket. (A) 700

Wood, Don (illus.). Heckedy Peg, by Audrey Wood. (K-3) 265, 266

———. King Bidgood's in the Bath, by Audrey Wood. (P-2) 587, 591

———. Napping House, by Audrey Wood. (P-2) 95, 254, 258, 587, 710, 1054

———. Quick as a Cricket, by Audrey Wood. (A) 700

Woods, Geraldine, and Harold Woods. United Nations, The. (5-6) 588

Woods, Harold, and Geraldine Woods. United Nations, The. (5-6) 588

Wright, Betty Ren. Dollhouse Murders, The. (3-6) 885

Yagawa, Sumiko. Crane Wife, The. (K-3) 419

Yarbrough, Camille. Cornrows. (3-5) 588

Yashima, Taro. Crow Boy. (1-3) 13, 31, 96, 255, 407, 587, 632, 979

Yates, Elizabeth. Amos Fortune, Free Man. (4-6) 2, 269, 417, 588, 750

———. My Diary, My World. (6) 413

Yeoman, John. Wild Washerwomen, The. (K-4) 271

Yep, Lawrence. Dragonwings. (5-6) 247, 411, 556, 910

Yolen, Jane. Commander Toad in Space. (1-2) 255, 259

If you are looking for ideas to use with specific children's books, check this section under title. Following the title, provided are the grade level and resource book codes that lead to idea books listed in the Literature Materials Guide beginning on page 171.

1, 2, 3 to the Zoo. (P-1) 1056
1787. (5-6) 417
18th Emergency, The. (4-6) 151, 870
329th Friend, The. (P-2) 271, 408
50 Simple Things Kids Can Do to Save the Earth. (4-6) 1026, 1048
500 Hats of Bartholomew Cubbins, The. (A) 255
A B See. (P-2) 11, 407
ABC Bunny. (P-1) 587
Abel's Island. (3-5) 47, 587, 668
Abraham Lincoln. (2-4) 1, 11, 269, 592
Across Five Aprils. (5-6) 48, 246, 413, 417, 549, 599, 749, 954
Action Contraptions. (2-6) 587
Adam Draws Himself a Dragon. (2-4) 259
Adam of the Road. (6) 269, 1053
Addie Across the Prairie. (2-4) 417, 588
Adventures of Ali Baba Bernstein, The. (3-4) 146, 274
Adventures of Pinnochio, The. (3-6) 587, 999, 1017
Adventures of Tom Sawyer. (5-6) 76, 205, 385, 550, 587
Aesop's Fables. (2-4) 591
After the Goat Man. (5-6) 414
Airmail to the Moon. (P-2) 587
Airplanes of the Future. (4-6) 588
Airport. (P-2) 588
Alamo, The. (4-6) 588
Alan and Naomi. (6) 367
Alaska. (4-6) 588
Albert's Toothache. (P-2) 255, 982
Aldo Applesauce. (4-6) 147
Alexander and the Terrible, Horrible, No Good Very Bad Day. (P-3) 11, 18, 19, 94, 133, 255, 265, 271, 407, 618, 716, 1008, 1054
Alexander and the Wind-up Mouse. (P-1) 12, 255, 271, 587, 715, 1003
Alexander the Great. (6) 595
Alexander Who Used to Be Rich Last Sunday. (P-3) 257, 267, 588, 1056
Alice Adventures in Wonderland. (4-6) 414, 587, 999
Alistair's Time Machine. (K-3) 1057
All About Baseball. (4-6) 587
All Butterflies. (P-1) 587
All By Myself. (P-1) 1030
All in a Day. (3-5) 588
All New Jonah Twist, The. (3-5) 270
All the Colors of the Race. (4-6) 587
All-of-a-Kind Family. (4-6) 308

Alligators Are Awful. (P-2) 419
Alphabatics. (P-1) 587
Alphabears: An ABC Book. (P-1) 587
Alphabet Soup. (P-2) 18
Alphie Gets In First. (P-2) 254
Altogether One at a Time. (4-6) 411
Always Gramma. (P-2) 416
Always Room for One More. (K-2) 1, 269
Amanda and the Witch Switch. (P-2) 271
Amazing Bone, The. (1-3) 420
Amazing Pig, The. (1-4) 271
Amazing Spiders. (1-4) 1054
Amelia Bedelia. (1-3) 11, 20, 97, 255, 421, 587, 591, 619, 712, 809, 1008, 1054, 1057
Amelia Bedelia and the Baby. (1-3) 3, 591, 997
Amelia Bedelia Goes Camping. (1-3) 135
Amelia Bedelia Helps Out. (1-3) 3, 591
American Family Farm, The. (4-6) 588
American Folk Songs for Children in Home, School and Nursery School. (A) 413
Amigo. (K-2) 409, 723
Aminal, The. (P-2) 271, 408
Amos and Boris. (1-3) 11, 407, 409
Amos Fortune, Free Man. (4-6) 2, 269, 417, 588, 750
Anansi the Spider. (1-3) 422
Anastasia Krupnik. (4-6) 49, 270, 309, 717, 866
Anatole and the Cat. (1-3) 11
And I Mean It, Stanley. (P-2) 129
And It Still Is that Way. (A) 588
And Now Miguel. (5-6) 269
And One for All. (5-6) 417
And Then What Happened, Paul Revere? (3-6) 51, 419
And to Think that I Saw It on Mulberry Street. (P-3) 587
Andy and the Lion. (1-3) 587
Angel Child, Dragon Child. (1-3) 977
Angelina's Birthday Surprise. (K-2) 1044
Angus and the Cats. (P-1) 11
Angus and the Ducks. (P-1) 587
Animal Fact/Animal Fable. (2-4) 1055
Animal Numbers. (P-1) 1056
Animal Song. (P-2) 587
Animal, Vegetable, and John D. Jones. (5-6) 414
Animals of the Bible. (3-6) 1, 269
Animals Should Definitely Not Wear Clothing. (P-1) 271
Anna, Grandpa and the Big Storm. (P-2) 588
Anne of Green Gables. (4-6) 201, 368, 413

Hokey-Pokey Man, The. (P-2) 417
Hole in the Dike, The. (P-2) 587
Hole Is to Dig, A. (P-2) 587
Home for a Bunny. (P-2) 1001
Homecoming, The. (5-6) 411, 560, 915 411
Homer Price. (3-6) 411, 518, 854, 1012
Homesick: My Own Story. (4-6) 373, 411, 587, 758
Honey, I Love and Other Love Poems. (2-4) 588
Hopeful Trout and Other Limericks, The. (2-4) 587
Horrible Harry in Room 2B. (1-3) 97
Horse of a Different Color, A. (4-6) 587
Horton Hatches the Egg. (P-3) 18, 419, 407
Horton Hears a Who. (P-3) 13, 590
Hosie's Alphabet. (A) 11, 587
Hot Air Henry. (K-2) 11, 1057
House Is a House for Me, A. (P-2) 267, 408, 588,
    793, 1056
House of Dies Drear. (5-6) 675, 1025
House of Sixty Fathers, The. (4-6) 417, 588
House of Wings. (5-6) 414
House on East Eighty-Eighth Street. (K-2) 590
How Big Is a Foot? (K-3) 415
How Little Porcupine Played Christmas. (K-3) 272
How Many Bugs in a Box? (P-2) 1056
How Many Days to America? A Thanksgiving Story.
    (1-3) 266, 588
How Many Snails? A Counting Book. (P-1) 1057
How Much Is a Million? (A) 1056
How My Library Grew. (P-2) 588
How My Parents Learned to Ear. (1-3) 968
How the Grinch Stole Christmas. (P-3) 266
How to Dig a Hole to the Other Side of the Earth.
    (2-4) 734, 1043
How to Eat Fried Worms. (4-6) 99, 259, 296, 414,
    418, 519, 676, 836, 1014, 1055
How to Make Pop-ups. (2-6) 587
Hubert's Hair Raising Adventure. (K-3) 271
Hugo at the Window. (P-2) 587
Humbug Potion: An ABC Cipher. (P-2) 410
Humbug Rabbit. (P-2) 408
Humbug Witch. (P-1) 271
Humphrey Lost Whale, The. (2-4) 410
Hundred Dresses, The. (3-5) 61, 297, 411, 520, 855,
    1015
Hundred Penny Box. (4-6) 471, 641, 719
Hungry Thing, The. (P-1) 794
Hungry, Hungry Sharks. (K-3) 598
Hunter and His Dog. (P-2) 419
Hunter and the Animals, The. (K-1) 587

I Am Phoenix. (4-6) 413, 587
I Can Blink. (P-1) 412
I Can Read With My Eyes Shut. (P-2) 11
I Dance in My Red Pajamas. (P-2) 588
I Forgot. (P-2) 588

I Go With My Family to Grandma's. (P-2) 588
I Have a Sister, My Sister Is Deaf. (1-4) 415
I Know a Lady. (K-2) 271, 986
I Know an Old Lady Who Swallowed a Fly. (P-3)
    271, 587
I Like Me. (P-2) 588
I Read Signs. (P-1) 588
I Should Have Stayed in Bed. (1-3) 587
I Speak English for My Mom. (1-3) 588
I Unpacked Grandmother's Trunk. (K-3) 410, 590
I Want a Dog. (P-2) 410
I Want to Be an Astronaut. (P-2) 588, 1057
I Was a Second Grade Werewolf. (1-3) 271
I Was So Mad. (P-2) 110
I Will Not Go to Market Today. (P-2) 271
I Wish I Were a Butterfly. (K-3) 588, 1011, 1054
I'm in Charge of Celebrations. (3-6) 257, 266, 588
I'm Telling You Now. (P-1) 271
I'm Terrific. (K-2) 255, 271, 408
I, Houdini: The Autobiography of a Self Educated
    Hamster. (4-6) 521
I, Juan de Pareja. (6+) 269
Ice Cream Cone Coot and Other Rare Birds. (P-2)
    408
Ida Early Comes Over the Mountain. (5-6) 414
Idle Bear, The. (P-2) 587
If At First You Do Not See. (K-3) 1057
If Dinosaurs Came Back. (P-2) 412
If Dinosaurs Were Alive Today. (P-2) 412
If I Could Work. (P-1) 588
If I Ran the Zoo. (P-3) 996
If I Were in Charge of the World and Other Worries.
    (2-5) 271, 588, 1018
If the Dinosaurs Came Back. (P-2) 408
If Wishes Were Horses. (P-2) 587
If You Give a Mouse a Cookie. (P-2) 18, 255, 258,
    271, 410, 795, 1004, 1056
If You Grew Up with George Washington. (2-4) 588
If You Made a Million. (3-6) 412
If You Take a Pencil. (1-3) 117
Iggie's House. (4-6) 260, 275
Ike and Mama and the Trouble at School. (4-6) 419
Imogene's Antlers. (P-2) 265, 271, 410, 713
Important Book, The. (P-K) 412, 1005, 1057
In a People House. (P-1) 998
In Coal Country. (1-3) 416, 588
In Shadowland. (1-4) 587
In the Dinosaur's Paw. (2-4) 274, 281
In the Face of Danger. (4-6) 417
In the Middle of a Puddle. (P-2) 587
In the Year of the Boar and Jackie Robinson. (3-6)
    14, 98, 268, 348, 411, 677, 719, 774, 917, 1020
In Trouble Again, Zelda Hammersmith? (3-5) 414
Inch Boy, The. (P-2) 410
Inch By Inch. (P-1) 258, 407, 1056
Incident at Hawk's Hill. (6) 561, 918

Magic Toyshop, The. (P-2) 1006
Magnificent Moo, The. (P-2) 271
Maia: A Dinosaur Grows Up. (2-4) 596
Mail Order Kid. (3-5) 414, 587
Mail Order Wings. (4-6) 411
Make It Special: Cards, Decorations and Party
  Favors for Holidays (4-6) 587
Make Way for Ducklings. (P-1) 1, 12, 95, 269, 271,
  272, 407, 415, 430, 646, 799, 1008
Mama One, Mama Two. (P-2) 588
Man Who Kept House, The. (K-3) 419
Many Lives of Benjamin Franklin, The. (P-5) 588
Many Moons. (2-4) 1, 269, 587, 987
Maps and Globes. (2-5) 416
Mare on the Hill. (P-2) 587
Mariah Delaney Lending Library Disaster, The. (4-6)
  419
Marianna May and Nursey. (P-2) 410
Mark Twain: What Kind of Name Is That? A Story of
  Samuel Langhorn Clemens. (6) 587
Mars. (K-3) 597
Martian Chronicles, The. (6) 1027
Martin Luther King: The Peaceful Warrior. (4-6)
  413, 1024
Mary McLeod Bethune. (5-6) 588
Mary of Mile 18. (P-3) 587
Mary, Mary Quite Contrary. (P-2) 1000
Master Puppeteer, The. (6) 413
Matchlock Gun. (2-4) 269
Matilda. (4-6) 8
Maude and Sally. (P-2) 271
Maurice's Room. (2-4) 301, 839
Max. (1-3) 121, 255
Maxillian: You Are the Greatest. (4-6) 413
May I Bring a Friend? (P-2) 1, 12, 269, 407, 710,
  800, 1004
McBroom and the Big Wind. (3-6) 271
Meet the Computer. (3-5) 1057
Mei Li. (1-3) 1, 269
Merry-Go-Round: A Book About Nouns. (A) 412
Michael Bird Boy. (K-3) 415
Michael Hague's Favorite Hans Christian Andersen
  Fairy Tales. (2-5) 593
Mickey's Magnet. (1-3) 1057
Midnight Farm, The. (P-K) 1056
Midnight Fox. (4-6) 414
Mike Mulligan and His Steam Shovel. (K-2) 11, 12,
  431, 709, 741, 998, 1010, 1057
Millie Cooper 3B. (2-4) 587
Millions of Cats. (P-2) 254, 265, 587, 997
Milton the Early Riser. (P-1) 267
Ming Lo Moves the Mountain. (K-2) 265, 1056
Miracles on Maple Hill. (4-6) 269
Miss Hickory. (4-6) 269
Miss Nelson Has a Field Day. (1-3) 273
Miss Nelson Is Back. (1-3) 432

Miss Nelson Is Missing. (1-3) 26, 96, 132, 265, 266,
  271, 410, 432, 647, 715, 822, 1008
Miss Rumphius. (K-3) 36, 265, 266, 271, 410, 419,
  407, 416, 433, 711, 1008
Missing. (5-6) 414
Misty of Chicoteague. (3-5) 14, 235
Mitten, The. (P-2) 257, 410, 801
Mixed Up Chameleon, The. (P-2) 1005
Moja Means One: A Swahili Counting Book. (1-3) 11
Molly's Pilgrim. (2-4) 267, 417, 588, 592
Monkey and the Crocodile, The. (1-3) 1004
Monster in the Third Dresser Drawer and Other
  Stories About Adam Joshua. (2-4) 283
Monticello. (4-6) 588
Moon Bear. (P-2) 258
Moon Seems to Change, The. (K-3) 597
Mooncake. (K-1) 597
Moonlight. (P-1) 992
More Stories Julian Tells. (2-4) 592
Morgan for Melinda, A. (4-6) 414
Morris the Moose Goes to School. (1-3) 273
Most Amazing Hide and Seek Alphabet Book, The.
  (P-1) 589
Most Amazing Hide and Seek Counting Book, The.
  (P-1) 1056
Mother Goose. (A) 587
Mother Goose Treasury. (K-3) 407
Mother's Day Mice, The. (P-2) 587, 1001
Mouse and the Motorcycle. (2-5) 37, 169, 259, 418,
  479, 587, 875
Mouse Paint. (P-2) 1005
Mouse Soup. (K-2) 840
Mousekin Takes a Trip. (P-2) 1057
Mousekin's Birth. (K-3) 415
Mousekin's Woodland Sleepers. (P-2) 1057
Moving In. (5-6) 414, 587
Moving Molly. (P-2) 265
Mr. and Mrs. Pig's Evening Out. (K-2) 11, 255
Mr. Griggs Work. (P-2) 416
Mr. Gumpy's Motorcar. (K-3) 415
Mr. Popper's Penguins. (3-5) 242, 324, 414, 527,
  876, 1042
Mr. Rabbit and the Lovely Present. (P-2) 12, 407, 1004
Mr. Revere and I. (5-6) 417, 528
Mr. Tamarin's Trees. (P-2) 408
Mr. Yowder and the Windwagon. (4-6) 588
Mrs Piggle Wiggle. (2-4) 271
Mrs. Dunphy's Dog. (P-2) 410
Mrs. Frisby and the Rats of NIMH. (4-6) 2, 16, 66, 99,
  213, 268, 269, 374, 414, 568, 681, 776, 925, 1021,
Mrs. Gaddy and the Fast Growing Vine. (1-3) 271
Mrs. Minetta's Car Pool. (K-2) 271, 419
Mrs. Peloki's Snake. (K-2) 271
Much Bigger Than Martin. (K-2) 1056
Mud Pony, The. (1-3) 587
Mufaro's Beautiful Daughter. (K-3) 257, 416, 1049

Literature Materials Guide

Materials in this section are first arranged by publisher and then alphabetically by author. Item numbers correspond to indexed numbers in the indexes.

BOOK LURES, INC.
P.O. Box 0455
O'Fallon, MO

1. Bernhardt, Edyth. *ABC's of Thinking with Caldecott Books.* Book Lures, Inc., 1988.

ABC's of Thinking with Caldecott Books is arranged by thinking skills based on Caldecott winners from 1938 to 1988. Skills such as creating analogies, brainstorming, creative thinking, compare/contrast, comprehension skills, and problem solving are included in this activity book. This activity book includes oral activities, art activities, and written activities.

Books included: *Animals of the Bible; Mei Li; Abraham Lincoln; They Were Strong and Good; Make Way for Ducklings; The Little House; Many Moons; Prayer for a Child; The Rooster Crows; The Little Island; White Snow, Bright Snow; The Big Snow; Song of the Swallows; The Egg Tree; Finders Keepers; The Biggest Bear; Madeline's Rescue; Cinderella; Frog Went-A-Courtin'; A Tree Is Nice; Time of Wonder; Chanticleer and the Fox; Nine Days to Christmas; Baboushka and the Three Kings; Once a Mouse...; The Snowy Day; Where the Wild Things Are; May I Bring A Friend?; Always Room for One More; Sam, Bangs & Moonshine; Drummer Hoff; The Fool of the World and the Flying Ship; Sylvester and the Magic Pebble; A Story, A Story; One Fine Day; The Funny Little Woman; Duffy and the Devil; Arrow to the Sun; Why Mosquitoes Buzz in People's Ears; Ashanti to Zulu; Noah's Ark; The Girl Who Loved Wild Horses; Ox-Cart Man; Fables; Jumanji; Shadow; The Glorious Flight; St. George and the Dragon; Polar Express; Hey, Al!; Owl Moon.*

2. Mealy, Virginia. *Newbery Books.* 2nd ed. Book Lures, Inc., 1991.

Newbery Books provides activities for thirty Newbery Medal winners from 1940 to 1991. Some activities accompany each winner. This activity book combined with other books will provide literary activities to enhance reading.

Books included: *Daniel Boone; Call It Courage; King of the Wind; Door in the Wall; Amos Fortune, Free Man; Witch of Blackbird Pond; Island of Blue Dolphins; A Wrinkle in Time; Shadow of a Bull; From the Mixed-up Files of Mrs. Basil E. Frankweiler; The High King; Summer of the Swans; Mrs. Frisby & the Rats of NIMH; Julie of the Wolves; Slave Dancer; The Grey King; Roll of Thunder, Hear My Cry; Bridge to Terabithia; The Westing Game; A Gathering of Days; Jacob Have I Loved; Visit to Wm. Blake's Inn; Dicey's Song; The Hero & the Crown; Dear Mr. Henshaw; Sarah, Plain & Tall; The Whipping Boy; Lincoln: A Photobiography; Number the Stars; Manic Magee.*

3. Polette, Nancy. *The Amelia Bedelia Thinking Book.* Book Lures, Inc., 1983.

The Amelia Bedelia Thinking Book is designed to extend productive and critical thinking skills based on the series Amelia Bedelia. This book contains some activities in fluency, flexibility, originality, elaboration, planning, forecasting, decision-making, problem solving, and evaluation. The activity book also contains writing activities, a gameboard, and opportunities for art.

Books included: *Amelia Bedelia Helps Out; Good Work, Amelia Bedelia; Teach Us, Amelia Bedelia; Amelia Bedelia and the Baby.*

4. Polette, Nancy. *The Frog and Toad Thinking Book.* Book Lures, Inc., 1982.

Activities in this book are based on Arnold Lobel characters in the Frog and Toad series. Five titles are included in the book. Activities in this book emphasize fluency, flexibility, originality, elaboration, planning, forecasting, decision making and problem solving. It also includes a gameboard, matrices, and limited art activities.

Books included: *Frog and Toad All Year; Days with Frog and Toad; Frog and Toad Together; Frog and Toad Are Friends; The Frog and Toad Coloring Book.*

5-9. Theme Related Novel Guides
This series offers thematic novel studies concerning the sea, survival, overcoming adversity, unforgettable characters and young heroines. Each book includes a variety of activities in the content areas, as well as activities that encourage critical thinking. Units also include semantic mapping, charts, additional reading lists, and excellent models for research which include actions, topics, and products. Interesting pre- and post-reading activities are also included.

5. Levine. Gloria. *Children of the Sea.* Book Lures, Inc., 1991.

Books included: *The Black Pearl; Call It Courage; The Eyes of Amaryllis; Greyling; The Wave.*

6. Polette, Nancy. *Survival.* Book Lures, Inc., 1991.

Books included: *Number the Stars; Sign of the Beaver; Sarah Bishop; Under the Hawthorn Tree; Wolves of Willoughby Chase; Young Nick and Jubilee.*

7.   Polette, Nancy. Trials: *Overcoming Adversity*. Book Lures, Inc., 1991.

Books included: *The Incredible Journey; Where the Red Fern Grows; Savage Sam; Stone Fox.*

8.   Polette, Nancy. *Unforgettable Characters*. Book Lures, Inc., 1991.

Books included: *The BFG; Charlotte's Web; Matilda; Pippi Longstocking; Stuart Little.*

9.   Polette, Nancy. *Young Heroines*. Book Lures, Inc., 1991.

Books included: *Calamity Kate; The Secret Garden; Strawberry Girl; Summer of the Swans; A Wrinkle in Time.*

*10.   Lance, Janice. *First Literature Experiences*. Book Lures, Inc., 1991.

First Literature Experiences is designed for very young children who are beginning to match the written word with their oral language. The book is based on five classic tales in a readers theatre format. Each story has material to make transparencies, blackline masters, and sensory activities. Each story is presented using all five senses to address each child's learning modality.

Books included: *Henny Penny; Three Little Pigs; Gingerbread Boy; Little Red Hen; The House That Jack Built.*

THE CENTER FOR APPLIED RESEARCH IN EDUCATION
A Division of Simon and Schuster
West Nyack, New York 10955

***11.   Stull, Elizabeth C. *Children's Book Activities Kit*. The Center for Applied Research in Education, 1988.

Children's Book Activities Kit contains over 200 activities designed to expose children to quality literature, increase their vocabulary, listening, and writing skills, and strengthen their ability to visualize and critically think. The kit is organized into 10 sections that cover different genres of children's books such as the alphabet, animals, and heroes and heroines. It focuses on 68 titles, many of which are award-winning, and provides activities for each that involve children in increasing their ability to think.

Books included:
ABC Books: *A Farmer's Alphabet; Hosie's Alphabet; The Guinea Pig ABC; ED Emberley's ABC; A, B, See!; On Market Street.*
Number Books: *Anno's Counting Book; The Very Hungry Caterpillar; Bicycle Race; Moja Means One; Swahili Counting Book; Shapes and Things; Through the Year with Harriet.*
Picture Books: *Hot Air Henry; Babar's Birthday Surprise; Strega Nona; When the Sky Is Like Lace; The Snowy Day; Town and Country; Where the Wild Things Are.*
Animal Books: *Angus and the Cat; Chickens Aren't the Only Ones; Bedtime for Frances; Swimmy; Curious*

George Goes to the Hospital; Anatole and the Cat; Pelican.
Fantasy Books: *Mike Mulligan and His Steam Shovel; A Pocket for Corduroy; Blueberries for Sal; The Pooh Story Book; Amos & Boris; The Garden of Abdul Gasazi; Charlotte's Web.*
Humorous Books: *Cloudy with a Chance of Meatballs; Madeline's Rescue; Jim and the Beanstalk; Petunia; Amelia Bedelia; Mr. and Mrs. Pig's Evening Out; I Can Read with My Eyes Shut.*
Monsters, Ogres, and Scary Things: *Wobble, the Witch Cat; Simon's Book; Arthur's Loose Tooth; The Very Worst Monster; There's A Nightmare in My Closet; What's Under My Bed?; Zarelda's Ogre; Python's Party.*
Heroes and Heroine: *Three Cheers for Mother Jones; Abraham Lincoln; The Story of Paul Bunyan; What's the Big Idea, Ben Franklin?; Runaway Slave; The Story of Harriet Tubman; Crazy Horse; Sioux Warrior; Bicycle Rider; Johnny Appleseed.*
Problem Solving: *Perfect Pigs; An Introduction to Manners; Ramona Quimby, Age 8; Everett Anderson's Friend; Alexander and the Terrible, Horrible, No Good, Very Bad Day; The Tenth Good Thing about Barney; It Could Always Be Worse; Say It!*
Poetry: *Rabbits, Rabbits; Speak Up; Hailstones and Halibut Bones; What I Did Last Summer; The Poetry Troupe; An Anthology of Poems to Read Aloud.*

CREATIVE TEACHING PRESS
Cypress, CA 90630

***12.   Wheeler, Sharon. *Activities for Enhancing Literature Books Included: K-1*. Creative Teaching Press, 1989.

This book contains 28 titles that were chosen by teachers, librarians, and students. Many are award-winning titles that encourage reading. Activities are on blackline masters and can be integrated with other resources into all content areas.

Books included: *Madeline; The Story of Babar; Mike Mulligan and His Steam Shovel; The Very Hungry Caterpillar; Freight Train; May I Bring A Friend?; Petunia; Ask Mr. Bear; Corduroy; Rosie's Walk; The Snowy Day; Leo the Late Bloomer; The Carrot Seed; Alexander and the Wind-Up Mouse; Brown Bear, Brown Bear, What Do You See?; Blueberries for Sal; Where the Wild Things Are; Caps for Sale; A Tree Is Nice; What Mary Jo Shared; Ira Sleeps Over; Harry the Dirty Dog; Mr. Rabbit and the Lively Present; William's Doll.*

***13.   Drew, Rosa, et. al. *Activities for Enhancing Literature. Books Included: 1-2*. Creative Teaching Press, 1989.

This collection of activities and reproducible pages provides extension activities for twenty-one children's trade titles and integrates language arts, math, social studies, and science with reading. These activities also incorporate critical thinking, writing, and communication skills into the curriculum. Open-ended questions and easily constructed projects provide many opportunities to develop critical thinking and creativity.

Books included: *Little Rabbit's Loose Tooth; Stone Soup; The Little House; The Happy Lion; Dandelion; Bread and Jam for Frances; Danny and the Dinosaur; Whose Mouse Are You?; Frog and Toad Are Friends; Winnie the Pooh; The Day Jimmy's Boa Ate the Wash; Strega Nona; Chester the Worldly Pig; The Nicest Gift; Horton Hears a Who; Sylvester and the Magic Pebble; Stevie; The Tenth Good Thing about Barney; The Biggest Bear; Crow Boy; My Grandson Lew.*

***14. Young, Janet, et al. *Activities for Enhancing Literature Books Included: 3-4*. Creative Teaching Press, 1989.

This book was designed to encourage children to increase their written and oral communication skills, develop an appreciation of literature, and increase their ability to critically think. The book contains nine units filled with background information about the literature, vocabulary development activities, and blackline masters to provide enrichment. Activities are designed to facilitate individual students or to be incorporated into cooperative learning. Some units are designed to integrate language arts with math, science, and social studies.

Books included: *Why Mosquitoes Buzz in People's Ears; The Elephant's Child; The Steadfast Tin Soldier; The Velveteen Rabbit; Ramona the Pest; Sadako and the Thousand Paper Cranes; Misty of Chincoteague; James and the Giant Peach; In the Year of the Boar and Jackie Robinson.*

***15. Weber, Gail, et al. *Activities for Enhancing Literature Books Included: 3-4. Volume II.* Creative Teaching Press, 1990

Books included: *Koko's Kitten; Jumanji; Annie and the Old One; Aesop's Fables; Yeh-Shen, A Cinderella Story from China; Stone Fox; Charlotte's Web; What's the Big Idea, Ben Franklin?*

***16. Engles, Jennifer, et al. *Activities for Enhancing Literature Books Included: 5-6*. Creative Teaching Press, 1989.

Books included: *The Sign of the Beaver; From the Mixed-Up Files of Mrs. Basil E. Frankweiler; The Cay; Freaky Friday; Mrs. Frisby and the Rats of NIMH; The Indian in the Cupboard; The Lion, the Witch, and the Wardrobe; Where the Red Fern Grows.*

***17. Young, Janet. *Activities for Enhancing Literature Books Included: 5-6. Volume II.* Newbery Award Books. Creative Teaching Press, 1990.

Books included: *Sarah, Plain and Tall; Dear Mr. Henshaw; Call It Courage; The Summer of the Swans; Bridge to Terabithia; Island of the Blue Dolphins; A Wrinkle in Time; Roll of Thunder, Hear My Cry.*

*18. Bruno, Janet. *Book Cooks.* Creative Teaching Press, Inc., 1991.

Book Cooks is a literature-based cooking book that provides thirty-five opportunities for learning math, reading, science, cooperative learning, and activities to build self-esteem. Each recipe provides a list of related literature and extension activities.

Books included: *Alexander and the Terrible, Horrible, No Good, Very Bad Day; Alphabet Soup; Bread and Jam for Frances; Caps for Sale; The Carrot Seed; Chicken Soup with Rice; Cinderella; Clifford, the Big Red Dog; Cloudy with a Chance of Meatballs; The Day Jimmy's Boa Ate the Wash; Frog and Toad Are Friends; The Gingerbread Man; Goldilocks and the Three Bears; Gregory the Terrible Eater; Hansel and Gretel; Happy Birthday, Moon; Horton Hatches the Egg; If You Give a Mouse a Cookie; Ira Sleeps Over; It Looked Like Spilt Milk; Johnny Appleseed; Katy No-Pocket; Little Rabbit's Loose Tooth; Owl Moon; Pancakes for Breakfast; The Popcorn Book; Pumpkin, Pumpkin; Rosie's Walk; The Snowy Day; Strega Nona; The Tale of Peter Rabbit; The Three Little Pigs; The Very Busy Spider; The Very Hungry Caterpillar; Where the Wild Things Are.*

ECONOCLAD
A Division of the American Companies
P.O. Box 1777
Topeka, Kansas 66601

**19-93. *Story Strategies* Series
These guides provide individual and cooperative learning activities, questions about the literature, writing topics, projects, and assessment tools. Each guide is divided into introducing the book, activities for each chapter of the book, post-reading activities, and evaluations.

Story Strategies—Grades 1 and 2
19. *Alexander and the Terrible, Horrible, No Good Very Bad Day*
20. *Amelia Bedelia*
21. *Annie and the Old One*
22. *Chair for My Mother*
23. *Corduroy*
24. *Frog and Toad Are Friends*
25. *Ira Sleeps Over*
26. *Miss Nelson Is Missing*
27. *Where the Wild Things Are*

Story Strategies—Grades 2, 3, 4
28. *Blackberries in the Dark*
29. *The Boxcar Children*
30. *Charlotte's Web*
31. *Crow Boy*
32. *The Drinking Gourd*
33. *Freckle Juice*
34. *J. T.*
35. *Little House in the Big Woods*
36. *Miss Rumphius*
37. *The Mouse and the Motorcycle*
38. *Nate the Great and the Sticky Case*
39. *Pippi Longstocking*
40. *Ramona Quimby, Age 8*
41. *Sam, Bangs and Moonshine*

42. *Stone Fox*
43. *Stuart Little*
44. *Tales of a Fourth Grade Nothing*
45. *Tenth Good Thing about Barney*
46. *White Stallion*

Story Strategies — Grades 4, 5, 6

47. *Abel's Island*
48. *Across Five Aprils*
49. *Anastasia Krupnik*
50. *And Now Miguel*
51. *And Then What Happened, Paul Revere?*
52. *Ben and Me*
53. *Blue Willow*
54. *The Borrowers*
55. *Bridge to Terabithia*
56. *Call It Courage*
57. *Cricket in Times Square*
58. *Dear Mr. Henshaw*
59. *Enormous Egg*
60. *From the Mixed-Up Files of Mrs. Basil E. Frankweiler*
61. *Hundred Dresses*
62. *Indian in the Cupboard*
63. *Island of the Blue Dolphins*
64. *James and the Giant Peach*
65. *The Lion, the Witch and the Wardrobe*
66. *Mrs. Frisby and the Rats of NIMH*
67. *Phantom Tollbooth*
68. *Phillip Hall Likes Me, I Reckon, Maybe*
69. *Pinballs*
70. *Rabbit Hill*
71. *Ramona and Her Father*
72. *Rascal*
73. *Return of the Indian*
74. *Roll of Thunder, Hear My Cry*
75. *Sarah, Plain and Tall*
76. *Tom Sawyer*
77. *Trumpet of the Swan*
78. *Tuck Everlasting*
79. *Witch of Blackbird Pond*
80. *Wrinkle in Time*

Story Strategies — Grades 6, 7, 8

81. *Call of the Wild*
82. *The Cay*
83. *Anne Frank: Diary of a Young Girl*
84. *Dicey's Song*
85. *Hatchet*
86. *Incredible Journey*
87. *Jacob Have I Loved*
88. *Julie of the Wolves*
89. *The Pearl*
90. *Sounder*
91. *Treasure Island*
92. *Where the Red Fern Grows*
93. *Winter Room*

THE EDUCATION CENTER
1410 Mill Street
Greensboro, NC 27408

94-99. *Learning Through Literature* Series

This series of resource books utilizes renowned children's literature to develop critical thinking and creative writing skills. Extension activities within each unit provide a multitude of opportunities for children to "experience" the stories. These units also include vocabulary development, synopses of the books and activities sheets designed to develop comprehension skills.

94. Andrews, Becky, et al. *Learning through Literature, Books Included: K-1. Book One.* The Education Center, Inc. 1990.

Books included: *The Very Hungry Caterpillar; Brown Bear, Brown Bear, What Do You See?; Corduroy; There's A Nightmare in My Closet; If You Give a Mouse a Cookie; Are You My Mother?; The Tale of Peter Rabbit; Bread and Jam for Frances; Ira Sleeps Over; Alexander and the Terrible, Horrible, No Good, Very Bad Day.*

95. *Learning through Literature Books Included: K-2.* The Education Center, Inc., 1991.

Books included: *The Little House; Frederick; If I Ran the Zoo; Curious George; Nana Upstairs, Nana Downstairs; Make Way for Ducklings; The Napping House; Whistle for Willie; The Little Engine That Could; Where the Wild Things Are.*

96. Allaire, Audrey, et al. *Learning Through Literature Books Included: 2-3. Book Two.* The Education Center, Inc., 1990.

Books included: *Nate the Great; Stone Soup; Bedtime for Frances; Frog and Toad Are Friends; Kermit the Hermit; Miss Nelson Is Missing!; Crow Boy; Freckle Juice; Did You Carry the Flag Today, Charlie?; Beezus and Ramona.*

97. Badden, Diane, et al. *Learning through Literature Books Included: 2-3. Second Series.* The Education Center, Inc., 1991.

Books included: *Strega Nona; Sylvester and the Magic Pebble; Big Bad Bruce; Amelia Bedelia; The One in the Middle Is the Green Kangaroo; Cam Jansen and the Mystery of the Circus Clown; Arthur's Eyes; Horrible Harry in Room 2B; Keep the Lights Burning; Charlotte's Web.*

98. Andrews, Becky, et al. *Learning through Literature Books Included: 4-5.* The Education Center, Inc., 1991.

Books included: *Charlie and the Chocolate Factory; Where the Red Fern Grows; The Pinballs; Sign of the*

Beaver; Tales of a Fourth Grade Nothing; Sideways Stories from Wayside School; In the Year of the Boar and Jackie Robinson; The Indian in the Cupboard.

99. Andrews, Becky, et al. *Learning through Literature Books Included: 4-6. Book Three.* The Education Center, Inc., 1990.

Books included: *Soup; Sarah, Plain and Tall; The Summer of the Swans; How to Eat Fried Worms; Island of the Blue Dolphins; Mrs. Frisby and the Rats of NIMH; James and the Giant Peach; Sounder.*

ENGINE-UITY, LTD.
P.O. Box 9610
Phoenix, AZ 85068

***100-249. Porta Center Kits.**
These kits are intended to aid the study of books by basing activities on Bloom's Taxonomy. Each center has a worksheet based on the knowledge and comprehension levels of Bloom's books including: answer key and eight task cards, 2 each from application to evaluation. Each center comes with directions for constructing the folder that will house the material. Porta-centers are designed to be used in conjunction with the basal, or as one aspect of collection of literature-based activities.

Bac-Packs
100. *Frog Goes to Dinner*
101. *Pancakes for Breakfast*
102. *The Snowman*
103. *Hiccup*
104. *Deep in the Forest*
105. *Bear and the Fly*
106. *Changes, Changes*

Porta Centers Grades K-1
107. *Clifford, the Big Red Dog*
108. *There's a Nightmare in My Closet*
109. *Chicken Soup with Rice*
110. *I Was So Mad*
111. *Leo the Late Bloomer*
112. *Rosie's Walk*
113. *Blackboard Bear*
114. *Little Bear's Visit*
115. *My Mom Travels a Lot*
116. *Pinkerton Behave*
117. *If You Take a Pencil*

Porta Centers Grades 1-2
118. *Where the Wild Things Are*
119. *Ira Sleeps Over*
120. *The Day Jimmy's Boa Ate the Wash*
121. *Max*
122. *Curious George*
123. *The Very Hungry Caterpillar*
124. *Bread and Jam for Frances*
125. *Arthur's Honey Bear*
126. *My Teacher Sleeps in School*
127. *Danny and the Dinosaur*
128. *The Snowy Day*
129. *And I Mean It, Stanley*

130. *Nate the Great Stalks Stupidweed*
131. *A Porcupine Named Fluffy*

Porta Centers Grades 2-3
132. *Miss Nelson Is Missing*
133. *Alexander and the Terrible, Horrible, No Good, Very Bad Day*
134. *No Roses for Harry*
135. *Amelia Bedelia Goes Camping*
136. *Regards to the Man in the Moon*
137. *The Girl Who Loved Wild Horses*
138. *Madeline's Rescue*
139. *Frederick*
140. *Gila Monsters Meet You at the Airport*
141. *The Pain and the Great One*
142. *The Biggest Bear*
143. *Something Queer Is Going On*
144. *Sylvester and the Magic Pebble*
145. *Why Mosquitoes Buzz in People's Ears*

Porta Centers Grades 3-4
146. *Adventures of Ali Baba Bernstein*
147. *Aldo Applesauce*
148. *Beezus and Ramona*
149. *Bunnicula*
150. *The Cybil War*
151. *The 18th Emergency*
152. *Frankenstein Moved In on the Fourth Floor*
153. *Freaky Friday*
154. *Henry Huggins*
155. *Jennifer and Josephine*
156. *Legend of the Bluebonnet*
157. *Pippi Longstocking*
158. *Ramona the Pest*
159. *Rich Mitch*
160. *Sam, Bangs and Moonshine*
161. *Stuart Little*

Porta Centers Grades 4-5
162. *Behind the Wall*
163. *The Best Christmas Pageant Ever*
164. *Cat Walk*
165. *The Great Brain*
166. *Hank the Cowdog*
167. *Harriet the Spy*
168. *The Hoboken Chicken Emergency*
169. *The Mouse and the Motorcycle*
170. *Nothing's Fair in the Fifth Grade*
171. *Otherwise Known as Sheila the Great*
172. *Owls in the Family*
173. *Runaway Ralph*
174. *Snow Treasure*
175. *Superfudge*
176. *Tales of a Fourth Grade Nothing*
177. *Taste of Blackberries*
178. *Thirteen Ways to Sink a Sub*

Porta Centers Grades 5-6
179. *Ben and Me*
180. *Charlie and the Chocolate Factory*
181. *Incredible Journey*
182. *Indian in the Cupboard*
183. *James and the Giant Peach*
184. *Lost in the Barrens*

185. *The Phantom Tollbooth*
186. *Slake's Limbo*
187. *The Trumpet of the Swan*
188. *Tuck Everlasting*
189. *The White Mountains*

Classic Porta Centers Grades 3-4
190. *A Bear Called Paddington*
191. *The Velveteen Rabbit*
192. *Winnie the Pooh*

Classic Porta Centers Grades 4-5
193. *The Borrowers*
194. *The Light in the Forest*
195. *Little House in the Big Woods*
196. *The Wind in the Willows*

Classic Porta Centers Grades 5-6
197. *The Cay*
198. *Gentle Ben*
199. *The Lion, the Witch and the Wardrobe*
200. *The Secret Garden*

Classic Porta Centers Grades 6-7
201. *Anne of Green Gables*
202. *Cheaper by the Dozen*
203. *Old Yeller*
204. *Where the Red Fern Grows*

Classic Porta Centers Grades 7-8
205. *Adventures of Tom Sawyer*
206. *Anne Frank: The Diary of a Young Girl*
207. *The Call of the Wild*

Newbery Award Winners Porta Centers Grades 4-5
208. *Bridge to Terabithia*
209. *Caddie Woodlawn*
210. *Dear Mr. Henshaw*
211. *From the Mixed-Up Files of Mrs. Basil E. Frankweiler*
212. *Island of the Blue Dolphins*
213. *Mrs. Frisby and the Rats of NIMH*
214. *Sarah, Plain and Tall*
215. *The Whipping Boy*

Newbery Award Winners Porta Centers Grades 5-6
216. *Dicey's Song*
217. *The Door in the Wall*
218. *It's Like This, Cat*
219, *Jacob Have I Loved*
220. *Johnny Tremain*
221. *Julie of the Wolves*
222. *King of the Wind*
223. *Rabbit Hill*
224. *Roll of Thunder, Hear My Cry*
225. *Sounder*

Newbery Award Winners Porta Centers Grades 6-7
226. *Call It Courage*
227. *Slave Dancer*
228. *The Summer of the Swans*
229. *The Westing Game*
230. *Witch of Blackbird Pond*
231. *Wrinkle in Time*

Newbery Honor Porta Centers Grades 3-4
232. *Annie and the Old One*
233. *Charlotte's Web*
234. *Jennifer, Hecate, Macbeth, William McKinley and Me, Elizabeth*
235. *Misty of Chincoteague*
236. *My Side of the Mountain*
237. *Ramona Quimby, Age 8*

Newbery Honor Porta Centers Grades 5-6
238. *The Black Pearl*
239. *The Cricket in Times Square*
240. *The Egypt Game*
241. *The Great Gilly Hopkins*
242. *Mr. Popper's Penguins*
243. *One-Eyed Cat*
244. *The Sign of the Beaver*
245. *Sing Down the Moon*

Newbery Honor Porta Centers Grades 6-7
246. *Across Five Aprils*
247. *Dragonwings*
248. *My Brother Sam Is Dead*
249. *Hatchet*

EVAN MOORE
9425 York Rd.
Monterey, CA 93940-6533

*250. Moore, Jo Ellen, and Leslie Tryon. *Aesop's Fables*. Evan Moore, 1988.

This literature mini unit has some art activities, writing suggestions, crossword puzzles, word searches, a poster, and drawing lessons based on six Aesop's Fables.

Books included: *The Country Mouse and the City Mouse; The Lion and the Mouse; The Goose That Laid the Golden Eggs; The Fox and the Grapes; The Fox and the Stork; The Tortoise and the Hare.*

*251. Moore, Jo Ellen, and Joy Evans. *Fun with Fairy Tales*. Evan Moore, 1987.

*252. Moore, Jo Ellen, and Joy Evans. *More Fun with Fairy Tales*. Evan Moore, 1987.

Fun with Fairy Tales and *More Fun with Fairy Tales* are literature mini packs that contain posters and reproducible pages for six fairy tales. Each mini pack contains a gameboard on the back cover.

Books included: *The Gingerbread Boy; The Three Bears; The Three Billy Goats Gruff; Henny Penny; The Three Little Pigs; The Little Red Hen.*

Books included: *Hansel and Gretel, Jack and the Beanstalk, Snow White and the Seven Dwarfs, Rumplestiltskin, Little Red Riding Hood, The Breman Town Musicians.*

*253. Moore, Jo Ellen, and Leslie Tryon. *Stories from Hans Christian Andersen.* Evan Moore, 1988.

Activities inspired by three of Hans Christian Andersen's timeless tales provide a springboard for reading, writing and art. This book includes two posters, resource pages for the teacher, story sequencing and art activities.

Books included: *The Ugly Duckling; The Princess and the Pea; The Emperor's New Clothes.*

*254. Evans, Joy, and Jo Ellen Moore. *Fun with Books.* Evans Moore, 1988.

This reproducible book utilizes 40 children's titles and includes some questions, art activities and a few generic activities for use with kindergarten and first graders.

Books included: *Caps for Sale; Where's Spot?; Drummer Hoff; Rosie's Walk; Pancakes for Breakfast; Corduroy; Ask Mr. Bear; The Blanket That Had to Go; The Mitten; The Very Hungry Caterpillar; The Mystery of the Missing Red Mitten; Millions of Cats; The Napping House; Harry the Dirty Dog; Lambs for Dinner; The Happy Day; The Lazy Bear; Clyde Monster; Harold and the Purple Crayon; Buzz Buzz Buzz; Springfellow; Moon Bear; Little Rabbit's Loose Tooth; Harry and the Terrible Whatzit; Ira Sleeps Over; There's a Nightmare in My Closet; Peter's Chair; Little Blue and Little Yellow; It Looked Like Spilt Milk; Round Robin; The Great Big Enormous Turnip; Alphie Gets in First; Goodnight Moon; Freight Train; On My Mother's Lap; Good Morning Chick; Benny Bakes a Cake; Rabbit's Morning; Timothy Goes to School; Oh, A Hunting We Will Go.*

*255. Moore, Jo Ellen, and Joy Evans. *More Fun with Books.* Evan Moore, 1987.

More Fun with Books is a reproducible book with activities for grades 1-3. Each title has approximately three activities.

Books included: *Hi, Cat!; No Ducks in Our Bathtub; Curious George Takes a Job; My Grandson Lew; Blueberries for Sal; Frog and Toad Together; Alexander and the Wind-Up Mouse; Annie and the Wild Animals; If You Give a Mouse a Cookie; Bread and Jam for Frances; Oh, Were They Ever Happy!; Tikki Tikki Tembo; A Chair for My Mother; Gilberto and the Wind; A Pair of Red Clogs; Stone Soup; Amelia Bedelia; Max; Katy and the Big Snow; Where the Wild Things Are; I'm Terrific; Strega Nona; Commander Toad in Space; George and Martha; Albert's Toothache; Crow Boy; The Biggest Bear; The Mysterious Tadpole; Sylvester and the Magic Pebble; Big Bad Bruce; Old Arthur; The 500 Hats of Bartholomew Cubbins; Do Not Open; Liza Lou and the Yeller Belly Swamp; The Relatives Came; Why Mosquitoes Buzz in People's Ears; Cloudy with a Chance of Meatballs; Mr. and Mrs. Pig's Evening Out; The Girl Who Loved Wild Horses; Alexander and the Terrible, Horrible, No Good, Very Bad Day.*

*256. Evans, Joy, and Jo Ellen Moore. *Even More Fun with Books.* Evan Moore, 1988.

This book is similar to its predecessor, but it has more questions about each title. It has oral, written activities and a section entitled, "Think About It" that provides some higher order questions.

Books included: *A Wrinkle in Time; Bridge to Terabithia; Bunnicula; Do Bananas Chew Gum?; James and the Giant Peach; The Indian in the Cupboard; Johnny Tremain; Little House on the Prairie; Ramona and Her Father; Sarah, Plain and Tall; Stuart Little; Tales of a Fourth Grade Nothing; The Teddy Bear Tree; Trouble River; The Whipping Boy.*

*257. Moore, Jo Ellen, and Leslie Tryon. *Never Too Old for Picture Books.* Evan Moore, 1989.

Never Too old for Picture Books contains twelve titles of children's picture books. Generic oral and written language activities are listed at the front of the book. Each title includes questions about the book, art activities and other language activities.

Books included: *Everyone Knows What a Dragon Looks Like; Wilfred Gordon MacDonald Partridge; Alexander Who Used to Be Rich Last Sunday; Faint Frogs Feeling Feverish; I'm in Charge of Celebrations; The Garden of Abdul Gasazi; Mufaro's Beautiful Daughter; The Treasure; Saint George and the Dragon; Knots on a Counting Rope; Yeh-Shen: A Cinderella Story from China; The Winter Wren.*

*258. Moore, Jo Ellen, and Joy Evans. *Read It Again.* Evan Moore, 1989.

Includes stories that can be read aloud. The activities include oral language, art projects, math readiness and creative dramatics.

Books included: *Brown Bear, Brown Bear; The Very Busy Spider; The Tale of Peter Rabbit; Moon Bear; The Mystery of the Missing Red Mitten; The Napping House; The April Rabbits; Corduroy; If You Give a Mouse a Cookie; Inch by Inch; Spiders in the Fruit Cellar; Peter's Chair.*

*259. Moore, Jo Ellen, and Joy Evans. *Sharing Chapter Books.* Evan Moore, 1989

Sharing Chapter Books consists of activities that correlate with read-aloud books. Each title includes language activities, art activities and questions about the story.

Books included: *Commander Toad in Space; How to Eat Fried Worms; The Chocolate Touch; Frog and Toad Together; George and Martha; My Father's Dragon; Little House in the Big Woods; The Mouse and the Motorcycle; Adam Draws Himself a Dragon; The Secret Moose; A Toad for Tuesday; The Josefina Quilt Story.*

GOOD APPLE
1204 Buchanan St.
Box 299
Carthage, IL, 62321-0299

***260. Palumbo, Thomas J. *Integrating the Literature of Judy Blume in the Classroom.* Good Apple, 1990.

The ten teaching components of a successful literature based program are integrated into the activities in this book making it an excellent teaching guide. This book provides a course outline for teaching literature based instruction. It is activity oriented and integrates the curriculum. The book contains literature motivators, short-term projects, critical thinking and writing activities, art extenders, and much more.

Books included: *Freckle Juice; Tiger Eyes; Blubber; Tales of a Fourth Grade Nothing; Otherwise Known as Sheila the Great; Superfudge; Iggie's House; The Pain and the Great One; Starring Sally J. Freedman as Herself; The One in the Middle is the Green Kangaroo; Then Again, Maybe I Won't; It's Not the End of the World.*

**261. Palumbo, Thomas J. *Integrating the Literature of Beverly Cleary in the Classroom.* Good Apple, 1991.

This guide to the works of Beverly Cleary offers eleven titles of Cleary and accompanying activities. It is designed to help build a classroom literature program based on the ten-step literature format. Each unit includes lead-ins to literature, vocabulary development, critical and creative thinking skills, and writing activities.

Books included: *Ramona and Her Father; The Ramona Quimby Diary; Henry and the Clubhouse; Dear Mr. Henshaw; Ribsy; Fifteen; Socks; The Luckiest Girl; The Ralph S. Mouse; Sister of the Bride; Ellen Tebbits.*

***262. Hackett, Christine Olivieri. *Little House in the Classroom.* Good Apple, 1989.

Designed to teach basic skills and provide enrichment for children, this book is divided into seven units based on Laura Ingalls Wilder's books. It successfully integrates children's literature into the curriculum, and provides relevant activities which include critical thinking, comprehension skills, and whole language activities. Most activities are intended for use with grades 3-5.

Books included: *Little House in the Big Woods; Little House on the Prairie; On the Banks of Plum Creek; By the Shores of Silver Lake; The Long Winter; Little Town on the Prairie; These Happy Golden Years.*

***263. Cinerelli, Sister Carol Joy. *Integrating Literature and the Language Arts Using the Tales of Hans Christian Andersen.* Good Apple, 1990.

This resource book contains activities related to thirteen titles of Hans Christian Andersen. Activities include questions based on Bloom's Taxonomy, art activities, writing and listening activities, drama, graphic organizers for critical thinking and reproducible materials.

Books included: *Hans Christian Andersen: His Life, His Works; The Life of Felix Mendelssohn; The Ugly Duckling; The Wild Swans; The Princess and the Pea: A Summary; Thumbelina: A Summary; The Steadfast Soldier: A Summary; The Snow Queen: A Summary; The Little Mermaid: A Summary; The Little Match Girl: A Summary; The Emperor's New Clothes: A Summary; A Fir Tree: A Summary.*

***264. Cincerelli, Sister Carol Joy. *Integrating Literature, Language and the Arts Using the Tales of the Brothers Grimm.* Good Apple, 1990.

Using the Tales of the Brothers Grimm, this resource book combines the tales of the Brothers Grimm with Bloom's Taxonomy. Each unit has background information on the story and several suggestions for utilization of activities with the story. Units include time lines, questions and worksheets based on Bloom's, task cards, and ideas for learning centers.

Books included: *Folklore; The Frog Prince; Rapunzel; Ashputtel (Cinderella); Snow White and Rose Red; Hansel and Gretel; Sleeping Beauty; Little Red Riding Hood; The Three Spinning Fairies; The Fisherman and His Wife; The Golden Goose; The Elves and the Cobbler.*

****265. Chapin, Laurie, and Ellen Flegenheimer-Riggle. *Leaping into Literature.* Good Apple, 1990.

Distinguished children's literature is a vehicle for developing higher order thinking skills, creativity, and creative problem solving in this book. Each of the thirty units is designed to provide open-ended activities that emphasize Bloom's Taxonomy as well as develop fluency, flexibility, originality, and elaboration. Blackline activity sheet are included with each lesson.

Books included: *Alexander and the Terrible, Horrible, No Good, Very Bad Day; Arthur's Christmas Cookies; Bea and Mr. Jones; Blueberries for Sal; A Chair for My Mother; Goldilocks and the Three Bears; Heckedy Peg; Imogene's Antlers; Ira Sleeps Over; Jumanji; Millions of Cats; Ming Lo Moves the Mountain; Miss Nelson Is Missing; Miss Rumphius; Moving Molly; The One in the Middle Is the Green Kangaroo; Owl Moon; The Pain and the Great One; The Patchwork Quilt; Patrick's Dinosaurs; A Pocket for Corduroy; The Relatives Came; The Snowy Day; Strega Nona; Sylvester and the Magic Pebble; The Tenth Good Thing about Barney; The Terrible Thing That Happened at Our House; Tight Times; The Very Hungry Caterpillar; Where the Wild Things Are.*

INCENTIVE PUBLICATIONS, INC.
3835 Cleghorn Ave.
Nashville, TN 37215-2532

***266. Forte, Imogene, and Joy MacKenzie. *Celebrate with Books.* Incentive Publications, Inc., 1991.

Popular children's holiday titles enable teachers to integrate literature into the holiday curriculum. The eleven units in this book are designed to help students acquire a love of literature, become better readers, and develop an appreciation of our holidays. Activities include teacher-directed projects, cooperative learning, art projects, integrated curriculum activities, and independent practice activities. These units accompanied with other resource materials will provide enough activities to successfully present each holiday.

Books included: *Cloudy with a Chance of Meatballs; Faint Frogs Feeling Feverish; Frederick; Heckedy Peg; How the Grinch Stole Christmas; How Many Days to America? A Thanksgiving Story; I'm in Charge of Celebrations; The Leprechaun's Story; Miss Nelson Is Missing!; Miss Rumphius; The Relatives Came; A Time to Keep; Wilfred Gordon MacDonald Partridge.*

****267. Cochran, Judith. *Insights to Literature, Primary.* Incentive Press, 1991.

This book utilizes the whole language and thematic approach to 29 popular titles with an interest and reading level that ranges from K-4. Every unit contains a Teacher's Guide that contains pre/post reading discussion questions/activities that link students' experiences to the story. These activities are interdisciplinary and integrate the literature into all content areas.

Books included: *Anno's Alphabet; Deep in the Forest; Bobo's Dream; Whistle for Willie; Green Eggs and Ham; Milton the Early Riser; Fish Is Fish; The Third Story Cat; There's a Nightmare in My Closet; One Fine Day; Nana Upstairs and Nana Downstairs; Too Many Books!; A House Is a House for Me; The Paper Crane; Once a Mouse; The Paper Bag Princess; Stevie; Alexander, Who Used to be Rich Last Sunday; A New Coat for Anna; The Island of the Skog; East O' the Sun and West O' the Moon; The Elephant's Child; The Girl Who Loved Wild Horses; Molly's Pilgrim; The One in the Middle is the Green Kangaroo; The Stories Julian Tells; The Littles; Lafcadio, The Lion Who Shot Back; Ramona and Her Father.*

****268. Cochran, Judith. *Insights to Literature.* Middle Grades. Incentive Press, 1991.

This resource book is thematically organized and is correlated to Bloom's Taxonomy with an emphasis on the higher order thinking skills for ten popular middle grade stories. Each piece of literature is introduced with a story frame that includes characters, setting, and a summary. Comprehension questions are identified as knowledge, comprehension, application, analysis, or evaluation level for an efficient way to question for critical thinking. Each unit contains activities and projects that pertain to the literature, journal writing activities, and integrated curriculum activities.

Books included: *The Velveteen Rabbit; Charlotte's Web; James and the Giant Peach; Sarah, Plain and Tall; In the Year of the Boar and Jackie Robinson; Mrs. Frisby and the Rats of NIMH; My Side of the Mountain; Bridge to Terabithia; A Wrinkle in Time; Island of the Blue Dolphins.*

**269. Comfort, Claudette Hegel. *Newbery & Caldecott Books in the Classroom.* Incentive Publications, Inc., 1991.

Discussion questions correlated with Bloom's Taxonomy for every Newbery and Caldecott winner through 1990 are included in this book. Generic activities and discussion questions that can be used with each book appear at the beginning of the book.

Books included:

Newbery: *The Story of Mankind; The Voyages of Doctor Doolittle; The Dark Frigate; Tales from SilverLands; Shen of the Sea; Smoky, the Cowhorse; Gay-Neck: The Story of a Pigeon; The Trumpeter of Krakow; Hitty: Her First Hundred Years; The Cat Who Went to Heaven; Waterless Mountain; Young Fu of the Upper Yangtze; Invincible Louisa; Dobry; Caddie Woodland; Roller Skates; The White Stag; Thimble Summer; Daniel Boone; Call It Courage; The Matchlock Gun; Adam of the Road; Johnny Tremain; Rabbit Hill; Strawberry Hill; Miss Hickory; The Twenty-one Balloons; King of the Wind; The Door in the Wall; Amos Fortune: Free Man; Ginger Pye; Secret of the Andes; ...And Now Miguel; The Wheel on the School; Carry On, Mr. Bowditch; Miracles on Maple Hill; Rifles for Watie; The Witch of Blackbird Pond; Onion John; Island of the Blue Dolphins; The Bronze Bow; A Wrinkle in Time; It's Like This, Cat; Shadow of a Bull; I, Juan De Pareja; Up a Road Slowly; From the Mixed-Up Files of Mrs. Basil E. Frankweiler; The High King; Sounder; Summer of the Swans; Mrs. Frisby and the Rats of NIMH; Julie of the Wolves; The Slave Dancer; M. C. Higgins the Great; The Grey King; Roll of Thunder, Hear My Cry; Bridge to Terabithia; The Westing Game; A Gathering of Days: A New England Girl's Journal 1830-32; Jacob Have I Loved; A Visit to William Blake's Inn; Dicey's Song; Dear Mr. Henshaw; The Hero and the Crown; Sarah, Plain and Tall; The Whipping Boy; Lincoln: A Photobiography; Joyful Noise: Poems for Two Voices; Number the Stars.*

Caldecott: *Animals of the Bible; Mei Li; Abraham Lincoln; They Were Strong and Good; Make Way for Ducklings; The Little House; Many Moons; Prayer for a Child; The Rooster Crows; The Little Island; White Snow, Bright Snow; The Big Snow; Song of the Swallows; The Egg Tree; Finders Keepers; The Biggest Bear; Madeline's Rescue; Cinderella, or The Little Glass Slipper; Frog Went A-Courtin'; A Tree Is Nice; Time of Wonder; Chanticleer and the Fox; Nine Days to Christmas; Baboushka and the Three Kings; Once A Mouse; The Snowy Day; Where the Wild Things Are; May I Bring a Friend?; Always Room for One More; Sam, Bangs, and Moonshine; Drummer Hoff; The Fool of the World and the Flying Ship; Sylvester and the Magic Pebble; A Story, A Story; One Fine Day; The Funny Little Woman; Duffy and the Devil; Arrow to the Sun; Why Mosquitoes Buzz in People's Ears; Ashanti to Zulu: African Traditions; Noah's Ark; The Little Girl Who Loved Wild Horses; Ox-Cart Man; Fables; Jumanji; Shadow; The Glorious Flight: Across the Channel with Louis Bleriot July 25, 1919; Saint George and the Dragon; The Polar Express; Hey, Al!; Owl Moon; Song and Dance Man; Lon Po Po: A Red Riding Hood Story from China.*

**270. Cook, Shirley. *Story Journal for Middle Grades.* Incentive Press, 1990.

Journal writing activities for 18 children's books are the focus of this book. A brief vocabulary list is provided with activity and the remainder of the page is the journal activity. Each journal question is designed to set a reading or listening purpose. At the end of each journal there are ten curriculum integration and creative thinking ideas.

Books included: *The All New Jonah Twist; Anastasia Krupnik; The Bears' House; The Family under the Bridge; Ferret in the Bedroom, Lizards in the Fridge; The Indian in the Cupboard; The Kid in the Red Jacket; The Kidnapping of Courtney Van-Allen and What's Her Name; The Night Swimmers; Nothing's Fair in the Fifth Grade; On My Honor; The Pinballs; The Remembering Box; Sarah, Plain and Tall; Stone Fox; Tuck Everlasting; A Wrinkle in Time.*

271. Cook, Shirley, and Kathy Carl. *Linking Literature and Writing.* Incentive Press, 1989.

Linking Literature and Writing is divided into three sections: fall, winter and spring. Within these sections there are activities for each month of the year. These activities include vocabulary building, writing activities, curriculum integration and visuals. Although there are few activities per literary selection, the activities are interesting and motivating.

Fall

September — Going to School
Herbie's Troubles; Miss Nelson Is Missing!; That Dreadful Day; The Other Emily

September — My Friends, My Family, Myself
A Chair for My Mother; Bea and Mr. Jones; Best Friends; The Big Orange Splot; I'm Telling You Now; If I Were in Charge of the World; Ira Sleeps Over; I'm Terrific; The Luckiest One of All; Maude and Sally; My Friend Jacob; Mother Told Me So; The Patchwork Quilt; The Relatives Came; Rolling Harvey Down the Hill; Rosie and Michael; The 329th Friend; I Was a Second Grade Werewolf

October — Let's Make Believe
The Baby Uggs Are Hatching; The Dream Eater; The Great Green Turkey Creek Monster; Harry and the Terrible Whatzit; The Island of the Skog; Joey Runs Away; No Such Things; The Queen of Eene; The Whingdingdilly

October — Halloween
Amanda and the Witch Switch; Arthur's Halloween; Cranberry Halloween; Dorrie and the Goblin; Harriet's Halloween Candy; Humbug Witch; The Teeny Tiny Woman; The Vanishing Pumpkin

November — Farm Animals-Pets
The Book of Pigericks; Can I Keep Him?; Chester the Worldly Pig; The Day Jimmy's Boa Ate the Wash; Gregory the Terrible Eater; I Will Not Go to Market Today; Louanne Pig in the Perfect Family; The Magnificent Moo; Pig, Pig Goes to Camp; The Story of Ferdinand.

November — Thanksgiving
Arthur's Thanksgiving; Cranberry Thanksgiving; It's Thanksgiving; One Terrific Thanksgiving; One Tough Turkey; Sometimes It's Turkey, Sometimes It's Feathers; Thanksgiving at the Tappletons; Thanksgiving Day; Things to Make and Do for Thanksgiving

Winter

December — Animals in the Wild
A Chocolate Moose for Dinner; Alexander and the Wind-Up Mouse; Animals Should Definitely Not Wear Clothing; Arthur's Nose; Bear Shadow; Big Bad Bruce; Helga High Up; Hubert's Hair Raising Adventure; If You Give a Mouse a Cookie; It Wasn't My Fault; Nosey Mrs. Rat; Pelican; Tangles; Zoo Doing

December — Christmas
Arthur's Christmas; Bah! Humbug?; The Christmas Cat; The Cobweb Christmas; Madeline's Christmas; The Polar Express

January — Humor
Begin at the Beginning; The Brothers Wrong and Wrong Again; Don't Forget the Bacon; King Wacky; Mister Gaffe; Mrs. Minetta's Car Pool; Mrs. Peloki's Snake; My Mom Hates Me in January; The Sheriff of Rottenshot; Ralph's Secret Weapon; There's Nothing to Do!; Today Was a Terrible Day; What's Under My Bed?

January — Mindbender and Mysteries
Demi's Find the Animal A B C; Jumanji; Take Another Look; Unriddling; Where's Waldo?; The Wreck of the Zephyr

February — Valentine's Day
A Sweetheart for Valentine; A Valentine for Cousin Archie; Bee My Valentine; The Best Valentine in the World; Freckles and Willie; The Great Valentine's Day Balloon Race; The Mysterious Valentine; Some Things Go Together; The Valentine Bears

February — Groundhog's Day
Wake Up, Groundhog

February — Tall Tales
Big Mose: Hero Fireman; Grandpa's Farm; The Great Big Especially Beautiful Easter Egg; John Henry and Paul Bunyan Play Baseball; McBroom and the Big Wind; Mrs. Gaddy and the Fast Growing Vine; Pecos Bill Catches a Hidebehind; Whoppers: Tall Tales and Other Lies

Spring

March — March Holidays
The Country Bunny and the Little Gold Shoes; The Easter Pig; Leprechauns Never Lie; The Leprechaun's Story; The Pinkish Purplish Bluish Egg

March — Folklore and Fables
The Amazing Pig; Bubba and Babba; Fables; The Frog Princess; I Know an Old Lady Who Swallowed a Fly; The Jolly Postman; Once A Mouse; The Paper Crane; Sylvester and the Magic Pebble; Strega Nona; The Thief Who Hugged a Moonbeam; Three Aesop Fox Fables; The Three Sillies; The Wild Washerwomen

April—Character Study
Alexander and the Terrible, Horrible, No Good, Very Bad Day; Blueberries for Sal; Encyclopedia Brown Boy Detective; The Giving Tree; I Know a Lady; Lentil; Loudmouth George and the Sixth Grade Bully; Mrs. Piggle Wiggle; Ramona the Pest; Miss Rumphius; Stevie; Through Grandpa's Eyes; White Dynamite and the Curly Kid

April—April Fool's Day
April Fool

April—Cook Up a Story
Chicken Salad Soup; Chicken Soup with Rice; The Giant Jam Sandwich; Jam; The Popcorn Book; Stone Soup

May—Award Winners
Annie and the Old One; The Biggest Bear; The Girl Who Loved Wild Horses; The Glorious Flight: Across the Channel with Louis Bleriot; Hey, Al!; Madeline's Rescue; Make Way for Ducklings; Ox-Cart Man; Sam, Bangs and Moonshine; Where the Wild Things Are

May—Stories Too Good to Miss
The Aminal; Brave Irene; Doctor De Soto; The Garden of Abdul Gasazi; The Hating Book; Imogene's Antlers; Sidney Rella and the Glass Sneakers; Tikki Tikki Tembo; The Velveteen Rabbit

**272. Rommel, Carol A. *Integrating Beginning Math & Literature*. Incentive Press, 1991

Teachers looking for a source integrating children's literature with mathematics will enjoy the 32 units in this book. These units contain activities that are developmentally appropriate for young children. The math activities are concrete and provide opportunities for children to interact with varying stages of complexity. Each unit combines literature and math in such a way that children are forming a foundation for problem solving. Activities are designed for small groups and whole groups. Language concepts are divided into three categories: exposure concepts, mastery concepts, review concepts. These units combined with other resource books will provide a complete study of each literature piece.

Books included: *Johnny Appleseed; Going to the Doctor; The Biggest Nose; The Witch Who Lives Down the Hall; Pumpkin, Pumpkin; Willis; Sylvester and the Magic Pebble; Our Garage Sale; The Twelve Days of Christmas; The Sandman; The Post Office Book; How Little Porcupine Played Christmas; January Brings the Snow; Time; Curious George; Lion Dancer: Ernie Wan's Chinese New Year; The Boy Who Hated Valentine's Day; Little Rabbit's Loose Tooth; Get Ready for Robots; Teddy Bears Cure a Cold; A Birthday for Frances; The Berenstain Bears' Trouble with Money; The Littlest Dinosaurs; A Drop of Blood; The Grouchy Ladybug; A Bargain for Frances; Make Way for Ducklings; Alice's Adventures in Wonderland; The Story about Ping; Bunches and Bunches of Bunnies; The Funny Little Woman*

INSTRUCTIONAL FAIR
2400 Turner Ave., NW
Grand Rapids, MI 45904

***273-277. *Literature Based Reading* Series
This series of activity books is arranged by grade levels. Each book offers activities that include critical thinking, writing, art, group projects, and comprehension skills. Answers to questions and activity sheets are included in the back of the book. Combined with other activity books, these books provide enough activities to comprehensively teach a selection.

273. *Literature-Based Reading (Gr. 1-2)*. Instructional Fair, Inc.

Books included: *Miss Nelson Has a Field Day; The Mysterious Tadpole; Corduroy; Clifford at the Circus; Are You My Mother?; Nimby; Morris the Moose Goes to School; Nate the Great and the Phony Clue; Arthur's Tooth.*

274. *Literature-Based Reading (Gr. 2-3)*. Instructional Fair, Inc.

Books included: *Good Work, Amelia Bedelia; Frog and Toad Together; Freckle Juice; In the Dinosaur's Paw; Lyle Finds His Mother; The Terrible Thing That Happened at Our House; Camp Ghost-a-Way; The Magic School Bus at the Waterworks; The Adventures of Ali Baba Bernstein.*

275. *Literature-Based Reading (Gr. 3-4)*. Instructional Fair, Inc.

Books included: *Charlotte's Web; Ramona Quimby, Age 8; Tales of a Fourth Grade Nothing; Encyclopedia Brown, Boy Detective; Iggie's House; The Wonderful Wizard of Oz.*

276. *Literature-Based Reading (Gr. 4-5)*. Instructional Fair, Inc.

Books included: *The Phantom Tollbooth; The Return of the Indian; Soup; Tuck Everlasting; Hang Tough, Paul Mather; Wait Till Helen Comes.*

277. *Literature-Based Reading (Gr. 5-6)*. Instructional Fair, Inc.

Books included: *The Westing Game; The Lion, the Witch and the Wardrobe; Number the Stars; My Brother Louis Measures Worms; Julie of the Wolves; The Cay.*

LEARNING LINKS
2300 Marcus
New Hyde Park, NY 11042

*278-404. *Novel Ties* Series

Novel Ties are reproducible study guides that can be used with specific novels. These guides provide an excellent supplementary tool to be used with other materials. They are written on a chapter-by-chapter format and they contain a synopsis, pre-reading activities, comprehension and extension activities. These guides are designed to be used in whole group reading or cooperative groups.

Level 2

278. *Annie and the Old One*
279. *Busybody Nora*
280. *Freckle Juice*
281. *In the Dinosaur's Paw*
282. *Julian's Glorious Summer*
283. *Monster in the Third Dresser Drawer and Other Tales of Adam Joshua*
284. *Next Spring an Oriole*
285. *The One in the Middle Is the Green Kangaroo*
286. *Rip-Roaring Russell*
287. *Seven Kisses in a Row*

Level 3

288. *Be a Perfect Person in Just Three Days*
289. *Ben and Me*
290. *Cam Jansen and the Mystery of the Dinosaur Bones*
291. *Chalk Box Kid*
292. *Chocolate Touch*
293. *Felita*
294. *A Gift for Mama*
295. *Helen Keller*
296. *How to Eat Fried Worms*
297. *The Hundred Dresses*
298. *J. T.*
299. *Jacob Two-Two Meets the Hooded Fang*
300. *The Littles*
301. *Maurice's Room*
302. *Nate the Great and the Missing Key*
303. *O'Diddy*
304. *Ramona the Brave*
305. *Silver*
306. *A Taste of Blackberries*
307. *Witch of Fourth Street*

Level 4

308. *All of a Kind Family*
309. *Anastasia Krupnik*
310. *The Big Wave*
311. *Bunnicula*
312. *Charlie and the Chocolate Factory*
313. *Charlotte's Web*
314. *Cricket in Times Square*
315. *Dear Mr. Henshaw*
316. *The Enormous Egg*
317. *Fantastic Mr. Fox*
318. *The Great Brain*
319. *The Indian in the Cupboard*
320. *James and the Giant Peach*
321. *Journey to Jo'burg*
322. *The Lion, the Witch and the Wardrobe*
323. *Maggie Marmelstein for President*
324. *Mr. Popper's Penguins*
325. *My Brother Stevie*
326. *Pippi Longstocking*
327. *Sadako and the Thousand Paper Cranes*
328. *Sarah, Plain and Tall*
329. *Shoeshine Girl*

330. *Socks*
331. *Stone Fox*
332. *Superfudge*
333. *Tales of a Fourth Grade Nothing*
334. *Trouble River*
335. *Velveteen Rabbit*

Level 5

336. *Bridge to Terabithia*
337. *The Cabin Faced West*
338. *Caddie Woodlawn*
339. *Call It Courage*
340. *The Cay*
341. *Daphne's Book*
342. *Edgar Allen*
343. *The Fighting Ground*
344. *Freaky Friday*
345. *From the Mixed-Up Files of Mrs. Basil E. Frankweiler*
346. *The Great Gilly Hopkins*
347. *Incredible Journey*
348. *In the Year of the Boar and Jackie Robinson*
349. *Island of the Blue Dolphins*
350. *Little House on the Prairie*
351. *Luke Was There*
352. *My Side of the Mountain*
353. *On My Honor*
354. *Phantom Tollbooth*
355. *The Pinballs*
356. *Sign of the Beaver*
357. *Silver Coach*
358. *Sign Down the Moon*
359. *Slake's Limbo*
360. *Summer of the Swans*
361. *Tuck Everlasting*
362. *The Twenty-One Balloons*
363. *War with Grandpa*
364. *Welcome Home, Jellybean*
365. *The Whipping Boy*
366. *The Wish Giver*

Level 6

367. *Alan and Naomi*
368. *Anne of Green Gables*
369. *The Door in the Wall*
370. *Follow My Leader*
371. *Hatchet*
372. *The High King*
373. *Homesick: My Own Story*
374. *Mrs. Frisby and the Rats of NIMH*
375. *Number the Stars*
376. *The One-Eyed Cat*
377. *Park's Quest*
378. *The Pushcart War*
379. *The Secret Garden*
380. *Snow Treasure*
381. *The Westing Game*
382. *The White Mountains*
383. *The Wind in the Willows*
384. *The Witch of Blackbird Pond*

Level 6-12

385. *Adventures of Tom Sawyer*
386. *Anne Frank: The Diary of a Young Girl*
387. *The Black Pearl*
388. *Come Sing, Jimmy Jo*
389. *The Dark Is Rising*
390. *Dicey's Song*
391. *The Hobbit*
392. *Johnny Tremain*
393. *Julie of the Wolves*
394. *The Light in the Forest*
395. *The Little Prince*
396. *My Brother Sam Is Dead*
397. *The Pearl*
398. *Roll of Thunder, Hear My Cry*
399. *Sounder*
400. *The Summer of My German Soldier*
401. *Treasure Island*
402. *The Wave*
403. *Where the Red Fern Grows*
404. *A Wrinkle in Time*

LIBRARIES UNLIMITED
P.O. Box 6633
Englewood, CO 80155-6633

****405. Mohr, Carolyn, Dorothy Nixon, and Shirley Vickers. *Books That Heal: A Whole Language Approach.* Libraries Unlimited, Inc./Teacher Ideas Press, 1991.

Using a multidimensional array of reading activities, this book focuses on bibliotherapy and self understanding. Included are activities that promote literal thinking, critical thinking, creative thinking, interpretive thinking, and multidisciplinary activities that integrate the curriculum. This book also includes cooperative learning and activities that promote working with resource people and facilitators. This book is designed to teach reading through the whole language approach which integrates reading, writing, listening, and speaking.

Books included:
Coping: *The Silent Storm; A Family Apart; Island of the Blue Dolphins*

Death: *On My Honor; Sadako and the Thousand Paper Cranes; Bridge to Terabithia*

Differences: *Harriet the Spy; Julie of the Wolves; Freedom Train*

Divorce: *It's Not the End of the World; Dear Mr. Henshaw; DeDe Takes Charge!*

Poverty: *Sounder; No Promises in the Wind; The Noonday Friends*

Relationships: *Between Friends; Where the Red Fern Grows; The Bears' House*

Self Concept: *Edith Herself; From the Mixed-Up Files of Mrs. Basil E. Frankweiler; Call It Courage*

Storytelling and Reading Aloud: *A Taste of Blackberries; The Big Wave; Sarah, Plain and Tall*

***406. Somers, Albert B. and Janet Evans Worthington. *Candles and Mirrors.* Libraries Unlimited, Inc. 1984.

The key to successful reading, according to the authors, is correctly selecting literature for children according to their reading level and interest level. Each of the 35 selections begins with a summary of the literature, followed by an appraisal of the book. Themes and literary concepts are included, as well as related problems and opportunities. These guides contain prereading activities, discussion questions, writing activities, and other activities. Combined with other resources, this book will help provide a stimulating and interesting study of the literature.

Books included:
6-8:   *Julie of the Wolves*
6-9:   *Sounder*
7-8:   *A Day No Pigs Would Die; The Light in the Forest; The Diary of Anne Frank*
7-9:   *The Witch of Blackbird Pond; Jacob Have I Loved; The Pearl*
7-10:   *The Contender*
8-10:   *The Pigman; The Outsiders; The Miracle Worker; The Call of the Wild*
8-11:   *My Brother Sam Is Dead*
9-10:   *Animal Farm; To Kill a Mockingbird; Great Expectations; Romeo and Juliet; Antigone; A Raisin in the Sun*
9-11:   *The Red Badge of Courage*
9-12:   *The Old Man and the Sea*
10-11: *The Catcher in the Rye*
11:     *Death of a Salesman; The Glass Menagerie; Our Town; Billy Budd; Sailor (An Inside Narrative); The Scarlet Letter*
11-12: *Black Boy; Lord of the Flies; The Chocolate War; A Separate Peace*
12:     *Macbeth; Wuthering Heights*

****407. Olsen, Mary Lou. *Creative Connections: Literature and the Reading Program.* Libraries Unlimited, Inc., 1987.

Fun activities for children's trade titles that correlate with the basal as well as provide extension activities for basal skills are included in this guide. This book provides activities that integrate literature into the curriculum, and connect literature with math, science, social studies, art. Each unit contains information about the book and author, as well as student objectives, suggestions for media centers, computer programs that correlate with the unit, and additional reading lists. Enrichment activities for gifted students are also included in each unit. Each unit also contains activities that promote parent involvement! This resource book can be used in conjunction with other materials to provide a balanced approach to literature.

Books included:

Grade 1: *Anno's Counting Book; Mother Goose Treasury; Will I Have a Friend?; A, B, See!; Make Way for Ducklings; What Mary Jo Shared; The Snowy Day; The Carrot Seed; Peter Spier's Rain; The Very Hungry Caterpillar; The Sky Is Full of Song; Little Rabbit's Loose Tooth; Petunia; Where the Wild Things Are; Alexander and the Terrible, Horrible, No Good, Very Bad Day.*

Grade 2: *Story of Babar; Horton Hatches the Egg; Amos and Boris; Corduroy; Winnie-the-Pooh; Ira Sleeps Over; Story of Johnny Appleseed; The Popcorn Book; May I Bring a Friend?; Gung Hay Fat Choy; Song of the Swallows; Mr. Rabbit and the Lovely Present; The Little House; Miss Rumphius; Tale of Peter Rabbit.*

Grade 3: *Bananas: From Manolo to Margie; The Post Office Book: Mail and How It Moves; Talking Leaves; The Story of Sequoyah; Bunnicula: A Rabbit-Tale of Mystery; Leo the Late Bloomer; Fables; Columbus; Jack Jouett's Ride; Little House in the Big Woods; Why Mosquitoes Buzz in People's Ears; Cricket Songs; Fool of the World and the Flying Ship; Crow Boy; Island of the Skog; Inch by Inch*

408. Polkingharn, Anne T., and Catherine Toohey. *Creative Encounters.* Libraries Unlimited, 1983.

Full of creative activities for fifty renowned literary titles. Each title includes a very brief synopsis, materials needed and an activity which enables the student to appreciate various author's styles and develop comprehension/problem solving skills.

Books included: *If the Dinosaurs Came Back; The Princess and the Pea; The King's Flower; Harold and the Purple Crayon; Please Send a Panda; Corduroy; A Pocket for Corduroy; Flat Stanley; The Little Red Balloon; The 329th Friend; Mr. Tamarin's Trees; A House Is a House for Me; The Pumpkin Smasher; The Bump in the Night; There's an Ant in Anthony; A Perfect Nose for Ralph; The Maggie B.; The Bed Just So; Santa Makes a Change; A Book of Hugs; The Christmas Cookie Sprinkle Snitcher; Families; I'm Terrific; The Whingdingdilly; A Color of His Own; Elmer: The Story of a Patchwork Elephant; Harlequin and the Gift of Many Colors; Eight Ate: A Feast of Homonym Riddles; One Fine Day; Tooth-Gnasher Superflash; The Aminal; My Very Own Octopus; Strega Nona; Rapunzel; There's Nightmare in My Closet; Owl's New Cards; Pezzettino; My Daddy's Mustache; The Field of Buttercups; Annie's Rainbow; Dear Hildegarde; The Biggest Sandwich Ever; Crictor; The Lonely Skyscraper; Humbug Rabbit; Benjamin's 365 Birthdays; Look Again; Red Riding Hood: Retold in Verse for Boys and Girls to Read Themselves; Would You Rather; The Seamstress of Salzburg; The Ice Cream Cone Coot and Other Rare Birds; True or False?*

****409. Kruise, Carol Sue. *Learning through Literature.* Libraries Unlimited, Inc./Teacher Ideas Press, 1990.

The activities in the book are designed to help children become better readers, writers, and thinkers through a blending of whole language and critical thinking. This book interrelates reading and writing; thus, it provides excellent whole language activities that are based on critical thinking processes. The literature in this resource book is based on a variety of genre which includes fantasy, mysteries, science fiction, adventure, and realism. Each unit contains a summary of the story, prereading activities, activities for predicting, postreading activities, and thinking activities, writing activities, and et cetera activities. Most activities and stories are intended for grades 1-3, but some activities could be incorporated into the intermediate grades.

Books included: *Amigo; Amos and Boris; The Beast in Ms. Rooney's Room; Binky Brothers, Detectives; Cherries and Cherry Pits; Chester the Worldly Pig; Chicken Little; The Cloud Book; The Fallen Spaceman; The Funny Little Woman; The Laziest Robot in Zone One; Rosie's Walk; The Stories Julian Tells; A Story, A Story; Swamp Monsters.*

*410. Polkingharn, Anne T., and Catherine Toohey. *More Creative Encounters.* Libraries Unlimited, Inc., 1988.

More Creative Encounters is a children's literature idea book for elementary grades that provides activities for specific book titles. This book has response-based literature activities that cover fifty-one titles of renowned children's literature. Each literary selection contains a summary of the book, the purpose for reading, materials needed, and activities designed so that each child's response is unique.

Books included: *Marianna May and Nursey; The Very Busy Spider; Arthur's Eyes; I Unpacked My Grandmother's Trunk; Owl Lake; The Jolly Postman or Other People's Letters; When Panda Came to Our House; A, My Name Is Alice; Need a House? Call Ms. Mouse; Humbug Potion: An A B Cipher; Lion; If You Give a Mouse a Cookie; Check It Out! The Book about Libraries; Our Snowman; Bird's New Shoes; Boo!; The Quilt Story; Who Want a Cheap Rhinoceros?; Let's Make Rabbits; Large as Life; Nighttime Animals; Miss Nelson Is Missing!; Father Time and the Day Boxes; Seven Eggs; The Little Old Lady Who Was Not Afraid of Anything; Darkness and the Butterfly; Clyde Monster; The Magic School Bus at the Waterworks; Golly Gump Swallowed a Fly; The Rebus Treasury; Old Henry; Mrs. Dunphy's Dog; What a Catastrophe!; The Paper Crane; The Mitten; Imogene's Antlers; Pig Pig and the Magic Photo Album; Paper John; Hattie and the Fox; Humphrey the Lost Whale: A True Story; The Inch Boy; Claude and Sun; At This Very Minute; On Market Street; Burt Dow Deep-Water Man; I Want a Dog; The Doorbell Rang; A Three Hat Day; Miss Rumphius; Frosted Glass; Doctor Change; Winnie the Witch.*

***411. Jenkins, Christine, and Sally Freeman. *Novel Experiences.* Libraries Unlimited, Inc./Teacher Ideas Press, 1991.

This text is for teachers who want to enhance their curriculum through discussions of contemporary children's literature. *Novel Experiences* contains leader discussion guides for 35 books, seven for each grade, two through six. The children's titles include a variety of genres, writing styles and reading levels. Each unit includes a summary of the literature, prereading, motivation, art, vocabulary, discussion questions, enrichment activities and a list of related books.

Books included:
Grade 2
The Beast in Ms. Rooney's Room; The Gingerbread Rabbit; Julian's Glorious Summer; Jumanji; Nate the Great and the Fishy Prize; Something Queer at the Library; Wagon Wheels.

Grade 3
Altogether, One at a Time; The Celery Stalks at Midnight; The Hundred Dresses; On the Banks of Plum Creek; Sidewalk Story; Stone Fox; A Taste of Blackberries.

Grade 4
Follow My Leader; Homer Price; Jennifer, Hecate, Macbeth, William McKinley and Me, Elizabeth; Knight's Castle; Mrs. Piggle-Wiggle's Magic; Sadako and the Thousand Paper Cranes; Song of the Trees.

Grade 5
The Egypt Game; Gone-Away Lake; Harriet Tubman; Conductor on the Underground Railroad; In the Year of the Boar and Jackie Robinson; The Indian in the Cupboard; Mail Order Wings; On My Honor.

Grade 6
Dragonwings; The Hero and the Crown; Homecoming; Homesick; My Own Story; Nobody's Family Is Going to Change; Roll of Thunder, Hear My Cry; Sing Down the Moon.

**412.   Carroll, Joyce Armstrong.   *Picture Books: Integrated Teaching of Reading, Writing, Listening, Speaking, Viewing, and Thinking. Jackdaws Series 1.* Libraries Unlimited, Inc./Teacher Ideas Press, 1991.

Jackdaws are curious birds who carry objects away and conceal them. In this activity book, jackdaws are artifacts, concepts, and activities. There are twenty-eight jackdaws in this book that include everything from spiders to clay pots. Selections include reading/writing connections, library connections, math connections, science connections, social studies connections, art connections, and sometimes drama and poetry connections.

Books included: *The Very Busy Spider; Brown Bear, Brown Bear, What Do You See?; When the Clay Sings; The Blue Balloon; The Important Book; Chicka Chicka Boom Boom; Eating the Alphabet; The Pottery Place; Jambo Means Hello: A Swahili Alphabet Book; Leonardo Da Vinci; If Dinosaurs Were Alive Today; Stringbean's Trip to the Shining Sea; Merry-Go-Round; I Can Blink; A Mediterranean City through the Ages; Five Secrets in a Box; Surprise Party; A Trip to Mars; The Very Quiet Cricket; Too Many Eggs: A Counting Book; Frank and Ernest; The Enormous Watermelon; The Furry News: How to Make a Newspaper; Who Said Red?; The Jolly*

Postman or Other People's Letters; The Book of Shadowboxes: The Story of the ABC's; If You Made a Million; Earth Circles.

***413.   Blass, Rosanne J., et al. *Responding to Literature Activities for Grades 6, 7, 8.* Libraries Unlimited, Inc./Teacher Ideas Press, 1991.

This supplementary resource was designed to be used by teachers, librarians, media specialists, and supervisors. Ten different literature-based activities have been developed to be used with any literary selection. Activities such as read-aloud titles included compare and contrast, personal responses, reflective thinking, reconstructing the story, sample/predict/confirm; game titles included fiction boards, riddle races, sports stumpers, trivial treasures and trash; music and dance titles included selecting background music, music through the ages, choreography, new lyrics, favorite songs of famous people; drama titles included puppetry, skits, readers' theater, plays; writing titles included journals, anthologies, word plays, etc; art titles included characterization, descriptive scenes, listen and respond, poetry; oral expression titles included storytelling, conducting interviews, choral reading, world news, monologues; discovery learning/group problem solving titles included solving problem situations, story puzzles, unsolved mysteries, suggesting solutions, bookish bulletin boards. Each activity has a related reference and resource list.

Books included: *The Sign of the Beaver; The Big Wave; The Case of the Baker Street Irregular; On My Honor; Unidentified Flying Riddles; The Story of Basketball; Still More Tell Me Why; Let the Circle Be Unbroken; Dogsong; Heaven to Betsy; American Folksongs for Children; Martin Luther King: The Peaceful Warrior; The Master Puppeteer; A Hero Ain't Nothin but a Sandwich; Hatchet; My Diary, My World; Speak Roughly to Your Little Boy; The King's Fifth; Across Five Aprils; The Secret Garden; The Grey King; Anne of Green Gables; The Owl Service; Talking to the Sun; The Tailypo: A Ghost Story; Rifles for Watie; Basketball: You Are the Coach; Maximillian, You're the Greatest; The Cybil War; Owls in the Family; The Indian in the Cupboard; Roll of Thunder, Hear My Cry; The Cay.*

**414.   Laughlin, Mildred Knight, and Kathy Howard Latrobe.   *Readers Theatre for Children: Scripts and Script Development.* Libraries Unlimited, Inc./Teacher Ideas Press, 1990.

This collection of scripts and script development allows children to become a part of quality literature. These scripts provide an entertaining alternative to book reports. Readers theater scripts require children to use the higher order thinking skills to develop and present the material. This is divided into four parts. Part I provides an overview of techniques that have been recommended by the author. Part II is a collection of completed scripts from classics, while Part III is a combination of scripts featuring ten novels. Part IV is a collection of forty-five scripts selected from children's literature. These scripts are designed to be easily read and performed. This book provides an abundance of activities that foster and encourage creativity.

Books included
Part I: No titles.

Part II: *Little Women; The Wonderful Wizard of Oz; The Secret Garden; Alice's Adventures in Wonderland; A Christmas Carol; Hans Brinker or the Silver Skates; "One-Eye, Two-Eyes, and Three-Eyes"; "The Water of Life"; "How the Camel Got His Hump"; Heidi; Treasure Island; Rebecca of Sunnybrook Farm.*

Part III: *After the Goat Man; The Animal, the Vegetable and John D. Jones; The Blossoms Meet the Vulture Lady; The Burning Questions of Bingo Brown; Cracker Jackson; The Cybil War; The House of Wings; The Midnight Fox; The Summer of the Swans; Trouble River.*

Part IV: *The Journey of the Shadow Bairns; Gray Boy; Mr. Popper's Penguins; Tuck Everlasting; Who Knew There'd Be Ghosts?; The Wish Giver; Shoeshine Girl; Ida Early Comes Over the Mountain; The Enormous Egg; Ellen Tebbits; Ramona and Her Father; The Get-Away Car; Thank You, Jackie Robinson; The House of Sixty Fathers; Missing; The Whipping Boy; Stone Fox; A Morgan for Melinda; To Catch a Crook; In Trouble Again, Zelda Hammersmith?; Brighty of the Grand Canyon; The Kelpie's Pearls; Blackberries in the Dark; From the Mixed-Up Files of Mrs. Basil E. Frankweiler; Rabbit Hill; A Wrinkle in Time; The Lion, the Witch, and the Wardrobe; Mail-Order Kid; Sarah, Plain and Tall; Winnie-the-Pooh; The Secret Language; The Borrowers; Mrs. Frisby and the Rats of NIMH; Jacob Two-Two Meets the Hooded Fang; How to Eat Fried Worms; Words by Heart; The Cricket in Times Square; Stinker from Space; Moving In; The Sign of the Beaver; A Dog on Barkham Street; Journey to Topaz; A Dog Called Kitty; Charlotte's Web; Little House on the Prairie.*

****415. Butzow, Carol M., and John W. Butzow. *Science through Children's Literature.* Libraries Unlimited, Inc./Teacher Ideas Press, 1989.

Teachers looking for ideas on how to integrate science and children fiction will find this book invaluable. This resource book is divided into two parts. Part I furnishes background information on integrating science with fiction, data on evaluating literature to assure it will accomplish the objective and successfully integrate with the science concepts, and information on implementation of science concepts through a whole language approach. It also provides a sample unit based on *Mike Mulligan and His Steam Shovel.* This sample unit contains a list of objectives, examples of concept mapping, writing activities, bulletin board ideas, an extensive bibliography that furnishes additional literature that could be utilized with these concepts, and suggestions for working with library media. Parts II, III, and IV of this book provide activities for teachers to use in the classroom. These sections are divided into thirty-five chapters that are based on science

concepts. Each chapter has a multitude of activities to reinforce the science concept, provide whole language activities, and encourage critical thinking.

Books included: *A Tree Is Nice; The Tiny Seed; Mousekin's Birth; Make Way for Ducklings; Two Bad Ants and Other Insects; The Very Busy Spider; The Grouchy Ladybug; Swimmy; Michael Bird-Boy; Chipmunk Song; Gregory, the Terrible Eater; I Have a Sister, My Sister Is Deaf; It's Mine; Hill of Fire; Everybody Needs a Rock; Simon Underground; Keep the Lights Burning, Abbie; The Very Last First Time; The Magic School Bus at the Waterworks; Space Songs; Spectacles; The Eye, Vision and Optics; Shadow: The Secret Birthday Message; How Big Is a Foot?; Choo, Choo; Who Sank the Boat?; Mr. Gumpy's Motorcar; Sadie and the Snowman; Strega Nona's Magic Lessons; The Big Balloon Race; The Glorious Flight; The Bionic Bunny Show; Dear Mr. Henshaw.*

***416. Fredericks, Anthony D. *Social Studies through Children's Literature: An Integrated Approach.* Libraries Unlimited, Inc./Teacher Ideas Press, 1991.

According to the authors, social studies should not be a "data regurgitation" program; it should be a process of learning from self to the world. The introduction of this book provides a valuable tool for developing whole language social studies activities, as well as providing a guide for developing thematic units and interdisciplinary integration. The book is divided into the seven social studies areas and provides activities, processes, and literature for each area. Each area has critical thinking questions and a list of related books and references. The thirty-two books included in this resource book were selected because of their social studies appropriateness; not because of reading levels. Each book can be adapted for use with all grade levels or can be utilized in more than one social studies area.

Books included:
Child and self: *Once There Were Giants; People; Sara Morton's Day.*

Family: *Always Gramma; Grandpa; Ox-Cart Man; The Wednesday Surprise; When I Was Young in the Mountains.*

Community and Neighborhood: *In Coal Country; Miss Rumphius; Mr. Griggs' Work; Shaker Lane.*

City and Country: *Grandpa Had a Windmill, Gramma Had a Churn; Night in the Country; Sam Johnson and the Blue Ribbon Quilt; Town and Country.*

States and Regions: *Aurora Means Dawn; Just Us Women; Your Best Friend Kate.*

Nation and Country: *Anno's U.S.A.; John Henry; A Picture Book of Abraham Lincoln; A Picture Book of Martin Luther King, Jr.; The Star-Spangled Banner; Those People in Washington.*

World: *All in a Day; The Great Kapok Tree; Jafta and the Wedding; Jambo Means Hello; Maps and Globes; Mufaro's Beautiful Daughters; My Sister Says.*

417. Laughlin, Mildred Knight, et al. *Social Studies Readers Theatre for Children.* Libraries Unlimited, Inc./ Teacher Ideas Press, 1991.

This title is designed to blend yesterday and today through reader's theater presentations of high interest historical fiction and biographies. The book is divided into four parts. Part I provides an overview of reader's theater. Part II includes fourteen complete tall-tale scripts. Part III gives suggested scripts for eight books by Laura Ingalls Wilder. Part IV contains sixty suggested scripts for students from books with settings spanning colonial America to twentieth century America.

Part I: No titles.

Part II: Tall Tales
Daniel Boone, Jim Bridger, Paul Bunyan, Annie Christmas, Davy Crockett, Febold Feboldson, Mike Fink, John Henry, Casey Jones, Joe Magarac, Gib Morgan, Pecos Bill, Windwagon Smith, Stormalong).

Part III: Laura Ingalls Wilder books
Little House in the Big Woods; Little House on the Prairie; On the Banks of Plum Creek; By the Shores of Silver Lake; The Long Winter; Little Town on the Prairie; These Happy Golden Years; The First Four Years.

Part IV: Colonial America
Encounter at Easton; Night Journeys; Charlie's House; A Lion to Guard Us; Squanto: Friend of the Pilgrims; The Courage of Sarah Noble; The Sign of the Beaver; The Witch of Blackbird Pond.

Independence Comes and the Nation Begins
1787; Johnny Tremain; The Cabin Faced West; Early Thunder; This Time, Tempe Wick?; Ben and Me; Mrs. Revere and I; Sarah Bishop.

The Nation Grows
Jenny's Corner; Caddie Woodlawn; Susanna of the Alamo: A True Story; Little Brother of the Wilderness: The Story of Johnny Appleseed; First Farm In the Valley: Anna's Story; Rachel and Obadiah; Amos Fortune: Free Man.

A Divided Nation
Charley Skedaddle; Turn Homeward, Hannalee; Zoar Blue; Across Five Aprils; Rifles for Watie; The Root Cellar; The Drinking Gourd; Nettie's Trip South.

Settling the West
Wagon Wheels; Riding the Pony Express; San Domingo: The Medicine Hat Stallion; Pioneer Cat; Addie across the Prairie; Caught in the Act; A Family Apart; In the Face of Danger; Zia; Trouble for Lucy; An Orphan for Nebraska; Grasshopper Summer

Twentieth-Century America
Shadrach's Crossing; Rain of Fire; Eight Mules from Monterey; Charlie Pippin; Molly's Pilgrim; The House of Sixty Fathers; Stone Fox; The Hokey-Pokey Man; Clara and the Bookwagon; Cave under the City; And One for All; Devil Storm; The Friendship; The Gold Cadillac; A Jar of Dreams; Journey Home; Journey to Topaz.

418. Mohr, Carolyn, et al. *Thinking Activities for Books Children Love: A Whole Language Approach.* Libraries Unlimited, Inc./Teacher Ideas Press, 1988.

Activities on Bloom's Taxonomy are included for 15 acclaimed children's titles. Each title is organized by chapters and includes questions, vocabulary words, interdisciplinary activities and bulletin board ideas. Also included are ideas for cooperative learning, partner reading centers, independent studies with contracts and creative problem solving ideas.

Books included: *Superfudge; Tales of a Fourth Grade Nothing; The Incredible Journey; The Pinballs; Shoeshine Girl; The Mouse and the Motorcycle; Ramona the Pest; Nothing's Fair in the Fifth Grade; Thirteen Ways to Sink a Sub; Bunnicula; Be a Perfect Person in Just Three Days; Summer of the Monkeys; How to Eat Fried Worms; Jelly Belly; The War with Grandpa.*

419. Kruise, Carol Sue. *Those Bloomin' Books: A Handbook for Extending Thinking Skills.* Libraries Unlimited, Inc., 1987.

Those Bloomin' Books is designed to provide activities, questions, and puzzles to promote growth in the cognitive and affective domains. This activity book applies Bloom's Taxonomy to children's literature that is to be read aloud orally to students. Each story begins with a summary of the story and pre-reading activities. Some of the titles are picture books that can be used at all grade levels. An annotated bibliography of classroom tested read-aloud books is included.

Books included: *Alligators Are Awful; And Then What Happened, Paul Revere?; Bea and Mr. Jones; The Butter Battle Book; The Castle in the Attic; The Crane Wife; The Elephant's Child; The Emperor's New Clothes; Estaban and the Ghost; Gila Monsters Meet You at the Airport; The Giving Tree; Going West; The Green Book; Horton Hatches the Egg; The Hunter and His Dog; Ike and Mama and the Trouble at School; The Legend of the Bluebonnet; The Lorax; The Man Who Kept House; The Mariah Delaney Lending Library Disaster; Miss Rumphius; Mrs. Minetta's Car Pool; My Brother Sam Is Dead; Nadia the Willful; One-Eyed Cat; A Pet for Mrs. Arbuckle; Pezzettino; The Sign of the Beaver; Small Pig; Sounder; The Story of Jumping Mouse; The Velveteen Rabbit; Watch the Stars Come Out; Wiley and the Hairy Man; The Wish Giver; The Witch Who Lives Down the Hall; The Wump World; You Look Ridiculous Said the Rhinoceros to the Hippopotamus.*

NOVEL UNITS
P.O. Box 1461
Palatine, IL 60078

***420-586. Novel Units Series
These comprehensive guides are designed to provide activities for many pieces of children's literature. Units are

organized by the chapters of a literature piece and each unit contains vocabulary strategies, prereading and motivational activities, art activities, graphic organizers, math activities, cooperative learning activities, comprehension questions, and activities that elicit critical thinking. Each Novel Unit contains bulletin board ideas, ideas for learning centers, and activities for discussion and independent practice. Each unit provides adequate activities to teach a literary selection.

Grades 1-2

420. *The Amazing Bone*
421. *Amelia Bedelia*
422. *Anansi the Spider*
423. *Arthur's Honey Bear*
424. *Bargain for Frances*
425. *Corduroy* and *Pocket for Corduroy*
426. *Curious George*
427. *Danny and the Dinosaur*
428. *Ira Sleeps Over*
429. *Lyle, Lyle, Crocodile*
430. *Make Way for Ducklings*
431. *Mike Mulligan and His Steam Shovel*
432. *Miss Nelson Is Missing/Miss Nelson Is Back*
433. *Miss Rumphius*
434. *Nate the Great and the Sticky Case*
435. *One Fine Day*
436. *Perfect the Pig*
437. *Pinkerton, Behave*
438. *Polar Express*
439. *Runaway Bunny*
440. *Stone Soup*
441. *The Story of Ferdinand the Bull*
442. This number not used.
443. *Swimmy/Frederick*
444. *Sylvester and the Magic Pebble*
445. *There's a Nightmare in My Closet*
446. Three Frog and Toad Books: Includes *Frog & Toad Are Friends; Frog & Toad Together; Frog & Toad All Year*
447. *Tikki Tikki Tembo*
448. *Ugly Duckling*
449. *Where the Wild Things Are*

Grades 3-4

450. *Be a Perfect Person in Just Three Days*
451. *Bear Called Paddington*
452. *Beezus and Ramona*
453. *Ben and Me*
454. *Best Christmas Pageant Ever*
455. *Can't You Make Them Behave, King George?*
456. *Charlie and the Chocolate Factory*
457. *Charlotte's Web*
458. *Chocolate Fever*
459. *Chocolate Touch*
460. *Courage of Sarah Noble*
461. *Cricket in Times Square*
462. *Encyclopedia Brown*
463. *Enormous Egg*
464. *Fairy Rebel*
465. *Fantastic Mr. Fox*
466. *Forgotten Door*
467. *Fourth Grade Celebrity*
468. *Freaky Friday*

469. *Freckle Juice*
470. *Henry and the Clubhouse*
471. *Hundred Penny Box*
472. *J. T.*
473. *James and the Giant Peach*
474. *Lion, the Witch and the Wardrobe*
475. *Little House in the Big Woods*
476. *Little House on the Prairie*
477. *The Littles*
478. *The Long Winter*
479. *The Mouse and the Motorcycle*
480. *The One in the Middle Is the Green Kangaroo*
481. *Owls in the Family*
482. *Pippi Longstocking*
483. *Ralph S. Mouse*
484. *Ramona the Brave*
485. *Ramona the Pest*
486. *Ramona Quimby, Age 8*
487. *Runaway Ralph*
488. *Sadako and the Thousand Paper Cranes*
489. *Sam, Bangs and Moonshine*
490. *Sarah, Plain and Tall*
491. *Secret Life of the Underwear Champ*
492. *Snow Treasure*
493. *Stone Fox*
494. *Stuart Little*
495. *Superfudge*
496. *Tales of a Fourth Grade Nothing*
497. *Tenth Good Thing about Barney*
498. *Trumpet of the Swan*
499. *Velveteen Rabbit*
500. *What's The Big Idea, Ben Franklin?*
501. *Where Was Patrick Henry on the 29th of May?*
502. *The Whipping Boy*

Grades 5-6

503. *Babe, the Gallant Pig*
504. *The Black Stallion*
505. *The Black Pearl*
506. *The Borrowers*
507. *Bridge to Terabithia*
508. *Brighty of the Grand Canyon*
509. *Bunnicula*
510. *Cabin Faced West*
511. *Caddie Woodlawn*
512. *Cat Ate My Gymsuit*
513. *Dear Mr. Henshaw*
514. *Door in the Wall*
515. *From the Mixed-Up Files of Mrs. Basil E. Frankweiler*
516. *Gentle Ben*
517. *The Great Brain*
518. *Homer Price*
519. *How to Eat Fried Worms*
520. *The Hundred Dresses*
521. *I, Houdini: Autobiography of a Hamster*
522. *Indian in the Cupboard*
523. *Island of the Blue Dolphins*
524. *It's Like This, Cat*
525. *Jelly Belly*
526. *Jennifer, Hecate, MacBeth, William McKinley and Me, Elizabeth*

527. *Mr. Popper's Penguins*
528. *Mr. Revere and I*
529. *Number the Stars*
530. *Old Yeller*
531. *The One-Eyed Cat*
532. *Otis Spofford*
533. *The Phantom Tollbooth*
534. *Phillip Hall Likes Me*
535. *The Pinballs*
536. *Rabbit Hill*
537. *Rascal*
538. *Return of the Indian*
539. *Roll of Thunder, Hear My Cry*
540. *Secret Garden*
541. *Secret of the Indian*
542. *Sing Down the Moon*
543. *Summer of the Monkeys*
544. *Summer of the Swans*
545. *Tuck Everlasting*
546. *War with Grandpa*
547. *Who Really Killed Cock Robin?*
548. *Wind in the Willows*

Grades 6-8
549. *Across Five Aprils*
550. *Adventures of Tom Sawyer*
551. *April Morning*
552. *Big Red*
553. *The Big Wave*
554. *Call It Courage*
555. *Anne Frank: Diary of a Young Girl*
556. *Dragonwings*
557. *The Great Gilly Hopkins*
558. *Hatchet*
559. *Hobbit*
560. *The Homecoming*
561. *Incident at Hawk's Hill*
562. *The Incredible Journey*
563. *Jacob Have I Loved*
564. *Johnny Tremain*
565. *Julie of the Wolves*
566. *King of the Wind*
567. *Light in the Forest*
568. *Mrs. Frisby and the Rats of NIMH*
569. *My Brother Sam Is Dead*
570. *My Side of the Mountain*
571. *Shadow of a Bull*
572. *Sign of the Beaver*
573. *Slave Dancer*
574. *Sounder*
575. *Soup*
576. *Summer of My German Soldier*
577. *Treasure Island*
578. *Where the Red Fern Grows*
579. *Witch of Blackbird Pond*
580. *Wrinkle in Time*

Grades 6-12
581. *Call of the Wild*
582. *The Cay*
583. *Cheaper by the Dozen*
584. *Dicey's Song*
585. *The Pearl*
586. *The Westing Game*

ORYX
4041 N Central at Indian School Rd.
Phoenix, AZ 85012

****587.   Laughlin, Mildred Knight, and Claudia Swiser. *Literature Based Reading*. Oryx Press, 1990.

Literature Based Reading has been arranged by levels from Kindergarten through fifth grade. Each level presents units with objectives appropriate to the students' abilities. Each unit begins with student objectives and an annotated bibliography that contains books that have been favorably reviewed and are deemed appropriate for the grade level indicated. Each unit is also introduced by a detailed group activity with objectives. Additional activities for other books and extending activities are included at each level.

Kindergarten/Transitional/First Grade
Visual Literacy
The Snowman; Do You Want to Be My Friend?; Sun's Up; Look! Look! Look!; Changes, Changes; The Trek; Dry or Wet; The Real Mother Goose Picture Word Rhymes; Feet!; Ten in a Bed; Animal Song; Dreams; Do Not Disturb; Junglewalk; Spots, Feathers and Curly Tails.

Predicting
Play Rhymes; The Runaway Bunny; What Is Beyond the Hill?; Shrewbettina's Birthday; Alphabears; Where's the Baby?; Hello, Goodbye; If Wishes Were Horses; The Box with Red Wheels; The Tale of Benjamin Bunny; A Place for Ben; Shoes; King Bidgood's in the Bath; But Not Billy.

Patterns in Literature
Wail Til the Moon Is Full; The Very Busy Spider; Drummer Hoff; Ask Mr. Bear; Henny Penny; The Three Bears; I Know an Old Lady Who Swallowed a Fly; It Looked Like Spilt Milk; The Three Billy Goats Gruff; Have You Seen My Duckling?; The Napping House; The Little Red Hen.

Sequencing
All Butterflies; The Pancake Boy; Eating the Alphabet; The Easter Bunny That Overslept; A B C Bunny; Millions of Cats; Chicken Little; Alphabatics; Blueberries for Sal; The Story of Chicken Licken; Sing a Song of Popcorn; Caps for Sale.

Characterization
Rockabye Crocodile; Annie and the Wild Animals; Big Al; Corduroy; Crusher Is Coming; The Hole in the Dike; Wild Robin; Peter's Chair; Frederick; The Little Engine That Could; Sylvester and the Magic Pebble; A Tiger Called Thomas

Plot Line
First Grade Can Wait; The Mother's Day Mice; Katie Morag Delivers the Mail; The Pirates of Bedford Street; James Marshall's Mother Goose; Leo the Late Bloomer;

A Visit from Dr. Katz; Tillie and the Wall; George and Martha; There's an Alligator under My Bed; Mother Goose; Katy No-Pocket; Hugo at the Window; Tomie de Paola's Mother Goose.

Vocabulary
One Crow; Stamp Your Feet; A Children's Zoo; Out and About; The Idle Bear; Up and Down on the Merry-Go-Round; Blackberry Ink; The Luckiest One of All; In the Middle of a Puddle; Hide and Seek Fog; Owl Moon; Sleepy Book

Second/Third Grade
Visual Literacy
Song and Dance Man; Each Peach, Pear, Plum; Where the Forest Meets the Sea; Hansel and Gretel; The Quilt; Jennie's Hat; Alexander and the Wind-Up Mouse; The Mare on the Hill; Growing Colors; Hailstones and Halibut Bones; Jolly Roger; A Dog of Hoboken; Sing a Song of Popcorn: Every Child's Book of Poems; Many Moons; The Bells of London; Hey, Al.

Predicting
It's So Nice to Have a Wolf around the House; Did You Carry the Flag Today, Charlie?; Helga's Dowry; Give Us a Great Big Smile, Rosey Cole; To Catch a Crook; Russell Sprouts; John Henry; The Quangle Wangle's Hat; What's the Matter with Carruthers?; Good Work, Amelia Bedelia; Never Trust an Ogre; The Z Was Zapped; Heckedy Peg.

Sequencing
The First Dog; Stopping by the Woods on a Snowy Evening; I Unpacked My Grandmother's Trunk; Cajun Night Before Christmas; Dogs and Dragons; Trees and Dreams; The Bunny Play; I Should Have Stayed in Bed; Why the Chicken Crossed the Road; The Night Before Christmas; Rapunzel; Chester; A Light in the Attic; The Night After Christmas; Casey at the Bat.

Characterization
Hanna's Hog; Mary of Mile 18; Ramona the Pest; The Mud Pony; Millie Cooper, 3B; Dinner at Alberta's; Class Clown; The Island of the Skog; Seven Kisses in a Row; Sam, Bangs and Moonshine; Amelia Bedelia Helps Out; Crow Boy.

Plot/Theme
Where the Buffaloes Begin; Dawn; The Mushroom Center Disaster; Cross-Country Cat; Andy and the Lion; Petunia; Leo, Zack and Emmie; Stone Fox; Rosy Cole's Great American Guilt Club; The Elephant's Child; Fables; Lentil; Annie and the Old One; Nate the Great Goes Down in the Dumps; Katherine's Doll.

Vocabulary
Hosie's Alphabet; Grandfather Twilight; Airmail to the Moon; A Pocketful of Cricket; The Scarebird; A Hole Is to Dig; Super Super Superwords; Listen to the Rain; Percy and the Five Houses; Beats Me, Claude; High in the Mountains; Step into the Night; Storm in the Night; Farmer Schulz's Duck; Wild Animals; Say It!

Discovering Information Books
Dinosaur Bones; Action Contraptions; Tornado Alert; The Popcorn Book; Rock Collecting; Sunken Treasure; Rock Collecting; How to Make Pop-Ups;

Taking My Dog to the Vet; At the Ballpark; Soap Bubble Magic; Storms; Young Lions.

Fourth/Fifth Grade
Becoming Visually Literate
The Little Match Girl; Anno's Aesop; Anno's Journey; Anno's Italy; In Shadowland; The Hunter and the Animals; Pigs from A to Z; Pecos Bill; The Twelve Dancing Princesses; Arrow to the Sun; The Stonecutter; The Water of Life; The Silver Pony; Rumplestiltskin; Duffy and the Devil.

Exploring Poetry
All the Colors of the Race; The Hopeful Trout and Other Limericks; Joyful Noise; I Am Phoenix; Seeing Things; Dogs and Dragons; Trees and Dreams; Celebrations; A Circle of Seasons; Paul Revere's Ride; A Sky Full of Song; Flower Moon Snow: A Book of Haiku; The Snopp on the Sidewalk and Other Poems; The Random House Book of Poetry for Children; Rainbows Are Made.

Analyzing Contemporary Realistic Fiction
Is Anybody There?; Cracker Jackson; The Summer of the Swans; Julie's Tree; Dear Mr. Henshaw; Between Friends; Throwing Shadows; Mail-Order Kid; Fourth Grade Is a Jinx; Bridge to Terabithia; The Great Gilly Hopkins; Moving In; A Taste of Blackberries; A Dog on Barkham Street; The Bully of Barkham Street.

Learning from Biographies and Autobiographies
A Grain of Wheat: A Writer Begins; A Girl from Yamhill; The Country Artist: A Story about Beatrix Potter; To the Point: A Story about E. B. White; Homesick: My Own Story (Jean Fritz); Self-Portrait: Trina Schart Hyman; Kipling: Storyteller of East and West; Little by Little: A Writer's Childhood; Bill Peet: An Autobiography; Mark Twain? What Kind of Name Is That?: The Story of Samuel Langhorn Clemens; Higher on the Door; When I Was Nine; Self-Portrait: Margot Zemach.

Enjoying Modern Fantasy
The Mouse and the Motorcycle; Bunnicula; The Phantom Tollbooth; Beloved Benjamin Is Waiting; The Gammage Cup; The Fledgling; The Lion, the Witch and the Wardrobe; The Borrowers; A Cricket in Times Square; Abel's Island; The Mysteries of Harris Burdick; The Stranger; The Castle in the Attic.

Introducing Classics
Peter Pan; The Wizard of Oz; The Story of Babar, the Little Elephant; The Secret Garden; Alice's Adventures in Wonderland; The Adventures of Pinocchio; A Christmas Carol; Angus and the Ducks; The Wind in the Willows; Rip Van Winkle; The Story of Ferdinand; The World of Pooh: The Complete Winnie-the-Pooh and House at Pooh Corner; And To Think That I Saw It on Mulberry Street; Heidi; The Adventures of Tom Sawyer.

Using Information Books
Sketching Outdoors in Autumn; Where Did You Get Those Eyes?; Racing Sled Dogs; One Day in the Prairie; String Games; Make It Special; Stamp Collecting as a Hobby; The News about Dinosaurs; Codes, Ciphers and Other Secrets; A Horse of a Different Color; All about Baseball; Barnstormers and Daredevils.

****588. Laughlin, Mildrid Knight, and Patricia Payne Kardeleff. *Based Social Studies: Children's Books and Activities to Enrich the K-5 Curriculum.* Oryx, 1991.

This title is organized to extend the social studies curriculum beyond the adopted text or the scope and sequence designed by local districts. *Literature Based Social Studies* is a tool all social studies teachers can use to enrich their content. Each unit contains student objectives, recommended readings, group introductory activities and follow-up activities.

Kindergarten/Transition/First Grade

Myself

Caps, Hats, Socks and Mittens; I Like Me!; Now One Foot, Now the Other; I Wish I Were a Butterfly; Cromwell's Glasses; Boris Bad Enough; The Growing Story; Harriet Reads Signs and More Signs; Goldilocks and the Three Bears; When I Get Bigger; New Baby; My Favorite Time of Year; I Forgot; Barney Is Big; One Step, Two.

Families

The Two of Them; Play Ball, Zachary; Dinosaurs Divorce; The Stories Julian Tells; Everett Anderson's Goodbye; Your Family, My Family; Katie-Bo; The Very Worst Monster; Mama One, Mama Two; Grandma's House; Breakfast with My Father; The Relatives Came; Sophie's Knapsack.

Economics of Family Living

Terrible Thing That Happened at Our House; Tight Times; You'll Soon Grow into Them, Titch; Another Mouse to Feed; This Year's Garden; Annie and Moon; Alexander Who Used to Be Rich Last Sunday; A Chair for My Mother.

Homes

Goodbye House; Building a House; Aunt Nina and Her Nephews and Nieces; Tool Book; Grandmama's Joy; A House Is a House for Me; From Blueprint to House; New House; Need a House? Call Ms. Mouse; 100 Words about My House; The Big Orange Splot; Let's Look All around the House; In My Treehouse.

Children and Their Families Near and Far

Bringing the Rain to Kapiti Plain; Where Children Live; Not So Fast, Songolo; Watch Out for the Chicken Feet in Your Soup; Summer; Honey, I Love and Other Love Poems; Count Your Way through Japan; Watch the Stars Come Out; Knots on a Counting Rope; The Chalk Doll; The Runaway Mittens; The Bicycle Man; Cooking the Japanese Way.

Friendship

We Are Best Friends; Rainy Day Kate; It's George; Grandma's Wheelchair; I Dance in My Red Pajamas; What Do You Say, Dear?; Nick Joins In; Through Grandpa's Eyes; A Playhouse for Monster; Rolling Harvey Down the Hil; The Tale of the Vanishing Rainbow; Let's Be Enemies; If I Were in Charge of the World; Lizzie and Harold.

Groups: Working and Playing Together

If I Could Work; What Is the Sign for Friend?; Changes, Changes; A Trip to the Dentist; A Trip to the Doctor; Swimmy; Fire Fighters; Whose Hat?; The Day Jimmy's Boa Ate the Wash; The Best Friends Club.

Transportation

Draw 50 Vehicles; Airport; I Want to Be an Astronaut; Dinosaurs Travel; Freight Train; Trains; Trucks; I Read Signs; I Go with My Family to Grandma's; Up in the Air; The Biggest Truck; Pig Pig Rides; 100 Words about Transportation; Richard Scarry's Cars and Trucks and Things That Go.

Holidays

A Picture Book of Abraham Lincoln; A Picture Book of George Washington; A Picture Book of Martin Luther King, Jr.; December 24th; Christmas Time; Thanksgiving Day; Spot's Birthday Party; Happy Father's Day; Happy Mother's Day; Trick or Treat, Danny!; Hanukkah; Birthday Presents; Peter Spier's Christmas; Over and Over.

Second/Third Grade

Native American Communities

And It Still Is That Way; Before Columbus; The Desert Is Theirs; When Clay Sings; The Legend of the Indian Paintbrush; Gift of the Sacred Dog; Squanto and the First Thanksgiving; First Came the Indians.

Pioneer Communities

Wagon Wheels; Party Rhymes; The Josefina Story Quilt; If You Grew Up with George Washington; Ox-Cart Man; Cassie's Journey; Log Cabin in the Woods; Pioneer Cat; Paul Bunyan; Pecos Bill; Clara and the Bookwagon; Hannah's Farm; Aurora Means Dawn; Dakota Dugout.

Rural and Small Town Living

The Best Town in the World; Island Boy; General Store; In Coal Country; Yonder; Frannie's Fruits; Family Farm; Shaker Lane; Oranges.

Urban Living

How My Library Grew; Pets without Homes; The Little House; Left Behind; The Post Office Book; Night Markets: Bringing Food to the City; City Seen from A to Z; Taxi: A Book of City Words; The Inside Outside Book of New York City; Anna, Grandpa and the Big Storm.

Being an American

The Many Lives of Benjamin Franklin; A Weed Is a Flower: The Life Story of George Carver Washington; The Life of George Washington Carver; Chang's Paper Pony; The Story of the Statue of Liberty; The Inside-Outside Book of Washington, D.C.; Quit Pulling My Leg!; A Story of Davy Crockett; The Long Way to a New Land; The Long Way Westward; The Star Spangled Banner; I Speak English for My Mom; Cornrows.

World Neighbors

Bananas: From Manolo to Margie; Very Last First Time; An Arabian Home; A, My Name Is Alice; The Way to Start a Day; Under the Sunday Tree; Count Your Way through Russia; The Boy Who Held Back the Sea; Our Home Is the Sea; Bread, Bread, Bread; Hats, Hats, Hats.

Celebrations

Dancing Is; All In a Day; I'm In Charge of Celebrations; Chinese New Year; Arbor Day; Molly's Pilgrim; The Family Christmas Tree Book; Nine Days to Christmas; April Fool's Day; Christmas Around the World; Happy New Year; Oh, What a Thanksgiving!; Rechenka's Eggs; It's Thanksgiving; Baboushka and the Three Kings.

Fourth/Fifth Grade

Early America
Encounter at Easton; Night Journey; Colonial American Crafts; The Home; The Double Life of Pocahontas; Baker's Dozen; A Colonial American Tale; From Path to Highway; Who Really Discovered America?; The Pilgrims of Plimoth; Fur Trappers and Traders; The Sign of the Beaver; Indians; From Abenaki to Zuni; Amos Fortune, Free Man.

Becoming a Nation
Thomas Jefferson, Father of Our Democracy; The Fighting Ground; At the Forge of Liberty; Jump Ship to Freedom; Black Heroes of the American Revolution; What Do You Mean? A Story about Noah Webster; Monticello; The Cabin Faced West; Can't You Make Them Behave, King George?; George Washington's Breakfast; Shh! We're Writing the Constitution; Where Was Patrick Henry on the 29th of May?; Where Was Patrick Henry on the 20th of May?; We the People: The Way We Were 1783-1793; Ben and Me; The Secret Soldier; Buttons for General Washington; George and Martha Washington at Home in New York.

The American Frontier
Pioneer Children of Appalachia; Klondike Fever; The Alamo; Buffalo Hunt; Children of the Wild West; Cowboys of the Wild West; Indian Chiefs; Death of the Iron Horse; Tree in the Trail; Susanna of the Alamo; Johnny Appleseed; Addie Across the Prairie; Little Brother of the Wilderness; Sarah, Plain and Tall; Who Let Muddy Boots into the White House?: A Story of Andrew Jackson; Mr. Yowder and the Windwagon; The Little House Cookbook; On the Banks of Plum Creek.

The Civil War Era
Turn Homeward Hannalee; Go Free or Die; Walking the Road to Freedom; Lincoln: A Photobiography; Stonewall; The People Could Fly; Jump Again!; The Battle of Gettysburg; The Tales of Uncle Remus; To Be a Slave; A Family Apart; Behind Rebel Lines; The Adventures of High John the Conqueror; Nettie's Trip South.

America: Land of Change
My Black Me; Extraordinary Black Americans from Colonial to Contemporary Times; The American Family Farm; Shadrach's Crossing; Charlie Pippin; How Many Days to America?: A Thanksgiving Story; The House of Sixty Fathers; Franklin Delano Roosevelt, President; Ellis Island; Long Ago in Oregon; Mary McLeod Bethune; The Black Snowman; We'll Race You, Henry; Don't You Dare Shoot That Bear!; Ragtime Tumpie; When I Grew Up Long Ago; Dancing Teepees; The Gold Cadillac; Journey to Topaz.

The United States Today and Tomorrow
To Live in Two Worlds; Airplanes of the Future; The Diane Goode Book of American Folk Tales and Songs; The National Air Space Museum A B C; The President's Car; Living in a Risky World; The Boy and the Ghost; Cross Your Fingers; Spit in Your Hat; Heartland; Alaska; Far Out; Stringbean's Trip to the Shining Sea; The United Nations.

THE PERFECTION LEARNING COMPANY
1000 North Second Avenue
Logan, Iowa 51546

****589-595. Fox, Carol, and Margery Sauer. *Celebrate Literature* Series. Perfection Form, 1990.

This curriculum guide and resource series is divided into five literature strands: poetry, traditional literature, picture books and fiction, biography and author study, and nonfiction, that can be utilized with any literary piece. Since the scope and sequence of the series is K-6, literary elements are introduced, reinforced, and reviewed. This series was developed to be a supplemental tool for teaching literature. Each unit begins with a stated objective and a list of featured books and resources. It is followed with motivational activities, ideas to focus children, then has activities for individual student involvement and whole group participation. Each unit also contains opportunities for creative responses, culminating activities, and suggestions for evaluating. An extensive bibliography accompanies each strand. This series can be combined with other resource materials to provide an excellent probe into children's literature.

589. Fox, Carol, and Margery Sauer. *Celebrate Literature, Grade K.* Perfection Learning, 1989.

Books included: Kindergarten
Anno's Counting; Changes, Changes; Chicken Little; The Complete Adventures of Peter Rabbit; A Great Big Ugly Man Came Up and Tied His Horse to Me; The Most Amazing Hide-and-Seek Alphabet Book; One Fine Day; Rosie's Walk; The Story about Ping; The Three Bears and Fifteen Other Stories; Tomie De Paola's Mother Goose; The Very Hungry Caterpillar.

590. Fox, Carol, and Margery Sauer. *Celebrate Literature, Grade 1.* Perfection Learning, 1989.

Books included: Grade 1
A Baby Sister for Frances; The Baby Uggs Are Hatching; A Bargain for Frances; Bedtime for Frances; Best Friends for Frances; A Birthday for Frances; Bread and Jam for Frances; The Cat in the Hat; Corduroy; Curious George; The Guinea Pig A B C; Horton Hears a Who; House on East Eighty-Eighth Street; I Unpacked My Grandmother's Trunk; The Lorax; Loveable Lyle; Lyle and the Birthday Party; Lyle Finds His Mother; Lyle, Lyle, Crocodile; Madeline; Madeline and the Bad Hat; Madeline and the Gypsies; Madeline in London; Madeline's Rescue; A Pocketful of Cricket; The Random House Book of Poetry for Children; The Tale of Peter Rabbit; The Three Bears and Fifteen Other Stories.

591. Fox, Carol, and Margery Sauer. *Celebrate Literature, Grade 2.* Perfection Learning, 1989.

Books included: Grade 2
Aesop's Fables; Amelia Bedelia; Amelia Bedelia and the Baby; Amelia Bedelia Helps Out; Cloudy with a Chance of Meatballs; Come Back, Amelia Bedelia;

Days with Frog and Toad; Fables; Father Bear Comes Home; Frog and Toad All Year; Frog and Toad Are Friends; Frog and Toad Together; The Gobblins'll Git You If You Don't Watch Out; Hiawatha; King Bidgood's in the Bathtub; A Kiss for Little Bear; Little Bear; Little Bear's Friend; Little Bear's Visit; Nothing Ever Happens on My Block; The Polar Express; The Random House Book of Fairy Tales; Teach Us, Amelia Bedelia; The Town Mouse and the Country Mouse; Whiskers and Rhymes; Wynken, Blynken, and Nod; Yeh-Shen: A Cinderella Story from China.

592. Fox, Carol, and Margery Sauer. *Celebrate Literature, Grade 3.* Perfection Learning, 1989.

Books included: Grade 3
Abraham Lincoln; Blackberries in the Dark; Favorite Fairy Tales Told around the World; Little House in the Big Woods; Molly's Pilgrim; More Stories Julian Tells; Now We Are Six; Owls in the Family; Ramona the Pest; Sarah, Plain and Tall; Socks; A Story, A Story; Tales of a Fourth Grade Nothing; When We Were Very Young.

593. Fox, Carol, and Margery Sauer. *Celebrate Literature, Grade 4.* Perfection Learning, 1989.

Books included: Grade 4
A Bear Called Paddington; The Borrowers; Charlotte's Web; East of the Sun, West of the Moon; Michael Hague's Favorite Hans Christian Andersen Fairy Tales; The New Kid on the Block; Peter Pan; Pippi Longstocking; Scary Stories to Tell in the Dark; There is a Carrot in My Ear and Other Noodle Tales; The Wizard of Oz.

594. Fox, Carol, and Margery Sauer. *Celebrate Literature, Grade 5.* Perfection Learning, 1989.

Books included: Grade 5
Bridge to Terabithia; Caddie Woodlawn; Call It Courage; The Cremation of Sam McGee; Dear Mr. Henshaw; The Illustrated Casey at the Bat; The Incredible Journey of Lewis and Clark; Island of the Blue Dolphins; The People Could Fly: American Black Tales; Rainbow in the Sky: Golden Anniversary Edition; The Witch of Blackbird Pond.

595. Fox, Carol, and Margery Sauer. *Celebrate Literature, Grade 6.* Perfection Learning, 1989.

Books included: Grade 6
Alexander the Great; D'Aulaire's Book of Greek Myths; The Door in the Wall; The Dream-Keeper and Other Poems; From the Mixed-Up Files of Mrs. Basil E. Frankweiler; The Lion, the Witch and the Wardrobe; Over Sea, Under Stone; Pierre-Auguste Renoir; The White Mountains; A Wrinkle in Time.

596-598. *Discovering Our World*

Designed to teach primary science with nonfiction books, the *Discovering Our World* teacher guides provide pre-reading activities to stimulate children's interest before they encounter the book. Activities during reading reinforce the concepts the books introduce. Each guide also has a fiction section that children can use to evaluate fictional writing about the same topics. This series includes teacher resource pages, reproducible art and take-home pages, a scope and sequence guide and a bibliography of related books.

596. *Dinosaurs Are Different; Digging Up Dinosaurs; Fossils Tell of Long Ago; My Visit to the Dinosaurs; What Happened to Patrick's Dinosaurs?; Last of the Dinosaurs; Maia: A Dinosaur Grows Up; Dinosaur Hunters; Whatever Happened to the Dinosaurs?; Tyrannosaurus Was a Beast; The Smallest Dinosaurs.*

597. *Mooncake; Is There Life in Outer Space?; The Moon Seems to Change; The Planets in the Solar System; Rockets and Satellites; The Sky Is Full of Stars; The Sun, Our Nearest Star; Sunshine Makes the Seasons; To Space and Back with Sally Ride; Jupiter; Mars; Saturn; Stars; Sun; Uranus.*

598. *Hungry, Hungry Sharks; Dolphins, Wonders of the Sea; Louis, the Fish; Where the Waves Break; Sharks.*

***599-617. *Portals to Reading* Series**

Delineates a host of adaptable ideas to get children and books together. These books include work attack skills, comprehension skills, study skills, and creative and critical thinking skills. All skills and activities are based on the literature and many skills require direct reading of the literature. Spelling and vocabulary lists are included along with supplementary activities.

599. *Across Five Aprils*
600. *Caddie Woodlawn*
601. *Call it Courage*
602. *Charlotte's Web*
603. *Incredible Journey*
604. *Island of the Blue Dolphins*
605. *Johnny Tremain*
606. *Julie of the Wolves*
607. *The Lion, the Witch and the Wardrobe*
608. *The Long Winter*
609. *My Side of the Mountain*
610. *Old Yeller*
611. *Roll of Thunder, Hear My Cry*
612. *Sounder*
613. *Summer of the Monkeys*
614. *Treasure Island*
615. *Where the Red Fern Grows*
616. *The Wind in the Willows*
617. *The Witch of Blackbird Pond*

***618-667. *Reading Beyond the Basal* Series**

Thoughtfully written guides that utilize children's literature to extend and enrich the basal programs. Activities that provide critical and creative thinking skills, comprehension skills are integrated into other content areas. Each guide contains an introduction to the author, a synopsis of the story, and many enrichment activities.

618. *Alexander and the Terrible, Horrible, No Good Very Bad Day*
619. *Amelia Bedelia*
620. *Annie and the Old One*
621. *Ashanti to Zulu: African Traditions*
622. *Bedtime for Frances*
623. *The Biggest Bear*
624. *Blueberries for Sal*
625. *Bread and Jam for Frances*
626. *Bringing the Rain to Kapiti Plain*
627. *Caps for Sale*
628. *A Chair for My Mother*
629. *Cloudy with a Chance of Meatballs*
630. *Corduroy*
631. *The Courage of Sarah Noble*
632. *Crow Boy*
633. *Dandelion*
634. *Doctor De Soto*
635. *The Emperor's New Clothes*
636. *Fables*
637. *Fantastic Mr. Fox*
638. *Frog and Toad Are Friends*
639. *Gregory the Terrible Eater*
640. *Hill of Fire*
641. *The Hundred Penny Box*
642. *Ira Sleeps Over*
643. *The Little House*
644. *Little House in the Big Woods*
645. *The Little Prince*
646. *Make Way for Ducklings*
647. *Miss Nelson Is Missing*
648. *Once a Mouse*
649. *One Fine Day*
650. *Paul Bunyan*
651. *Pippi Longstocking*
652. *Ramona Quimby, Age 8*
653. *Rosie's Walk*
654. *The Snowy Day*
655. *Stone Soup*
656. *The Story of Ferdinand*
657. *Strega Nona*
658. *Sylvester and the Magic Pebble*
659. *There's a Nightmare in My Closet*
660. *Tikki Tikki Tembo*
661. *The Ugly Duckling*
662. *The Velveteen Rabbit*
663. *We Are Best Friends*
664. *Where the Wild Things Are*
665. *Whistle for Willie*
666. *Why Mosquitoes Buzz in People's Ears*
667. *Yagua Days*

***668-694. *Reading Beyond the Basal Plus* Series

This series of activity books includes a summary of the specific novel, pre-reading activities that encourage critical thinking, transfer or experience to the literature, predicting and graphic organizers. A multitude of activities including questions, vocabulary, language development, critical thinking, creative dramatics, reading as a writer, reading-writing connections and interdisciplinary activities

in each unit. These activities are designed to develop an appreciation of literature and to encourage children to think.

668. *Abel's Island*
669. *The Best Christmas Pageant Ever*
670. *Blue Willow*
671. *Bridge to Terabithia*
672. *Bunnicula*
673. *Dear Mr. Henshaw*
674. *From the Mixed-Up Files of Mrs. Basil E. Frankweiler*
675. *The House of Dies Drear*
676. *How to Eat Fried Worms*
677. *In the Year of the Boar and Jackie Robinson*
678. *The Indian in the Cupboard*
679. *Ishi, Last of His Tribe*
680. *James and the Giant Peach*
681. *Mr. Frisby and the Rats of NIMH*
682. *One-Eyed Cat*
683. *The Pinballs*
684. *Queenie Peavy*
685. *Roll of Thunder, Hear My Cry*
686. *Sarah, Plain and Tall*
687. *The Sign of the Beaver*
688. *Sounder*
689. *Soup*
690. *Tuck Everlasting*
691. *The War with Grandpa*
692. *Where the Red Fern Grows*
693. *Wrinkle in Time*
694. *Zeely*

**695-704. *Story World—Hands On Activity Guide* Series

A Collection of ideas enhancing language development, drama, art, music and movement, math, science, and cooking activities that can be used in learning centers, groups, or both. They also provide suggestions for field trips and parent communications.

695. *Bedtime for Frances*
696. *Caps for Sale*
697. *Freight Train*
698. *Jamberry*
699. *Katy and the Big Snow*
700. *Quick as a Cricket*
701. *The Runaway Bunny*
702. *Swimmy*
703. *There's a Nightmare in My Closet*
704. *Where the Wild Things Are*

SCHAEFER PUBLICATIONS
P.O. Box 2853
Torrance, CA 70509

*705-722. *Literature Library*

Ranging from grades K-6, Schaeffer has developed several volumes of the *Literature Library*. Each book is based on four literary selections. Prereading activities, reading activities, and post-reading activities create the format of each selection. Most of Schaeffer's activities are worthy, but there are few per selection.

705-710. *Literature Library.* Grades 1-2

705. *Literature Library.* Volume 1
Freight Train, The Gingerbread Man, Good Night Moon, Very Hungry Caterpillar

706. *Literature Library.* Volume 2
Goldilocks and the Three Bears; Little Rabbit's Loose Tooth, Pocket for Corduroy, William's Doll

707. *Literature Library.* Volume 3.
Anno's Counting Book, Frog and Toad Are Friends, The Three Billy Goats Gruff, Will I Have a Friend?

708. *Literature Library.* Volume 4.
Brown Bear, Brown Bear, What Do You See?; The Little Red Hen; Sylvester and the Magic Pebble; Where the Wild Things Are

709. *Literature Library.* Volume 5.
Mike Mulligan and His Steam Shovel; My Grandson, Lew; Rosie's Walk; Umbrella

710. *Literature Library.* Volume 6
Ira Sleeps Over, Caps for Sale, May I Bring a Friend?, The Napping House

711-716. *Literature Library Grades 2-3*
711. *Literature Library.* Volume 1.
Bread and Jam for Frances, Little House in the Big Woods, Miss Rumphius, The Little Island

712. *Literature Library.* Volume 2.
Amelia Bedelia, Stone Soup, Stuart Little, Why Mosquitoes Buzz in People's Ears

713. *Literature Library.* Volume 3.
A Chair for My Mother, Imogene's Antlers, The Velveteen Rabbit, Why the Sun and the Moon Live in the Sky.

714. *Literature Library.* Volume 4.
Annie and the Old One, Big Bad Bruce, Ox-Cart Man, Strega Nona

715. *Literature Library.* Volume 5.
Alexander and the Wind-Up Mouse; Bringing the Rain to Kapiti Plain; Miss Nelson Is Missing!; Sam, Bangs and Moonshine

716. *Literature Library.* Volume 6.
Alexander and the Terrible, Horrible, No Good, Very Bad Day; Cinderella; Friday Night Is Papa Night; Moja Means One

717-722. *Literature Library Grades 4-5-6*
717. *Literature Library.* Volume 1.
Anastasia Krupnik; James and the Giant Peach; The Lion, the Witch and the Wardrobe; Sarah, Plain and Tall

718. *Literature Library.* Volume 2.
Bunnicula, The Indian in the Cupboard, Island of the Blue Dolphins, The Secret Garden

719. *Literature Library.* Volume 3.
Babe the Gallant Pig, Bridge to Terabithia, The Hundred Penny Box, In the Year of the Boar and Jackie Robinson

720. *Literature Library.* Volume 4.
Be a Perfect Person in Just Three Days, Charlotte's Web, Dear Mr. Henshaw, The Hot and Cold Summer

721. *Literature Library.* Volume 5.
Call It Courage, Charlie and the Chocolate Factory, From the Mixed-Up Files of Mrs. Basil E. Frankweiler, The Summer of the Swans

722. *Literature Library.* Volume 6.
A Wrinkle in Time, Blue Willow, Sounder, The War with Grandpa

SUNDANCE
A Division of Pharos Books, A Scripps Howard Company
P.O. Box 1326
Littleton, MS 01460

****723-748. *Connect Science* Series

Connect Science is a literature science series that not only contains scientific content but also provides many opportunities to learn the specific process. Each unit contains an excellent teacher's guide that includes content backgrounds, directions and answer keys for the activities. These units also include a variety of topics to link readings, themes, skills and studies in science and other curriculum areas. Activities that promote interdisciplinary studies and critical thinking skills comprise a major portion of the units. Bulletin board ideas and suggested readings are also available.

723. *Amigo*
724. *The Biggest Pumpkin Ever*
725. *Bringing the Rain to Kapiti Plain*
726. *The Caterpillar and the Polliwog*
727. *Cloudy with a Chance of Meatballs*
728. *Corn Is Maize*
729. *Doctor De Soto*
730. *Fireflies*
731. *Gilberto and the Wind*
732. *Gregory and the Terrible Eater*
733. *Hawk, I'm Your Brother*
734. *How to Dig a Hole to the Other Side of the World*
735. *Humphrey the Wayward Whale*
736. *Katy No Pocket*
737. *Koko's Kitten*
738. *The Lady and the Spider*
739. *The Little Island*
740. *The Magic School Bus at the Waterworks*
741. *Mike Mulligan and His Steam Shovel*
742. *Nothing Sticks Like a Shadow*
743. *Once There Was a Tree*
744. *Over in the Meadow*
745. *Regards to the Man in the Moon*
746. *Sugaring Time*
747. *Through Grandpa's Eyes*
748. *What Happened to Patrick's Dinosaurs?*

****749-769. *Connect Social Studies* Series

Designed for cooperative groups, whole groups or individuals, *Connect Social Studies* provides opportunities for children to use literature to make connections in social studies. Each unit contains a Teacher's Guide and ten reproducible student activity sheets. As students read the inquiry activities, they will process information, investigate issues, make decisions, think critically and participate in the political process. These units are designed to require the student to integrate and synthesize the fact and concepts they have acquired from the literature and connect them to their own lives. Units include prereading activities, vocabulary, book themes, social studies themes, critical/creative thinking activities, writing activities, projects and making connections. These units provide many interdisciplinary activities.

749. *Across Five Aprils*
750. *Amos Fortune, Free Man*
751. *Carry On, Mr. Bowditch*
752. *Charley Skedaddle*
753. *Chancy and the Grand Rascal*
754. *The Door in the Wall*
755. *The Double Life of Pocahontas*
756. *A Family Apart*
757. *Farmer Boy*
758. *Homesick: My Own Story*
759. *A Jar of Dreams*
760. *Johnny Tremain*
761. *Journey to Jo'burg*
762. *Journey to Topaz*
763. *Light in the Forest*
764. *Number the Stars*
765. *Plain Girl*
766. *Sadako and the Thousand Paper Cranes*
767. *Sing Down the Moon*
768. *War Comes to Willy Freeman*
769. *Where the Lilies Bloom*

***770-780. *Connect Writing* Series

Connect Writing provides students with eight sequential lessons that instruct and reinforce the writing process (prewriting, writing, revising/editing and proof-reading and publishing). Each lesson integrates a particular literary focus on the story with a reading and writing focus. The final lessons always introduce specific writing strategies and provide students with a personalized writing assignment. A skills matrix for each lesson is provided to help teachers integrate the skills. Each unit provides a teacher's guide with answers.

770. *Be a Perfect Person in Just Three Days*
771. *The Big Wave*
772. *The Courage of Sarah Noble*
773. *Dear Mr. Henshaw*
774. *In the Year of the Boar and Jackie Robinson*
775. *Julie of the Wolves*
776. *Mrs. Frisby and the Rats of NIMH*
777. *My Side of the Mountain*
778. *The Phantom Tollbooth*
779. *Sarah, Plain and Tall*
780. *The Whipping Boy*

**781-808. *Kinderbooks*

Designed to introduce young children to quality literature, *Kinderbooks* are activity packets that are based on a read-aloud, whole language approach. Activity cards and sheets are provided to build listening, speaking, thinking and prereading skills. Each activity packet contains five copies of a well-known children's book, six thematic activity cards, five reproducible activity sheets, creative activity cards, a comprehensive teacher's guide, and a take-home package. Activities are designed to elicit cognitive and affective responses and to meet a developmental range of abilities and needs in young children.

781. *Bear Shadow*
782. *The Bear's Toothache*
783. *The Biggest Pumpkin Ever*
784. *Blueberries for Sal*
785. *Caps for Sale*
786. *The Caterpillar and the Polliwog*
787. *A Chair for My Mother*
788. *Don't Forget the Bacon*
789. *Each Peach, Pear, Plum*
790. *Franklin in the Dark*
791. *The Grouchy Ladybug*
792. *Harry by the Sea*
793. *A House Is a House for Me*
794. *The Hungry Thing*
795. *If You Give a Mouse a Cookie*
796. *Joey Runs Away*
797. *The Little House*
798. *Lovable Lyle*
799. *Make Way for Ducklings*
800. *May I Bring a Friend?*
801. *The Mitten*
802. *Patrick's Dinosaurs*
803. *A Pocket for Corduroy*
804. *The Snowy Day*
805. *The Story of Johnny Appleseed*
806. *Sylvester and the Magic Pebble*
807. *Three Billy Goats Gruff*
808. *What Next Baby Bear?*

**809-897. *Leap* Series

Leap is a series designed to be used with paperback selections in grades two through six. Each packet contains prereading exercises that focus students' thinking and ignite an interest in the literature, questions, games, puzzles, drawing activities and writing skills. Postreading questions are designed to promote discussions that will elicit critical thinking. Each packet has extension and enrichment activities that provide interdisciplinary studies.

Grade 2

809. *Amelia Bedelia*
810. *A Bargain for Frances*
811. *The Beast in Ms. Rooney's Room*
812. *The Biggest Bear*
813. *Cam Jansen and the Mystery at the Monkey House*

814. *A Chair for My Mother*
815. *Curious George Flies a Kite*
816. *Dinner at Alberta's*
817. *Doctor De Soto*
818. *Freckle Juice*
819. *Harry and the Terrible Whatzit*
820. *Ira Sleeps Over*
821. *Lazy Lions, Lucky Lambs*
822. *Miss Nelson Is Missing*
823. *The One in the Middle Is the Green Kangaroo*
824. *The Pain and the Great One*
825. *Sam, Bangs and Moonshine*
826. *Something Queer Is Going On*
827. *The Story of Ferdinand*
828. *Troll Country*

Grade 3

829. *Blackberries in the Dark*
830. *Cam Jansen and the Mystery at the Monkey House*
831. *Cam Jansen and the Mystery of the Dinosaur Bones*
832. *The Case of the Nervous Newsboy*
833. *The Chalk Box Kid*
834. *The Chocolate Touch*
835. *A Hippopotamus Ate the Teacher*
836. *How to Eat Fried Worms*
837. *The Legend of the Bluebonnet*
838. *Lily and the Runaway Baby*
839. *Maurice's Room*
840. *Mouse Soup*
841. *Nate the Great and the Phony Clue*
842. *No One Is Going to Nashville*
843. *The Paper Bag Princess*
844. *Pippi Longstocking*
845. *A Promise Is a Promise*
846. *Ramona Quimby, Age 8*
847. *Sarah, Plain and Tall*
848. *What's the Big Idea, Ben Franklin?*

Grade 4

849. *Be a Perfect Person in Just Three Days*
850. *The Best Christmas Pageant Ever*
851. *The Big Wave*
852. *Charlie and the Chocolate Factory*
853. *Charlotte's Web*
854. *Homer Price*
855. *The Hundred Dresses*
856. *J. T.*
857. *Little House on the Prairie*
858. *Maggie Marmelstein for President*
859. *Skinnybones*
860. *Stone Fox*
861. *Superfudge*
862. *Tales of a Fourth Grade Nothing*
863. *A Taste of Blackberries*
864. *Where Do You Think You're Going, Christopher Columbus?*
865. *The Whipping Boy*

Grade 5

866. *Anastasia Krupnik*
867. *The Black Stallion*
868. *Bunnicula*
869. *Cricket in Times Square*
870. *The 18th Emergency*
871. *Freaky Friday*
872. *The Great Brain*
873. *Helen Keller's Teacher*
874. *The Lion, the Witch and the Wardrobe*
875. *Mouse and the Motorcycle*
876. *Mr. Popper's Penguins*
877. *My Side of the Mountain*
878. *Owls in the Family*
879. *The Phantom Tollbooth*
880. *The Search for Grissi*
881. *Top Secret*

Grade 6

882. *Arthur for the Very First Time*
883. *Ben and Me*
884. *Bridge to Terabithia*
885. *The Dollhouse Murders*
886. *The Enormous Egg*
887. *Gentle Ben*
888. *Harriet the Spy*
889. *King of the Wind*
890. *Phillip Hall Likes Me, I Reckon, Maybe*
891. *Song of the Trees*
892. *Sounder*
893. *There's a Boy in the Girls' Bathroom*
894. *Trouble River*
895. *The Twenty-One Balloons*
896. *The Witch of Blackbird Pond*
897. *A Wrinkle in Time*

***Lift**

Designed to provide students with practice in critical-creative thinking and language skills, *Lift* is a literature-based program that serves as a tool to integrate skills and promote a love of literature. Each packet develops and reinforces thinking skills; thus, listening, speaking, reading and writing are improved. *Lift* packets contain a comprehensive teacher's guide and activity sheets that include a primary and secondary skill. *Lift* provides many opportunities for a whole language approach to reading as integrates listening, speaking, reading, writing and literary analysis. The activities in *Lift* are designed to promote the acquisition of skills and concepts throughout the reading of each book and provide multiple opportunities for synthesis.

898. *A Banner in the Sky*
899. *The Black Pearl*
900. *The Borrowers*
901. *Call It Courage*
902. *Carry On, Mr. Bowditch*
903. *The Cat Ate My Gymsuit*
904. *The Cay*

905. *Cheaper by the Dozen*
906. *Dear Mr. Henshaw*
907. *Dicey's Song*
908. *Dogsong*
909. *Door in the Wall*
910. *Dragonwings*
911. *The Facts and Fictions of Minna Pratt*
912. *From the Mixed-Up Files of Mrs. Basil E. Frankweiler*
913. *The Great Gilly Hopkins*
914. *Harriet Tubman*
915. *The Homecoming*
916. *The House with a Clock in Its Walls*
917. *In the Year of the Boar and Jackie Robinson*
918. *Incident at Hawk's Hill*
919. *The Incredible Journey*
920. *The Indian in the Cupboard*
921. *Island of the Blue Dolphins*
922. *James and the Giant Peach*
923. *Julie of the Wolves*
924. *The Lottery Rose*
925. *Mrs. Frisby and the Rats of NIMH*
926. *My Brother Sam Is Dead*
927. *On My Honor*
928. *The One-Eyed Cat*
929. *The Pinballs*
930. *The Pushcart War*
931. *Racing the Sun*
932. *Rascal*
933. *Sarah Bishop*
934. *The Secret Garden*
935. *Shadow of a Bull*
936. *The Sign of the Beaver*
937. *Sing Down the Moon*
938. *Slake's Limbo*
939. *The Slave Dancer*
940. *Snow Treasure*
941. *Sounder*
942. *A Stranger Came Ashore*
943. *Summer of the Monkeys*
944. *Summer of the Swans*
945. *Tuck Everlasting*
946. *The War with Grandpa*
947. *The Westing Game*
948. *Where the Lilies Bloom*
949. *Where the Red Fern Grows*
950. *The Witch of Blackbird Pond*
951. *The Wizard of Oz*
952. *The Wolves of Willoughby Chase*
953. *Words by Heart*

**Novel Aids*

Novel Aids, Literature/Language Arts Program, is an integrated approach to the whole novel. This series is designed for grades 4-8, is based on popular adolescent titles, and includes prereading, reading and postreading activities that promote thoughtful literary analysis. Each *Novel Aid* contains reproducible activity sheets, a two-page test, a comprehensive teacher's guide and answer key, and a glossary. Packets also include projects, writing activities and related readings.

954. *Across Five Aprils*
955. *April Morning*
956. *Dicey's Song*
957. *Incredible Journey*
958. *Island of the Blue Dolphins*
959. *Johnny Tremain*
960. *No Promises in the Wind*
961. *Old Yeller*
962. *Roll of Thunder, Hear My Cry*
963. *Summer of My German Soldier*
964. *Treasure Island*
965. *Where the Red Fern Grows*

**Project People*

Project People is a literature based series of packets that are designed to explore issues that children may encounter in real life. Each packet integrates one read-aloud story with many interdisciplinary activities and learning experiences. The packets have open-ended discussions that challenge creative and critical thinking. *Project People* is designed to increase students' awareness, acceptance and adjustment to sensitive situations that children commonly experience. The activities in these packets are classified by outcome. A comprehensive teacher's guide includes a book synopsis, a list of story themes, step-by-step instruction, management strategies and creative activities. Reproducible activity sheets motivate cooperative learning or they can be used individually. Each packet includes a skills matrix that matches specific activities with affective and cognitive skills.

Grade 1

966. *The Balancing Girl*
967. *Bea and Mr. Jones*
968. *How My Parents Learned to Eat*
969. *Something Special for Me*
970. *We Are Best Friends*

Grade 2

971. *My Mother's Getting Married*
972. *A New Coat for Ana*
973. *Stevie*
974. *The Tenth Good Thing about Barney*
975. *The Terrible Thing that Happened at Our House*
976. *William's Doll*

Grade 3

977. *Angel Child, Dragon Child*
978. *Annie and the Old One*
979. *Crow Boy*
980. *Keep the Lights Burning, Abbie*
981. *The Long Way to a New Land*

**Wise Owl*

Wise Owl is a read-aloud program that promotes creative and critical thinking in very young children. These series are based on distinguished stories that children love. They include open-ended questions about such topics as the nature of bravery, loneliness and friendship. Each packet includes copies of the related paperback book, reproducible activity cards with philosophical discussion questions based on the book and a teacher's guide.

982. *Albert's Toothache*
983. *The Bear That Wasn't*
984. *The Bee-Man of Orn*
985. *Frog and Toad Together*
986. *I Know a Lady*
987. *Many Moons*
988. *The Real Thief*

**Wordless Books

Preschool and primary teachers will appreciate this series devoted entirely to stories without words. *Wordless Books: An Early Language Development Program*, is designed to help children develop an interest in literature, to stimulate their thinking, and to enhance their language development. Each *Wordless Book* packet includes seven copies of a wordless book, a teacher's guide, children's worksheets and a letter to parents with suggested extensions.

989. *Anno's Counting Book*
990. *A Boy, a Dog and a Frog*
991. *Changes, Changes*
992. *Moonlight*
993. *Pancakes for Breakfast*
994. *The Snowman*

TEACHER CREATED MATERIALS
6421 Industry Way
Westminster, CA 92683

*995-1006. *Literature Activities for Young Children* Series

Reinforce basic skills through multi-sensory activities for young children in this series. Reproducible sheets make it easy to use best-loved stories as a basis for imaginative projects.

995. *Literature Activities for Young Children.* TCM 298

Read-Aloud Rhymes for the Very Young; You Read to Me, I'll Read to You; The Sky Is Full of Song; Chicken Soup with Rice; A Child's Garden of Verses.

996. *Literature Activities for Young Children.* TCM 299.

Now We Are Six; If I Ran the Zoo; The Book of Pigericks; Sing a Song of Popcorn: Every Child's Book of Poems; The Real Mother Goose, The Random House Book of Poetry for Children.

997. *Literature Activities for Young Children.* TCM 300.

The Story about Ping; Caps for Sale; Madeline; Goodnight Moon; Nana Upstairs, Nana Downstairs; Lyle, Lyle Crocodile; The Little Engine That Could; Little Toot; Brown Bear, Brown Bear, What Do You See?; Amelia Bedelia and the Baby; Millions of Cats; Dandelion.

998. *Literature Activities for Young Children.* TCM 301

Blueberries for Sal, The Very Hungry Caterpillar, Green Eggs and Ham, Winnie-the-Pooh, Clifford's Birthday Party, The Carrot Seed, Mike Mulligan and His Steam Shovel, Harry the Dirty Dog, The Snowy Day, Big Bad Bruce, Are You My Mother?, In a People House.

999. *Literature Activities for Young Children.* TCM 302

Pinocchio, Cinderella, Alice in Wonderland, The Gingerbread Boy, Sleeping Beauty, Jack and the Beanstalk, Little Red Riding Hood, The Three Bears, Hansel and Gretel, The Little Red Hen, Snow White and the Seven Dwarfs, The Three Little Pigs.

1000. *Literature Activities for Young Children.* TCM 303

Jack and Jill, Baa Baa Black Sheep, Hickory Dickory Dock, Humpty Dumpty, Little Bo Peep, Three Little Kittens, Little Boy Blue, Peter Peter Pumpkin Eater, Little Miss Muffet, Mary Mary Quite Contrary, Little Jack Horner, Old Mother Hubbard.

1001. *Literature Activities for Young Children.* TCM 304

The Biggest Pumpkin Ever; Little Witch's Big Night; Sometimes It's Turkey, Sometimes It's Feathers; It's Thanksgiving; The Littlest Angel; Twas the Night before Christmas; The Valentine Bears; The Best Valentine in the World; The Mother's Day Mice; Leprechauns Never Lie; Home for a Bunny; The Country Bunny and the Little Gold Shoes.

1002. *Literature Activities for Young Children.* TCM 305

The Lion and the Mouse, The Goose that Laid the Golden Egg, The City Mouse and the Country Mouse, The Rabbit and the Turtle, The Fox and the Grapes, The Ants and the Grasshopper, The Bee and the Dove, The Proud Turtle, The Crow and the Pitcher, The Pelican and the Crane, The Camel Dances, The Baboon's Umbrella.

1003. *Literature Activities for Young Children.* TCM 306

A Pocket for Corduroy, Frog and Toad Together, Whistle for Willie, There's a Nightmare in My Closet, Bread and Jam for Frances, The Very Busy Spider, The Biggest Bear, Katy and the Big Snow, The Tale of Peter Rabbit, Harold and the Purple Crayon, Alexander and the Wind-Up Mouse, Cloudy with a Chance of Meatballs.

1004. *Literature Activities for Young Children.* TCM 307

There's an Alligator under My Bed, The Grouchy Ladybug, Leo the Late Bloomer, Rosie's Walk, If You Give a Mouse a Cookie, May I Bring a Friend?, Little Rabbit's Loose Tooth, The Little House, Spot Goes to the Farm, The Monkey and the Crocodile, Where's Waldo?, Mr. Rabbit and the Lovely Present.

1005. *Literature Activities for Young Children.* TCM 308

Mouse Paint; The Mixed-Up Chameleon; Two Bad Ants; Rain; Ask Mr. Bear; The Important Book; Now One Foot, Now the Other; Danny and the Dinosaur; The King Who Rained; Carl Goes Shopping; Do You Want to Be My Friend?; The Jolly Postman.

1006. *Literature Activities for Young Children.* TCM 309

Papa, Please Get the Moon for Me; The Lorax; The Magic Toyshop; Deep in the Forest; Lifetimes; Petunia; Over in the Meadow; Chester the Worldly Pig; Nelli: A Cat on Her Own; What Do You Do, Dear?; Timothy Goes to School; Arthur's Nose.

***1007-1027. *Literature and Critical Thinking* Series.

This series combines renowned children's literature with Bloom's Taxonomy to elicit critical thinking skills. Each book averages 96 pages and presents units based on six children's books. Each of the reproducible units focuses on one children's book title with activities ranging from knowledge to evaluation. These books provide teachers with art projects, bulletin boards, writing activities, science projects, social studies projects, and independent thinking activities.

1007. *Literature and Critical Thinking, Primary.* TCM 356

Frog and Toad Are Friends, Bedtime for Frances, Ira Sleeps Over, The Whingdingdilly, The Velveteen Rabbit, The Emperor's New Clothes.

1008. *Literature and Critical Thinking, Primary.* TCM 357

Alexander and the Terrible, Horrible, No Good, Very Bad Day; Corduroy; Amelia Bedelia; Miss Nelson Is Missing; Miss Rumphius; Make Way for Ducklings.

1009. *Literature and Critical Thinking, Primary.* TCM 361

William's Doll, Where the Wild Things Are, Stone Soup, The Tenth Good Thing About Barney, Love You Forever, Sylvester and the Magic Pebble.

1010. *Literature and Critical Thinking, Primary.* TCM 311

The Tale of Peter Rabbit, Why Mosquitoes Buzz in People's Ears, The Quarreling Book, Oliver Button Is a Sissy, Mike Mulligan and His Steam Shovel, Tikki Tikki Tembo.

1011. *Literature and Critical Thinking, Primary.* TCM 317

I Wish I Were a Butterfly, Song and Dance Man, The Great Kapok Tree, Cloudy with a Chance of Meatballs, Caps for Sale, The Jolly Postman.

1012. *Literature and Critical Thinking, Intermediate.* TCM 355.

Stone Fox, Charlotte's Web, Ramona the Pest, Chocolate Fever, Homer Price, James and the Giant Peach.

1013. *Literature and Critical Thinking, Intermediate.* TCM 358

The Giving Tree; Dear Mr. Henshaw; Stuart Little; The Sign of the Beaver; King of the Wind; Sarah, Plain and Tall.

1014. *Literature and Critical Thinking, Intermediate.* TCM 359

The Whipping Boy, Call It Courage, Be a Perfect Person in Just Three Days, Help! I'm a Prisoner in the Library, How to Eat Fried Worms, The Trouble with Tuck.

1015. *Literature and Critical Thinking, Intermediate.* TCM 362.

The Hundred Dresses, The Cay, The Great Brain, Owl Moon, On My Honor, The Reluctant Dragon.

1016. *Literature and Critical Thinking, Intermediate.* TCM 312

Danny: The Champion of the World, The Polar Express, Shoeshine Girl, The Enormous Egg, The Little Prince, Annie and the Old One.

1017. *Literature and Critical Thinking, Intermediate.* TCM 313.

A Taste of Blackberries, The Wump World, From the Mixed-Up Files of Mrs. Basil E. Frankweiler, The Adventures of Pinocchio, The Summer of the Swans, Henry Bear's Park.

1018. *Literature and Critical Thinking, Intermediate.* TCM 315

Where the Sidewalk Ends, Casey at the Bat, Hailstones and Halibut Bones, Joyful Noise, If I Were in Charge of the World, The Random House Book of Poetry for Children.

1019. *Literature and Critical Thinking, Challenging.* TCM 360.

The Black Stallion, Where the Red Fern Grows, Bridge to Terabithia, The Secret Garden, Island of the Blue Dolphins, The Indian in the Cupboard.

1020. *Literature and Critical Thinking, Challenging.* TCM 363.

Roll of Thunder, Hear My Cry; In the Year of the Boar and Jackie Robinson; My Side of the Mountain; Tuck Everlasting; The Lion, the Witch and the Wardrobe; Little House on the Prairie.

1021. *Literature and Critical Thinking, Challenging.* TCM 364.

The Twenty-One Balloons, Caddie Woodlawn, A Wrinkle in Time, Lassie Come Home, Mrs. Frisby and the Rats of NIMH, The Witch of Blackbird Pond.

1022. *Literature and Critical Thinking, Challenging.* TCM 310

The Call of the Wild, The Pearl, Little Women, The Prince and the Pauper, The Hobbit, Kidnapped.

1023. *Literature and Critical Thinking, Challenging.* TCM 314

Sing Down the Moon, Johnny Tremain, The Slave Dancer, The Friendship, Sadako and the Thousand Paper Cranes, Snow Treasure.

1024. *Literature and Critical Thinking, Challenging.* TCM 316

Child of the Silent Night: The Story of Laura Bridman, Ishi: The Last of His Tribe, Lincoln: A Photobiography, Martin Luther King: The Peaceful Warrior, Anne Frank: The Diary of a Young Girl, The Land I Lost.

1025. *Literature and Critical Thinking, Challenging.* TCM 318

Wolf Rider, The House of Dies Drear, The Egypt Game, The Stalker, The Westing Game, The Case of the Baker Street Irregular.

1026. *Literature and Critical Thinking, Challenging.* TCM 319

Do Animals Dream?, Ashanti to Zulu, Steven Caney's Invention Book, Junk in Space, Bird, 50 Simple Things Kids Can Do to Save the Earth.

1027. *Literature and Critical Thinking, Challenging.* TCM 320

The Search for Delicious, The Martian Chronicles, The Castle in the Attic, Stinker from Space, Weird Henry Berg, The Hero and the Crown.

1028-1053. *Thematic Unit Series*

Thematic units are whole language, literature-based units that include the interdisciplinary activities necessary for integration. These units include literature selections and questions that often emphasize critical thinking, poetry, planning guides, writing activities, bulletin board ideas, curriculum connections, cooperative learning activities, culminating activities, and a bibliography. The units are well organized and contain many more suggestions than needed.

Young Children

1028. Animals. TCM 250

Dear Zoo, Nature's Footprints: In the Barnyard, The Pop-Up Pet Shop, Spot Goes to the Circus.

1029. Seasons. TCM 251.

My Spring Robin, The Seasons of Arnold's Apple Tree, Something Is Going to Happen, When Summer Ends.

1030. My World. TCM 252

All by Myself, Mommies at Work, My Family, Richard Scarry's Book of Things that Go, The New Baby.

1031. Bears. TCM 267.

Goldilocks and the Three Bears, Good as New.

1032. Self Esteem. TCM 269

George and Martha.

1033. Five Senses. TCM 270

The Little Red Hen, The Town Mouse and the Country Mouse.

Primary

1034. Apples. TCM 266

The Giving Tree, Johnny Appleseed.

1035. Creepy Crawlies. TCM 268.

Over the Steamy Swamp, The Very Hungry Caterpillar

1036. Dragons and Dinosaurs. TCM 271

Beware the Dragons!, What Happened to Patrick's Dinosaurs?

1037. Our Environment. TCM 272

The Great Kapok Tree, The Wartville Wizard.

1038. Weather. TCM 273

Cloud Book, Cloudy with a Chance of Meatballs

1039. Friendship. TCM 274

Best Friends, Friends

1040. Bubbles. TCM 275

Never Snap at a Bubble, Professor Bubbles' Official Handbook.

1041. Native Americans. TCM 276

Arrow to the Sun, Legend of the Bluebonnet, Rainbow Crow.

1042. Penguins. TCM 277

A Penguin Year, Mr. Popper's Penguins

Intermediate

1043. Rocks and Soil. TCM 265

The Magic School Bus Inside the Earth; How to Dig a Hole to the Other Side of the Earth.

1044. Birthdays. TCM 264

Angelina's Birthday Surprise; Happy Birthday, Dear Duck; The Secret Birthday Message.

1045. Jungle. TCM 283

A Story, A Story; Why Mosquitoes Buzz in People's Ears.

1046. Oceans. TCM 284

The Cay, The Crab that Played with the Sea.

1047. Native American. TCM 285

Annie and the Old One, The Gift of the Sacred Dog.

1048. Ecology. TCM 286

One Day in the Tropical Rain Forest, The Wump World

1049. Multicultural Folktales.

Mufaro's Beautiful Daughter, Song of Sedna.

1050. Friends.

Charlotte's Web, Bridge to Terabithia.

Challenging

1051. Civil War. TCM 290

Behind Rebel Lines, Charley Skedaddle.

1052. The Revolutionary War

The Fighting Ground, Johnny Tremain.

1053. Medieval Times

Robin Hood of Sherwood Forest, Adam of the Road, Door in the Wall.

**1054. Carratello, John, and Patty Carratello. *Literature Activities for Reluctant Readers.* Teacher Created Materials, Inc., 1991.

The authors have chosen literature of high interest to motivate those children who don't like to read, but the activities are limited. There are seven areas of this book and each area relates to self esteem and enjoyment. Combined with other resources, this resource book provides some interesting alternatives to the basal.

Books included: *The Day Jimmy's Boa Ate the Wash; Amelia Bedelia; The Napping House; I Wish I Were a Butterfly; Leo the Late Bloomer; The Carrot Seed; Franklin in the Dark; Alexander and the Terrible, Horrible, No Good Very Bad Day; Starring First Grade; The Little Old Lady Who Was Not Afraid of Anything; The Vanishing Pumpkin; Humbug Witch; My Grandson Lew; The Tenth Good Thing about Barney; Now One Foot, Now the Other; Amazing Spiders; Chicka Chicka Boom Boom; Poem Stew; He Bear, She Bear; The Bears' Vacation; The Berenstain Bears and Too Much Junk Food.*

1055. *Literature Activities for Reluctant Readers, Intermediate.*

Amazing Poisonous Animals; Animal Fact/Animal Fable; Annie and the Old One; Be a Perfect Person in Just Three Days; Ben and Me; The Black Stallion; Cowardly Clyde; Hatchet; How to Eat Fried Worms; Jumanji; Kermit the Hermit; Lila on the Landing; The Magic Schoolbus Inside the Earth; Runaway to Freedom; Skinny-bones; Stone Fox; A Taste of Blackberries; The War with Grandpa; Where the Sidewalk Ends; Will You Sign Here, John Hancock? The Wump World.

**1056. Carratello, John, and Patty Carratello. *Connecting Math & Literature Books Included: Primary.* Teacher Created Materials, Inc., 1991.

Mathematical skills such as numbers, measurement, problem solving, and geometry are correlated with children's literature in this resource. The book also provides suggestions for developing counting centers and additional literature to use with each unit. It is reproducible and activities are easily assimilated into the curriculum.

Books included: Counting Center: *Anno's Counting Book; Bears on Wheels, 1, 2, 3; To the Zoo; How Many Bugs in a Box?; The Most Amazing Hide-and-Seek Counting Book; When Sheep Cannot Sleep; Animal Numbers; One Wooly Wombat.*

Relationships

The Midnight Farm, The Wolf's Chicken Stew.

Place Value

How Much Is a Million?

Operations

Annie's One to Ten, Ten Bears in My Bed, Bunches and Bunches of Bunnies, Emma's Christmas, The Doorbell Rang.

Estimation

Moira's Birthday.

Size

Much Bigger Than Martin, Inch by Inch.

Mass

Who Sank the Boat?

Capacity

The Giant Jam Sandwich

Time

A Circle of Seasons, The Year at Maple Hill Farm, The Very Hungry Caterpillar, The Grouchy Ladybug.

Money

Alexander, Who Used to be Rich Last Sunday; Where the Sidewalk Ends.

Pattern Center

There Was an Old Lady Who Swallowed a Fly; Drummer Hoff; The Rose in My Garden; Brown Bear, Brown Bear, What Do You See?; If You Give a Mouse a Cookie; Bringing the Rain to Kapiti Plain; The Napping Mouse.

Sorting, Classification, Graphing

Harriet's Halloween Candy, Frog and Toad Are Friends, A House Is a House for Me.

Logic

Q Is for Duck, Ming Lo Moves the Mountain.

Shapes

The Secret Birthday Message

Relationships between Shapes

Grandfather Tang's Story.

**1057. Cerbus, Deborah Plona, and Cheryl Feichtenbiner Rice. *Connecting Science and Literature.* Teacher Created Materials, 1991.

Designed to provide specific strategies and activities for integrating early elementary science and literature, this book is divided into sections of life science, earth science, physical science, and process skills with the accompanying literature. Each section contains descriptions of picture books, specific science concepts, and integrated language arts activities. Some activities are designed for cooperative learning groups.

Books included:

Life Science

Birthday Presents; Dear Zoo; The Enormous Watermelon; Germs Make Me Sick; Have You Seen Birds?; The Magic School Bus Inside the Human Body; Pumpkin, Pumpkin; The Seasons of Arnold's Apple Tree; A Small World; The Tiny Seed; A Tree Is Nice; The Very Hungry Caterpillar; The Year at Maple Hill Farm

Earth Science

Grasslands; Mousekin Takes a Trip; Mousekin's Woodland Sleepers; Hot Air Henry; I Want to Be an Astronaut; January Brings Snow; The Magic School Bus Inside the Earth; Patrick's Dinosaurs; Rain; Rainbow of My Own; The Snowy Day; Sun Up, Sun Down; Swimmy.

Physical Science

Alistair's Time Machine, Bear Shadow, Berenstain Bears' Science Fair, Meet the Computer, Mickey's Magnet, Mike Mulligan and His Steam Shovel.

Process Skills

Amelia Bedelia, How Many Snails?, If at First You Do Not See, The Important Book, My Presents, Spectacles, The Five Senses.

1058-1061. *Literature Unit* Series

In order to help teachers utilize quality literature in the classroom, this series provides support ideas for individual children's novels. Each reproducible book contains vocabulary activities, interdisciplinary activities, cooperative learning activities and unit tests.

1058. *Bridge to Terabithia*
1059. *Sign of the Beaver*
1060. *Where the Red Fern Grows*
1061. *A Wrinkle in Time.*